CAMBRIDGE STUDIES IN
MODERN POLITICAL ECONOMIES

Editors
SUZANNE BERGER, ALBERT O. HIRSCHMAN, AND CHARLES MAIER

State, market, and social regulation:
new perspectives on Italy

Suzanne D. Berger, editor: *Organizing interests in Western Europe: pluralism, corporatism, and the transformation of politics*

Charles F. Sabel: *Work and politics: the division of labor in industry*

Judith Chubb: *Patronage, power, and poverty in southern Italy: a tale of two cities*

Angelo Panebianco: *Political parties: organization and power*

Charles S. Maier, editor: *Changing boundaries of the political: essays on the evolving balance between the state and society, public and private in Europe*

Charles S. Maier: *In search of stability: explorations in historical political economy*

State, market, and social regulation

New perspectives on Italy

Edited by

PETER LANGE AND MARINO REGINI

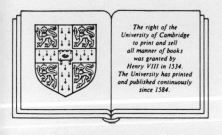

The right of the
University of Cambridge
to print and sell
all manner of books
was granted by
Henry VIII in 1534.
The University has printed
and published continuously
since 1584.

CAMBRIDGE UNIVERSITY PRESS

Cambridge
New York   Port Chester   Melbourne   Sydney

Published by the Press Syndicate of the University of Cambridge
The Pitt Building, Trumpington Street, Cambridge CB2 1RP
32 East 57th Street, New York, NY 10022, USA
10 Stamford Road, Oakleigh, Melbourne 3166, Australia

First published 1989

Printed in the United States of America

Library of Congress Cataloging-in-Publication Data

State, market and social regulation : new perspectives on Italy /
edited by Peter Lange and Marino Regini.
p. cm. – (Cambridge studies in modern political economies)
Bibliography: p.
Includes index.
ISBN 0-521-35453-6
1. Italy – Economic policy – Congresses. 2. Industry and state –
Italy – Congresses. 3. Labor policy – Italy – Congresses. 4. Italy –
Social policy – Congresses. I. Lange, Peter Michael. II. Regini,
Marino, 1943– . III. Series.
HC305.S636 1989
338.945–dc19   89-30796
                                                              CIP

British Library Cataloguing in Publication Data

State, market and social regulation : new perspectives
on Italy. – (Cambridge studies in modern political
economies)
1. Italy. Economic conditions
I. Lange, Peter II. Regini, Marino
330.945′0928

ISBN 0-521-35453-6 hard covers

Contents

vi   *Contents*

Contributors

GIANPRIMO CELLA
Professor of Sociology, University of Brescia

ANTONIO CHIESI
Assistant Professor of Sociology, University of Trieste

BRUNO DENTE
Associate Professor of Political Science, University of Bologna

GERALD A. EPSTEIN
Assistant Professor of Economics, University of Massachusetts at Amherst

MAURIZIO FERRERA
Associate Professor of Political Science, University of Pavia

ELENA GRANAGLIA
Assistant Professor, Institute of Economics and Finance, University of Rome

PETER LANGE
Professor of Political Science, Duke University

ALBERTO MARTINELLI
Professor of Political Science, University of Milan

MASSIMO PACI
Professor of Sociology, University of Ancona

GIANFRANCO PASQUINO
Professor of Political Science, University of Bologna, and Senator of the Italian Republic

MARINO REGINI
Professor of Sociology, University of Trento

GLORIA REGONINI
Associate Professor of Political Science, University of Florence

EMILIO REYNERI
Professor of Sociology, University of Parma

vii

JULIET B. SCHOR
   Associate Professor of Economics, Harvard University
SONIA STEFANIZZI
   Ph.D. Candidate, European University Institute, Florence
SIDNEY TARROW
   Professor of Political Science, Cornell University

Preface

This volume is the product of a seminar organized in April 1986 by the Conference Group on Italian Politics and Society (Congrips) and the Italian journal of political economy, *Stato e Mercato*. The conference was held at the Villa Serbelloni of the Rockefeller Foundation in Bellagio, Italy, and was attended by twenty-seven U.S. and Italian scholars. The theme of the seminar was "The State and Social Regulation in Italy," much the same as the title of this volume. This should not suggest, however, that the reader is about to examine the "acts" of the meeting. Rather, the essays collected here represent the fruit of a collective effort that lasted over many months both before and after the meeting at the lake. Its aim was to develop a relatively systematic and integrated study of *il caso italiano* in comparative perspective. This seemed particularly useful in light of past treatments of Italy as an anomalous and confusing, if not contradictory, "case" when compared to other advanced industrial democracies, an excessive stress on the crisis-prone qualities of the Italian political economy, and a failure to appreciate how, and how much, a close look at Italy might contribute to an understanding of developments elsewhere.

The seminar was, in fact, organized around a set of specific questions posed by the editors in preliminary form in the "call for papers." Their focus was on how the role of the Italian state was changing relative to other forms and institutions for regulating economic and social interaction. Policy pronouncements and political changes elsewhere suggested a declining role for the state and a new emphasis on the market. Was this also true in Italy? Was the role of the Italian state declining, or growing, or just changing? And what might we learn about how to examine and understand developments outside of Italy by a more detailed look at the Italian "case"?

The twenty-one papers selected for presentation at the seminar were discussed in detail over four days by the participants. Those subsex   *Preface*

quently selected because of their relative compatibility and greater relevance to the theme (itself partially redefined) were then rewritten by their authors on the basis of comments made at the conference and detailed commentaries made by the editors. Most of these edited and reworked articles were first published in the volume *Stato e regolazione sociale: nuove prospettive sul caso italiano* (Bologna: Il Mulino, 1987) and are translated here. A short article by Sabino Cassese that appeared in Italian has not been reproduced, and Sonia Stefanizzi and Sidney Tarrow prepared a piece for English-language publication. Two articles growing out of the conference were also published in *Stato e Mercato* (articles by Ida Regalia and Elisabetta Addis in issue no. 19, April 1987) but do not appear in this volume.

This recounting of the history of this collection is certainly not intended to be self-congratulatory. It is, instead, meant to indicate the extent to which efforts were made by all of our collaborators to create a collective volume that would nonetheless be relatively integrated and systematic. Beyond the many reciprocal references contained in the various chapters, the attempt by the editors to use the Introduction to provide a shared set of analytical concepts and working hypotheses, and the willingness of our collaborators to follow our lead, we feel that the chapters present a relatively unified, if not uniform, interpretation of *il caso italiano*. We also feel that this interpretive framework is both relatively rich and innovative; but these are issues about which only the reader can decide.

We want here to thank the various institutions and persons without whose contributions this volume would not have been possible. The Rockefeller Foundation provided us with a magnificent setting and excellent meals and lodging, which contributed immensely to the pleasure of our week of intense work together. The National Science Foundation's U.S.-Italy Cooperative Science Program (grant no. INT-8516199) provided financial support for travel and conference costs and for preparation of the Italian- and English-language volumes. Grants from the Consiglio Nazionale di Ricerca (no. 84.01151.09) and from the National Science Foundation (no. INT-8415549) enabled Marino Regini and Peter Lange, respectively, to conduct research that contributed to the Introduction and Conclusion to this volume as well as permitting Lange to spend six months in Italy at the time the conference was being prepared and initial editing of the volume begun. And of course we are indebted to Congrips and *Stato e Mercato*, whose close collaborators – above all Sidney Tarrow – contributed to the development of the conference theme. Suzanne Berger gave us invaluable assistance in securing an English-language publisher. In addition to the authors whose essays appear here and those whose work appeared in *Stato e Mercato* and in the Italian volume, we want to extend special thanks to the participants in the seminar who are not represented in this volume. Their participation made a substantial contribution to the ultimate success of our efforts. In alphabetical order they are: Arnaldo Bagnasco, Suzanne Berger, Carlo Donolo, Miriam Golden, Michael Lewis-Beck, Michelle Miller, Raffaella Nanetti, Gianni Nardozzi, Robert Putnam, Michele Salvati, Gustave Schachter, Carlo Trigilia, and Douglas Wertman.

Finally, Richard Locke devoted weeks of detailed work to preparing the translations of all the essays except those by the editors and by Schor and Epstein. His assistance was invaluable. In addition, we want to thank Bonnie Banks, Pamela Camerra-Rowe, Nadia Carelli, and Mary Umstead for their editorial, bibliographical, and clerical assistance.

P.L. and M.R.

Introduction: interests and institutions – forms of social regulation and public policy-making

PETER LANGE AND MARINO REGINI

Since the late 1960s, an important debate has developed in the social sciences concerning the changing role of the state in the regulation of relationships among social classes and groups. The general question has been whether there has been a shift in the boundaries and balance between state, market, and various social institutions in the creation and maintenance of social order. More specifically, how have the roles of these institutions in the coordination of economic activities and the management of conflicts over the allocation of scarce resources changed in the postwar period?

The first, and in many ways still exemplary, comparative contribution to this debate was Andrew Shonfield's *Modern Capitalism* (1965). Shonfield challenged the prevalent tendency to undervalue the potentially autonomous and positive role of the state in the capitalist economy, maintaining instead that such a role was widespread and in many cases desirable in the advanced industrial democracies. The dimensions and complexity of state intervention – particularly in countries like France, Great Britain, and Italy – lent considerable support to his argument. Yet, as so often happens in the social sciences, Shonfield's observations took considerable time to be fully absorbed. Thus, just when scholars decided to "bring the state back in" to their analyses (Skocpol 1985), the phenomenon itself was in decline. In fact, in many countries opposing trends appeared to have taken hold.

Nonetheless, a more careful reading of the literature shows that it often contains generalizations based on relatively fragile theoretical propositions or on highly selective examples which not infrequently correspond to the normative predispositions of the authors. This volume instead seeks to address the theme of the changing role of the state and of the balance between state regulation and the different forms of social regulation more systematically. In this introductory chapter we offer an analytical and conceptual framework and suggest

1

some interpretations for which the subsequent chapters provide plausible support. Being solely analytical, this chapter itself should be read in conjunction with our conclusions in the final chapter, where we try to apply concepts and interpretations to the Italian case.

To begin, how can we bring some order to the plurality of approaches that have characterized the recent discussion of trends in the state's role and its relationship to other modes of regulation? Simplifying, we can identify three types of approaches:

1. Some authors have sought to develop broad international comparisons, seeking to identify the "changing boundaries" (Maier 1987) between what has traditionally been treated as "public" and thus subject to direct regulation or control of the state and that which has been thought more appropriately regulated by the market, by community norms, or by other forms of social regulation. Such an approach offers the breadth and richness of the historical-comparative method and has the merit of identifying general trends over long periods of time. The use of this particular analytical lens, however, can mask the possibility (or probability, as we shall suggest subsequently) that what we see today are shifts in opposing directions in different areas of state regulation. Furthermore, the extensive historical reconstructions often do not permit identification of the crucial causal variables and thus do not provide an adequate explanatory framework.

2. A more specialized though still comparative approach looks at specific *policy* areas – health or wage policy, for instance – and compares different countries in order to identify and explain the variations in the modes of regulation in these areas. Research of this type has flourished in recent years, leading to a much better understanding of how specific policies – or their absence – emerge and change. The strengths of this approach have led us to rely on it in structuring the present volume, in which we have given ample space to sectoral analysis of economic and welfare policies and industrial relations. If considered in isolation, however, such studies also run considerable risks, above all that of leaping to generalizations about trends and their explanations based on specific areas of activity and relationships. No matter how interesting and politically salient, any one of these areas represents only a limited part of the activities subject to regulation. Furthermore, precisely because of the concentrated attention on a specific area, there is a danger of missing the interconnections between developments in different policy areas. Finally, such sectoral studies run the risk of underestimating the role of actors who have structural power that is only partially visible in the roles which these actors play in the decisions concerning *specific* policies.

3. A third approach, characteristic of many studies in the field of public policy, has both more restricted empirical bases and more prescriptive ambitions, since it examines single countries and the costs and benefits of different forms of regulation in a specific area of activity. Analyses of this type often implicitly assume some national peculiarity (for example, American "exceptionalism" or the Italian "anomaly"); or, conversely, the existence of universal characteristics (for example, the economistic assumptions built into much of American public policy analysis). Doubt is cast on both types of assumptions by international comparisons of decisional processes and their outcomes. In addition, these studies often are underlain by a type of "voluntarism" that originates in an excessive belief in a form of rationality which is little constrained by either structures of power or the existence of profoundly divergent preferences among the individuals and groups affected by the policy.

The objective of this volume is to contribute to an understanding of the questions raised by the first two approaches through systematic case studies of the most important areas of regulation in Italy. We would maintain that studies of different policy areas, centered on a specific country but carried out with an historical-comparative perspective, are, given the present state of knowledge and resources, best able to identify the tendencies and processes at work in different sectors of the relationship between the state and society and, above all, to specify their causes. This type of study allows us to establish to what extent one can speak of a "general trend" towards the spread of one or another mode of regulation across policy areas and what may be the reasons for such a trend if it exists. We cannot, of course, develop cross-national generalizations based on a study of this type. We can, however, offer a framework for such comparative research as well as insights from intra-national comparisons, which will, we hope, further stimulate international research as well as offer a better understanding of contemporary Italy.

Moving to the substance of the volume, we need first to identify the conceptual underpinnings common to the individual chapters.

1. Regulation: some concepts

To begin, what are the objects of the "regulation" with which we are concerned? What exactly is "regulated" in the specific policy areas analyzed in the subsequent chapters?

The literature on forms of regulation (see section 2 below) treats "social order" as the object of regulation and takes up the question of "how society holds together."[1] The concept of social order is, however, too sweeping for our purposes.

Another major thread in the literature, of which Shonfield's already cited work remains emblematic, poses the problem of the relationships between state and economy, between public and private. It considers the market economy as the critical mechanism for the allocation of resources and the principal source of conflicts and contradictions *and* as a potential object of regulation by the state, operating in conjunction with or as substitute for the market. This theme has stimulated an important debate but presents two difficulties from our perspective. First, it considers only the state and the market as regulative mechanisms of the economy, thereby ignoring the possible importance of other institutions. Second, taking the "market economy" as its object of study, it loses sight of the fact that significant economic activities take place outside of the market (for example, in the so-called "third" or voluntary sector) but nonetheless require regulation.

For the purposes of this volume, the object of regulation can be defined as a particular set of *activities* and *relationships between actors:* those which pertain to the sphere of production and distribution of economic resources.[2]

Having identified our object of study, we need now to specify what we mean by "regulation." The use of this concept is far from uniform in the literature. The French "regulation" school uses this concept with a far broader significance than we intend (e.g., Boyer 1979; Boyer and Mistral 1978). We define as regulation the mode or form (or better, as we will see in a moment, the different modes) by which a determinate set of activities and/or relationships among actors is coordinated, the related resources allocated, and the related conflicts, whether real or potential, structured (that is, prevented or reconciled). There are, therefore, three dimensions to the concept of regulation as we use it: the coordination of activities or relationships, the allocation of resources, and the structuring of conflicts. These dimensions are not always closely examined or given equal importance in the different policy areas examined in the essays, but they constitute the ideal scope of our discussion of the trends in regulation.

When can we consider regulative activities to have been successful? "Successful" regulation implies the relatively stable production and reproduction of relationships between social groups such that the allocation of resources among them occurs in accordance with shared expectations and without recourse to "illegitimate" means or the frequent and diffuse use of force. In this sense, effective regulation of economic activities (which are the primary focus of this volume) contributes to the creation of not only economic but also social regulation.[3]

The discussion to this point implies that we do not expect regulation to take place in similar ways and with similar degrees of success in the different areas of activities and relationships examined. On the contrary, we begin with the assumption that the production and reproduction of social order, and of order in the areas of economic activity examined here, always represents – when it occurs – the composite result of different ways of regulating real or potential conflicts of interest. Several implications relevant to the analyses that follow derive from this general perspective.

The first is that the modes of regulation can be different in different areas of activities and relationships since they reflect variations in the structures of power, decision processes, and preferences of the actors involved. Second, and somewhat in tension with the preceding, although the decision process is broken up into different policy areas, some actors (e.g., mass political parties, class trade unions) may pursue more general objectives that extend across several policy areas. They can, therefore, expect that the outcomes in one policy area will condition their capacity to satisfy their preferences in others. It follows that it is quite possible (as we discuss further in section 5) that the conduct of conflicts over the modes of regulation in a particular area may be subject to more general strategies pursued by actors conscious of their interests in other areas. Third, variations in this "mix" of segmentation and interdependence between different areas of activity and relationship – above and beyond the variability in the degree of "rationality" and strategic capacity of the actors – imply that it is quite unlikely that the overall social order is the outcome of a "grand design"; more limitedly, it is also unlikely that the outcome of regulation in any specific area fully reflects more general underlying power relationships.[4] It is doubtless an excessive generalization to speak, as do numerous authors, of "statist" or "pluralist" or "neo-corporatist" systems (see, for example, Lehmbruch and Schmitter 1982; Steiner 1981) or even of a "national style of policy making" (Richardson 1982). Obviously, in a given country certain forms of regulation may predominate. But, if we keep in mind the plurality of policy areas in any country, it is difficult to imagine a single coherent and consistent form of regulation.

2. Modes of regulation

The attempts to identify the different modes or forms of social regulation, their consequences, and the reasons they change has a long history and a well-respected theoretical tradition. We certainly cannot here repeat that history or pretend to make a fully original theoretical contribution. Some specifications are, however, necessary in order to frame the essays which follow and to clarify the objectives of the volume.

The discussion can begin from the difference (often poorly understood) between modes or principles of regulation and the institutions by which these modes are most commonly employed. An overview of the vast literature on regulation shows a notable degree of consistency and continuity in the typologies proposed.

Basically, there are three principles or modes of social regulation – that is, means by which activities are coordinated, resources allocated, and conflicts structured – on which there is a vast consensus: authority or hierarchical control; exchange; and solidarity, i.e., cooperation based on shared norms and values. These principles, each of which has its "classic" presentation (Hobbes, Adam Smith, and Durkheim, respectively), have been discussed together, although with somewhat different names, by Karl Polanyi and more recently by numerous authors including Poggi, Crouch, Lindblom, and Ouchi among others.[5] They are taken up by various essays in this volume.

It nonetheless appears clear that each of these principles has historically come to be identified with different institutions. Authority has generally been considered the constitutive principle of the state and of other bureaucratic organizations, exchange of the market, and solidarity or normative regulation of communities (whether of the traditional type such as the family and clans or of new types such as social movements).[6] The identification of modes of regulation with specific institutions is a simplification that is often useful in examining trends in diverse areas of activity and relationships (we also do so at times below). Nonetheless, conflating them involves two risks that are worth considering.

First, the identification of modes of regulation with the traditional institutions with which they have become associated can, under conditions of social change and institutional innovation, lead to unnecessary analytical complications. When new institutions emerge or become particularly important, analysts are naturally inclined to expand the traditional typology and to seek to identify new principles or modes of regulation which these institutions supposedly incorporate.

This reasoning probably lies behind Streeck and Schmitter's (1985) most interesting recent effort to develop an analytical scheme for understanding the bases of social regulation. Impressed by the growth of concertative practices between large hierarchical associations in the advanced industrial democracies, they have proposed to add a fourth mode to the three traditional ones: the "associative" model of social order based on inter- and intra-organizational concertation.

There is little question that large interest associations have acquired an enormous importance in social regulation. What is less clear, however, is whether concertation really represents a new principle of social order or instead represents simply a different, and perhaps contingent, "mix" of the three traditional modes. More specifically, the associations enter into "inter-organizational concertation" when they use the combination of exchange, authority, and normative control that is discussed in the vast literature on "neocorporatism." In entering into concerted relationships, they face the problem of guaranteeing internal consent through the use of incentives and sanctions which differ from those traditionally used by organizations of representation. This internal problem of consent can also involve a particular "mix" of hierarchical control, exchange, and solidarity, but it seems to us to stretch the concept to treat this as "intra-organizational concertation" and consider it as a mode unto itself. The associations adopt particular mixes of the three principles of regulation that are certainly worthy of special attention. This does not, however, mean that a new mode of regulation or a new principle of social order has arisen with the growth in the importance of such concertative practices,[7] even if it may be convenient to discuss and analyze this mix under the name of organizational concertation.

This observation permits us to point out a second risk of too closely linking a mode of regulation with a particular institution. When this occurs, there is a tendency to think that the institution is based *solely* on the use of that mode, for example, that authority or hierarchical control is the only principle of regulation employed by the state. As we have suggested, and as is demonstrated in several of the essays which follow, this tendency can hide a fundamental characteristic of most, if not all, institutions: that their functioning is rooted in a mix of the three principles of regulation. What differentiates institutions from one another is the degree to which one or another of the modes of regulation is particularly characteristic, either because it is predominant or because the institution has historically been associated with that mode.

To assert that every institution incorporates a mix of regulative principles immediately implies a further important theoretical (and political) observation: that the proposition that certain modes of regulation are "inappropriate" to certain institutions is more a value judgment than a well-based analytical statement. Such judgments are, however, widespread in the recent literature on the relationship between state and society which points to "improper invasions" or "inappropriate blurring" of the boundaries between different regulative institutions. Those who emphasize the reduction of state policies to objects of exchange between private actors (Pizzorno 1981) or, in contrast, stress

the contradictions that arise out of the imposition of political considerations on the market (Offe 1982) often implicitly suggest that in some
institutions one mode of regulation is invading the "proper" sphere of
the other or that an area of activity or relationship is coming to be regulated by principles which are "inappropriate" to it. In doing so, they
point to, or at least evoke, profound changes, "contradictions," and
possible instability. In many cases, furthermore, the effort to identify
the sources of change gives way to more polemical purposes.

By contrast, the sectoral essays collected here demonstrate that
"invasions" and the use of "inappropriate" modes are the norm for
activities and relationships concerned with the production and distribution of economic resources. Furthermore, the norm in each of these
policy areas is one of intervention through a mix of institutions and
modes of regulation. The sources of the dysfunctions, contradictions,
and changes must be sought elsewhere; the simple presence of a "mix"
is insufficient.

Having made these theoretical specifications, we can now turn to a
description of the characteristic forms of regulation that are referred to
in various of the individual essays.[8]

Forms of state regulation

The state can coordinate activities, allocate resources, and
structure conflicts primarily through the exercise of its authority,
which, in the last analysis, is based on its monopoly of legitimate coer-
cion. In this case, regulative activity occurs primarily through the
means of laws and administrative rulings that are binding on the actors
involved. Salvati (1982) has discussed this type of regulation of economic activities as being "by decree" (as contrasted to by accord and
by the market), a term that captures well the oft-assumed characteristic
feature of state regulation. The state does not, however, exclusively use
its authority to regulate the vast scope of activities and relationships
that come under its purview. In many areas the success of its intervention depends on its ability also to use exchange and to call on shared
values. It would appear, in fact, that the latter two have probably
grown in importance in the last decade. In democratic and complex
societies the state has found the exclusive use of authority ever less
effective in the face of resistance from the individuals and groups
whose activity it is seeking to regulate.

Forms of social regulation

The market. The coordination of activities, allocation of
resources, and structuring of conflicts can also occur as the outcome of

exchanges based on prices determined by the interaction of supply and demand under conditions of competition. In the idealized market, competition is highly dispersed and is not influenced by normative linkages or the exercise of power and authority (except to establish the property rights essential for exchange to take place). An example of this idealized formulation is the assumption that the level of wages in an economy reflects the supply and demand for labor and the most efficient allocation of resources. As we know, however, this rarely, if ever, occurs in reality. Normative factors and/or authority relations "distort" the determination of prices and the destination of resources. In many markets, for instance, large organizations succeed in influencing prices through the use of internal hierarchies and the exercise of their power. The resultant "distortions," which reflect the desire of actors to alter what would be the outcomes of the market, are often considered as the causes of failures of neo-liberal experiments (Goldthorpe 1983). In addition, the functioning of the free market itself is made possible by preexisting norms that are generally ignored in the neo-classical market models (Goldthorpe 1978; Hirsch 1978).

Community. Where community institutions predominate, the coordination of activities and allocation of resources takes place primarily through forms of spontaneous solidarity. This can be rooted in norms, habits, or shared values of members of the community (whether it be a family, a clan, a subculture, a social movement, or the like) and is based on respect, trust, etc., or simply on identification with the community and thus its rules and hierarchy. Belonging to a community depends generally on ascriptive criteria or on processes of "collective identity formation" (Pizzorno 1978). Nonetheless, it is often noted that in many communities, relationships of authority and exchange play a supplemental role of sufficient importance to make it difficult to understand the functioning of norms without taking them into account.

Large interest associations. A wide range of activities appear to be regulated by the "public use of organized private interests" (Streeck and Schmitter 1985). This means that regulation occurs via accords reached between a few large interest associations that have a monopoly (or at least oligopoly) of representation of functional interests and a high level of disruptive power with respect to the interests of their bargaining partners and public order, and, as a result, are able to obtain privileged recognition from other associations and political authorities. In contrast to typical market contracts, "concerted" accords generally presuppose long-term strategic capacity on the part of the associations, which permits them to underutilize their market power and their disruptive power more generally (Schmitter 1974; Pizzorno 1978). These accords often require the exercise of legitimate authority to be implemented as well as the direct or implicit cooperation of the state to be effective. This is because they generally include a delegation of formally public functions to the private organizations that participate in concertation and the allocation of state resources to compensate those organizations for the costs and risks of their participation. Concerted accords can become highly unstable as the result of "crises of representation" that arise within the organizations. As a result, the success of such accords depends in large measure on the exercise of hierarchical control over associational members and often on the capacity of the former to provide "identity incentives," themselves based on shared values (Regini 1981; Lange 1977b).

These forms of regulation represent the basic models of structuring conflict, allocating resources, and coordinating activities in the economic policy areas in the advanced industrial democracies.

3. The role of the state and some initial hypotheses

Why should one assign a particular importance to the state among the regulative institutions just discussed? We can first observe that all of the activities and relationships examined in the chapters that follow have become objects or potential objects of state intervention in the postwar period. Conversely, in the 1980s economic *deregulation* has become a major topic of political discussion as a result of at least three developments: the so-called "perverse effects" of Keynesianism and of the expansion of the welfare state (fiscal crisis, excessive demands on the state, decommodification of labor, etc.); the new imperatives deriving from the intensification of international economic competition, which reduce the acceptability of inefficient or suboptimal national economic performance; and changes in the market, and sometimes also the political, power of labor and of the left more generally.

Thus, the most obvious and easiest question with which to begin an analysis of changes in the modes or forms of regulation in the sphere of the production and distribution of economic resources appears to be the following: overall, has there been an increase or decline in the role of the state in the last twenty years? Has there been a "retreat" of the state, as many have predicted (or hoped for), or has the pattern of increasing state intervention foreseen twenty years ago by Shonfield continued?

Italy is a particularly interesting case to examine from this perspective. On the one hand, for diverse historical reasons, state intervention has formally been very extensive and seemingly "authoritative" (see Cassese 1987) but at the same time highly inefficient and permeable to private interests. On the other hand, there have been intense and often contradictory developments in the power relationships among social classes and organizations in the last twenty years: roughly, in labor's favor in the 1970s, and away from labor and towards other social forces in the 1980s. We would expect, therefore, that these changing relationships would be reflected in the modes of regulating activities and relationships in the economic sphere.

For an interpretation of the Italian case, in light of the concepts and variables we have suggested and the findings of the different essays in this volume, we refer the reader to the Conclusions at the end of the volume. Here, however, we want to lay out the initial hypotheses we considered and explain the choice of the areas and themes the essays address.

The first hypothesis derives from our conviction that the issue of the increase or decline in the state's role is too generic and probably misleading; it needs to be reformulated and disaggregated. It is relatively easy and obvious to observe that changes in the forms of regulation in the policy areas in which the state potentially has a role have not been coherent and unidirectional in any country. This is so, because, as already suggested, the dominance of a form of regulation reflects the relative strength and distribution of politically relevant resources among social classes and groups, as well as their preferences; and these factors vary across policy areas. As a result, we chose to have our collaborators examine a wide range of economic and social policies. Within this framework, we hypothesized that each area of activity and relationship was regulated by a variable mix of regulative modes and institutions, and that such mixes were not necessarily expressions of internal contradictions.

The second hypothesis was based on the assumption that, even if one could identify unidirectional trends, an analysis that limited itself to showing a growth or decline of the regulatory role of the state would be insufficient for understanding how social interests influence the public allocation of resources and the structuring of social conflicts. In fact, such influence can occur in several ways. It is certainly widely agreed that classes and groups have greater or lesser influence over state action depending on their resources. But our hypothesis was somewhat less obvious because it pointed to another relationship: between the different types of interactions of social interests and political institutions that occur as part of the public policy-making process, on the one hand, and the variable capacities of these interests to condition the outputs, on the other. Put differently, the "weight" of different groups in society partially explains their capacity to condition public policy decisions; this capacity, however, is mediated by the structure of the societal and state institutions whose interaction produces the specific policies.

For this reason, two of the essays in this volume (Chapter 2 by Dente and Regonini and Chapter 1 by Pasquino) discuss the most appropriate "image" or "model" of policy-making in Italy and what role different actors generally play in the production of public policies. In section 5 of this Introduction we also propose a typology of policy-making based on a range of relationships between social interests and the institutions in different decisional arenas. The variation in the ways public policies are produced should contribute to explaining – as we have already said – why change in the relationships of strength between social classes and groups is not *directly* translated into shifts in the form of state regulatory policy, and why state action, provoked by such changes in the balance of power between interests, sometimes produces changes in the mix of regulatory modes and sometimes does not.

The studies in this volume generally support these initial hypotheses. They bring to light, however, the fact that the Italian reality is too complex to be captured by even the relatively articulated conceptual apparatus we have developed starting from the literature on regulation and policy-making. In synthesis, three further complexities need to be introduced.

1. "State regulation" has different meanings or, put another way, can take different forms. It is important to keep these differences in mind if we want to be clear about the implications of state intervention and its changes (see section 4).

2. As we expected, each area of activity or set of relationships among actors examined is regulated by a mix of regulative modes. There are very few activities or relationships in the sphere of the production and distribution of resources in which either the state norms or the market or community norms are *entirely* dominant. Their interpenetration is not an exception which necessarily leads to instability and contradictions, but the norm, at least for the cases we have examined. As we will see in the Conclusions, this mix is one of the reasons that most changes in the forms of regulation in Italy are both relatively invisible and at the same time relatively continual. What generally occur are marginal changes in the previous mix, determined not by grand decisions but by small adjustments; thus, change assumes primarily an incremental and adaptive form.

A more interesting and perhaps less expected feature of these mixes, however, is not that the different forms of regulation normally *coexist* in each of the areas examined. It is rather that in various of these areas we see particular *linkages* between state regulation (in one of the forms we discuss below) and the other forms of regulation, linkages that assume certain regular patterns.

3. Finally, the prevalence of one or another type of policy-making highlighted by our typology (see section 5) allows one to explain different capacities of the state to produce innovations in regulatory modes. But in the end this explains only a small part of the overall process of change. To understand the latter we need to take into account the linkages between forms of regulation which, as we have noted, characterize many areas of policy activity and economic and social relations. The possibilities and conditions for change are discussed at greater length in the Conclusions.

4. The levels of state regulation and linkages with other forms of regulation

The state has at its disposal a wide and articulated range of ways of intervening in society. It can use its authority and resources to regulate directly a set of activities and relations among actors or to condition (that is, to encourage or constrain) the functioning of other regulating institutions. The latter can, in turn, take different forms. Distinguishing between different levels of "intensity" or "directness" of state regulation is useful for analyzing more systematically the linkages between regulation by the state and by other institutions. To do so, we can identify four levels of state regulation.

1. The state can use its authority to establish directly how a set of activities and/or relationships among actors is to be coordinated and structured. The inherent nature of market or "mixed" economies, however, limits the scope and detail of state direction or direct control in the economic sphere.

2. The state can also use its authority to sanction or reinforce outcomes that result from other modes of regulation employed by other institutions. We can call this type of intervention the "lending of authority" to or legitimation of the modes by which activities and relations are regulated by institutions other than the state.

3. The authority of the state can be used to establish, that is, to create or modify, the rules of the game that allow or constrain the operation of other modes and institutions of regulation. We are dealing here with indirect intervention which is limited to conditioning the functioning of regulation by others. Often, however, the success of the latter depends on the indirect, rule-setting intervention of the state.

4. Finally, the state can intervene indirectly, thereby conditioning how other regulatory institutions function, not by using its authority to establish the rules but by using its economic resources. What is involved here is a purely allocative or supportive role (which does not mean that it is not crucial to the outcomes achieved), in which the state provides resources beyond those available to the institutions that are directly regulating the activities.

In Italy, the first and fourth types of intervention have traditionally been predominant. The extremely extended role of legislation and the "panoply of instruments available to the state" (Cassese 1987) have amplified the role of direct regulation of economic activities more than elsewhere. At the same time, the high permeability of public institutions to a multiplicity of interests has expanded the role of purely allocative and supportive intervention. By contrast, indirect regulation of a conditional character (Cassese 1987), characteristic of Anglo-American democracies, is decidedly weak in Italy.

As we have suggested previously, the essays in this volume demonstrate not only the co-presence of different forms of regulation in each of the areas of activity and relations examined (the "mix" foreseen in the original hypotheses) but also the importance of particular linkages between state regulation and the other regulatory modes and institutions. The multiplicity of these linkages results in good part from the varieties of ways the state can intervene and coordinate.

We see, for instance, examples of *regulation formally by the state* that, when its functioning is examined more closely, actually allow the market, or community ties or associative action, to extend its scope of influence beyond what it otherwise would be. We also see cases of regulation that *apparently occur without the state*, in which on closer inspection the state's intervention is essential if the other regulatory institutions are to operate. We can say that, in the first case, market, community, or associations operate *beneath the cover* of formal state regulation which takes form 1 or 2 discussed above. In the latter case, the other regulatory institutions can work *as an effect of* an intervention by the state, which in appearance does not have direct regulative intent – forms 3 and 4 above – but which is indispensable for regulation to take place.

We should perhaps add a third case in which market, community, or associations regulate *outside* the gambit of state intervention but in which it is how the state intervenes that favors their growth. We are thinking here, for example, of the development of supplemental insurance and private health care. At least in Italy, the development of the latter is strongly linked, on the one hand, to the inefficiency of public provision in these areas and, on the other hand, to the implicit or unintended treatment such private activities receive under the tax system (see Chapter 10 by Granaglia and Chapter 9 Paci). Or, better yet, we can think of the amply discussed cases of "non-decisions" (Bachrach and Baratz 1963), in which the state willingly avoids intervening despite the possibilities for doing so, in order to appease the unexpressed but predictable and potentially forceful demands of social actors, thereby leaving room for other modes of regulation. The development of "black" labor and the "underground economy" could be interpreted in this way (see Paci). We will, however, forgo discussion of this third, more disputable case here and examine instead how a large part of the activities and relations among actors analyzed in this volume are interpretable by the other two.

The first of these is *formal state regulation* under the cover of which other forms of regulation operate. The essays presented here, like other studies of Italian public policy, delineate two distinct groups of examples of this pattern.

One group involves cases of highly rigid legislation, predominantly based on binding and universalistic principles, which nonetheless allows (in fact often necessitates) "circumventions," that is, which leaves space for actors to "get around" the legal provisions through the operation of the market or communitarian ties. Examples include the failure to impose use of the public labor mobility institutions and, more generally, the evasion of the labor market norms established by law through the use of networks of solidarity (see Chapter 5 by Reyneri).

The other group includes instead those legislative or administrative provisions that do no more than accept and "legalize" accords reached among interest groups or norms established among "private governments," thereby lending, so to speak, the authority of the state to agreements reached among private actors. Examples include the so-called "contracted laws" reached between social partners or the ministerial sanctioning of decisions reached by self-governing bodies like the CUN (National University Council) or the National Council for Public Instruction to which public functions have been assigned. One might also include in this group the expansion of public welfare intervention that occurs through the "incorporation of blocs of private actors," which is discussed by Paci (Chapter 9).

The second case is *seemingly non-state regulation* that develops as the willed result of state intervention. Again, two separate subgroups can be identified.

One group includes all those situations in which activities seemingly regulated by the market (for example, the opening or closing of firms or factories), by solidarity relations (e.g., services provided through voluntary action in the so-called "third sector"), or by accords reached between associations (e.g., the agreements to modify the system of wage indexation) are, in reality, at least partially the result of interventions by public agencies that allocate resources under their control in order to facilitate the operation of other regulatory modes. Recall, for an example of the first, the role of financial incentives and transfers offered to firms (see Chapter 4 by Ferrera and Chapter 8 by Chiesi and Martinelli); for the second, the financial support provided by the state to voluntary organizations; and for the third, the compensations at the expense of the state that enable the "social partners" to reach concerted agreements (see Cella [Chapter 7] and Regini [1987a]).

The other group includes, instead, the "space" that is opened for market relations as a result of state intervention which alters the "rules of the game," that is, relations between forms of regulation. One example is the role played by a specific state institution, the Bank of Italy, in extending the role of market mechanisms at the time of the "divorce" of the Bank from the Treasury Ministry (see Epstein and Schor [Chapter 6] and Addis [1987]). Another example is the expansion of market rules – at the expense of public control – governing the hiring of workers which has recently become possible as a result of changes in previously existing legal norms on the criteria for hiring in the rules that allow apprenticeship contracts (see Chapter 5 by Reyneri).

5. The production of public policies: a typology of relationships between interests and institutions

If the different linkages between state and other forms of regulation are to an extent the outcomes of the balance of power between classes or social groups, there is also no question that the intervention by the state is itself somewhat conditioned by these balances of power. Nonetheless, as we already indicated in our discussion of our initial hypotheses and as many studies in this volume demonstrate, social interests influence state regulation in different ways. These differences partially reflect the character of the interest organizations and their relationship to the institutions where public decisions are made.

There are in the literature diverse "images" of policy-making that correspond in part to different analytical perspectives (e.g., the "public policy" approach; the "neo-corporatism" approach) or different disciplinary traditions. To bring some order into this diversity, it is useful to begin with two principal analytical dimensions, each one a continuum, which underlie the possible relationships between social interests and public institutions in the process of producing public policies.

1. The first dimension is the degree of "insulation," that is, the sep- arateness or seclusion of the decisional process from pressure by social interests. In a highly insulated policy-making process, inputs from soci- ety are highly filtered, if not profoundly altered, by the objectives and the culture of the decision-makers. As a result, the outputs do not so much reflect the diversity of social interests and relationships of strength between them as the way their organized representatives redefine them, subordinating them to what is considered the "institu- tional interest" or at least the set of shared values and interests among those who have to decide. A high degree of insulation need not signify that the representatives of social interests do not participate in the deci- sion process – in fact, they often are stable and institutionally sanc- tioned participants – but rather may signify that their action tends to adhere to the "institutional" logic which we have just suggested. Highly secluded decisional sites are particularly propitious for the development of "cooperative games" among the participants as con- trasted to "games of competition," which are distinguished by the effort to maximize the interests of the represented, but the two do not entirely coincide (Regini 1987b). As we will see, in fact, even in situa- tions of low isolation the actors can pursue a "satisficing," rather than "optimizing" (Simon 1947), logic in pursuit of their interests, thereby fostering "distributive collusion."

At the two extremes of the insulation–non-insulation continuum, the interaction between interests and institutions is almost nonexistent. Where insulation is at its maximum, the institutions pursue solely "public" objectives, from whose determination the representation of private interests is excluded. We rarely see this in democratic political systems; it is sometimes found in authoritarian ones. What Salvati (1982) has called "governing by decree," referring to the French case, is probably the closest one comes in modern democracies. On the other hand, minimum insulation suggests the "colonization" of the state by private interests. Or, in a markedly different form, it appears when selected private interests are granted the right directly to produce pub- lic policies. This is the case, often studied in the recent "neo-corpora- tist" literature and the study of some professions, of the "delegation" of public functions to private governments."[9] It should be said, how- ever, that these extremes have few if any empirical referents in Italy and can be set aside in our typology. The types of policy-making that need empirically to be identified and differentiated are those which fall between the extremes.

2. The second dimension is the degree of "comprehensiveness" (versus "segmentation") of the decisional process. Very comprehensive policy-making is characterized by a high degree of interest aggregation

in the inputs to the decision process and, above all, a high degree of interdependence among the outputs, in the sense that the policies are "global and intersectoral" (Regonini 1985) or closely intermeshed.

It is difficult to think of the logical extremes on this dimension and nonetheless provide empirically relevant examples. The most comprehensive policy-making is presumably attained in processes of interventionist planning. But this model is largely outside the Italian experience and the experience of the capitalist countries more generally. By contrast, the maximum of segmentation may be reached in distributive policy-making (see Chapter 2 by Dente and Regonini), which other authors have described as the result of clientalistic or spoils system governance (Amato 1976). There are, of course, also intermediate cases.

On the basis of these two dimensions it is obviously possible to construct a two-by-two matrix. Since we want to propose a typology which, at one and the same time, is simple, is useful for empirical analysis, and makes reference to the existing models in the literature, three (rather than four) types of policy-making are identified. The following typology seems effectively to capture the relationships between social interests and decisional sites for public policies in the advanced industrial democracies.

1. *Pluralistic pressure* is a well-known model in political science. Social interests are represented by a multiplicity of associations placing pressure on relatively permeable public institutions. Although the aggregative capacities of the interests vary considerably, the overall aggregation of inputs into the decision process is low. Outputs are relatively segmented as a result. They represent responses by institutions susceptible to pressures applied to fragmented interests, each of which is seeking to satisfy limited demands without paying much attention to linkages to other policy areas.

In this model, the permeability of the institutions – be they Parliament or parliamentary commissions, the government, or the public bureaucracies – means that, theoretically, each group succeeds in influencing policy in proportion to its strength, that is, as a reflection of the resources which it can bring to bear politically. In the Italian case, the political parties play a crucial role in mediating between the fragmented social demands and the decisional institutions (see Chapter 1 by Pasquino). But, when pluralistic pressure prevails, the parties do not substantially modify the structure of demands or their strength. Rather, they act more as instruments "weighing" the politically relevant resources of the interests and articulating their demands to the (often party-linked) decision-makers.

This is, therefore, a model of the production of public policies in which the structure of the decisional process has little direct impact on how social demands are translated into policy. The multiple social interests undergo a mediational process in which their resources are weighed and evaluated but in which there is little change in how the content of demands reaches decision-makers. In this model, competition among groups is conjunctural rather than structural, is occasional rather than permanent, and is expressed in a plurality of battles over how to divide public resources or condition the exercise of state authority. Furthermore, when it is possible, competition can give way to "distributive collusion" in which the actors succeed in each satisfying their basic demands while externalizing the costs of such collusion onto others.

2. The model of the *policy community* or *policy network* is one that is very common in the public policy literature.[10] Here too the production of public policies is assumed to be highly segmented. As is suggested by the term policy network, the decisional process is confined to a limited arena whose boundaries are defined by what is considered within a particular policy sphere and do not allow for extensions into other arenas. Corresponding to this high degree of segmentation is generally also a low degree of aggregation of interest inputs, but this issue is less important for the definition of this model of policy-making.

In fact – and this represents the fundamental difference with pluralistic policy-making – the decisional process in policy networks is highly insulated from external pressures. As we noted above, it need not be the case that representatives of external interests are excluded from the decisional process or have no influence within it. But these representatives, when they become participants in the network of relationships involved in a particular policy arena, alter their logic of action, as do other participants such as party representatives or public bureaucrats. As "experts" in specific policies, they become bearers of scarce resources that grant them a degree of potential autonomy. They also develop an interest in ensuring that the policies with which they are concerned assume prominence on the political agenda. Finally, they often engage in cooperative games with one another, which can lead to their redefining or abandoning some of their original objectives to bring them closer to those shared with other members of the network. Involvement in the construction and implementation of objectives particular to the network comes to predominate over the responsibility to pursue vigorously the goals and demands of those they ostensibly represent.

In this type of policy-making, therefore, the structure of decision-making sharply affects the likelihood that social demands will be translated directly into policies. Rather than occasional competition between interests and pressure by them on the decisional institutions, a logic of stable collusion prevails in the formulation of highly segmented, and generally distributive (rather than redistributive), policies. When such a logic is broken, the model itself breaks down and other modes of policy-making come to the fore.[11]

3. The final type is that of "oligopolistic bargaining" and is derived in part from the literature on neo-corporatism but need not be strictly limited to systems characterized by neo-corporatist arrangements.

What distinguishes this type of policy-making from the preceding two is, in the first place, that the relevant interests are not fragmented when they become politically relevant. In fact, there are some large, "encompassing" organizations that are capable of "pre-mediating" or aggregating among a multiplicity of interests before they reach the decision-making arena. Much the same occurs as the result of the action of "mass political parties," which continue to be able to aggregate social demands rather than becoming "catch-all" parties (Kirchheimer 1966). When they participate in the decisional process, these associational or party actors can follow a logic that takes into account interdependencies between choices made in one policy area and those made in another. In contrast to fragmented interest groups or sectoral experts, it can be advantageous for them to privilege the congruence of decisions in different areas. This is most likely when such encompassing actors – who are few in number and see the advantage of excluding others – are the only ones with access to the public policy process. Under these conditions one can speak of "oligopolistic bargaining"[12] among actors with privileged access to the state.

A second difference is that the actors follow a logic of interest representation rather than the pursuit of institutional objectives. They need, therefore, to transmit at least in part the demands of their members and/or electorates. Alongside the representative function, however, encompassing associations or mass parties need also perform the function of control or filtering of such demands. This is the case for two reasons. On the one hand, the high degree of interest aggregation requires that intra-organizational decision processes be protected from "excessive" influence by the represented. On the other hand, to successfully retain their oligopoly status and privileged access to state resources, these organizations need to be able to assure their counterparts that those they represent will consent to decisions taken at the peak. The degree of insulation of the decision process from social demands in this type is, therefore, intermediate with respect to the other two types. The need to represent and the need to control are in dynamic tension; and when this tension is not successfully managed, it can lead to instability in the type of decision-making itself.

In public policy-making by oligopolistic bargaining, then, the decisional process partially modifies social demands. The relationships among the actors representing social interests and between these actors and the institutions are permeated by a mixture of competition (or conflict) and cooperation.

It is important to repeat that the typology we have developed seeks to capture the relationship between the ways social interests are articulated and expressed concerning specific policies, and the state institutions or decisional sites that have responsibility for those policies. In other words, it is concerned with the *structure of interactions* between interests and institutions that produce policies. Thus, it says nothing about which actors might dominate one or the other type of policy-making, or about the role that different public institutions may have in the production of policies. Since other essays in this volume refer to these issues, however, a short discussion seems in order to prevent confusion.

First, the institutions that are entitled to decide in certain policy areas and with which relevant social interests will establish relationships – be they of pluralistic pressure, intra-network cooperation, or concerted bargaining – can obviously vary. The type of institution, that is, the decisional site, will largely determine the degree of permeability to external interests. It is generally the case that Parliament and parliamentary commissions – and sometimes, notably in Italy, also the public administration – are more permeable than the executive or restricted ministerial committees. This implies that the degree of insulation of policy-making in different policy areas will vary along with the public institutions with which, in different countries or at different times, the relevant interests need to interact to pursue policy goals.

Second, for each of the three types of policy-making we have sketched, actors other than those we have discussed may play a role. In particular, the leaderships of political parties and/or technical bureaucrats may become important. Theoretically, each of these may succeed in dominating the decisional process, if by dominance we mean control of the agenda and the availability of the resources necessary to secure the outcome. Our typology does not aim at predicting the influence likely to be exercised by different actors, although in some cases it implies that certain actors may be unable to become predominant because of the structure of the relationship between actors and institutions in that particular policy arena.[13] The latter observation, further, suggests that it is also improbable that one actor will become predominant across a wide range of public policies handled in different types of institutional structures unless one structural type is pervasive throughout the political system.[14]

We will leave a full discussion of the Italian case to the Conclusions. It is, nonetheless, useful here to indicate how the typology presented enables us to capture the policy-making process in Italy. For years, the Italian system has been described as being highly conflictual and ideologically polarized (Sartori 1966) but characterized by distributive practices that cement the dominant social bloc, while partially compensating those excluded from direct decisional authority (Amato 1976). The type of public policy production best characterizing such a political system would seem to be that of pluralistic pressure. This is, in fact, the type often used by different authors – with different labels – to describe the system. And it is the case that in Italy interests appear to be relatively fragmented and public institutions highly permeable. Even the widespread role of parties would not seem in conflict with this image, for as we have noted, they can both be the principal agent of social mediation and fundamentally condition how the public institutions function. Even with their mediation, if the parties are not highly aggregative, fragmented social demands would have a good chance of being translated fairly directly into the policy-making process; and that process would itself reflect the balance of power among interests without significant filtering by the decision-making institutions.

From the studies collected here, this image would seem relatively appropriate for some policy areas, for example, industrial policy (Ferrera, Chapter 4; see also Maraffi [1987] on local policies), but not for others. First of all, in the last ten years there have been significant attempts to establish a model of oligopolistic bargaining alongside that of pluralistic pressure in various policy areas (from incomes policies, to industrial and labor policies, to pension policy). The history of these efforts – which took on particular prominence from 1977 to 1984 – has been recounted by many (including the editors of this volume), with often divergent interpretations. In synthesis one can, however, say that this model was never fully put in place. The organized interests were not sufficiently strong to impose it, either on the other organized actors or on those they represented; and/or the state never was able adequately to provide the guarantees and compensations necessary for such oligopolistic bargaining to succeed (Lange 1984; Regini 1987a). Oligopolistic bargaining, however, is certainly not dead; it is likely to be proposed again when deemed by some actors to serve their interests.

Second, in several policy areas the policy network model seems at times to have predominated (see, for instance, several chapters in this volume and Regonini [1985] and Addis [1987]; see also Regalia [1987b] and Regonini [1987] for studies at the local level). As we have already indicated, this does not imply that the parties have not continued to play a central policy role, even in these cases. But the logic of action of their representatives has tended more toward relatively stable, distributive cooperation with the other public and private actors than toward competition based on political allegiance, affirmation of ideological differences, and reinforcement of narrow partisan interests.

This seems in contrast with the conflictual and polarized vision of Italian politics. But one can suggest that the two images are, in fact, tightly linked to each other. A theoretically highly conflictual and polarized system, with the characteristics of the Italian one, would risk stalemate or incessant crisis and uncertainty even if the production of individual public policies followed a logic of partisan competition and redistribution. Instead, as we have suggested and the following chapters document, the party representatives in different policy areas often follow a different logic, based on segmentation and separation of issues and characterized within issue areas by distributive cooperation. This could, perhaps, be the result of "goal displacement" (Selznick 1957) by one or more of the organizations. Or instead, it may be the expression of the fact that in many policy areas, the partisan representative does not have a precise ordering of preferences and therefore finds it more "rational" to privilege his membership in the policy network in which he is an "expert" and based on which he can influence the positions of the party or organization to which he belongs. This is all the more the case since the party may often be ill-equipped to evaluate the actions taken by their representatives in specific policy arenas (see Dente and Regonini, Chapter 2).

Finally, it may also be the result of the strategies of the parties and encompassing organizations (themselves often with close partisan linkages). While they rhetorically stress competition and confrontation, in the practice of policy-making they consent to and encourage cooperative games. They thereby avoid decisional stalemate or polarization and crisis and gain some resources, at least until such behavior creates costs greater than those which would result from a more confrontational approach. Thus, *il caso italiano* provides a complex and often seemingly contradictory image, not only of the mixes and linkages between modes of state and social regulation but also of the ways private interests succeed in conditioning public policies – and therefore of how regulation occurs in Italy. The essays that follow assist us in developing a more up-to-date, informed, and rich analytical understanding of the Italian regulatory and policy processes. This is indispensable for insight into contemporary Italian affairs and into how Italy "holds together." It can also enrich and enliven our understanding of regulation, how it is achieved, when it succeeds and fails, and how and why it changes in other national settings.

Notes

1 An ancient question but one that has been repeatedly raised in recent years with respect to the Italian case.

2 More particularly, the essays in this volume are concerned with the forms of regulation of: (1) activities that influence the production and distribution of resources via the manipulation of macro-economic aggregates (Chapter 6); (2) relations between capital and labor and within the organizations that represent them (Chapters 3, 7, and 8); (3) activities related to the distribution of welfare benefits (Chapters 9 and 10); and (4) activities connected to the regulation, promotion, management, etc., of the processes for the production of goods (Chapters 4 and 5).

3 Regulation in this sense can be thought of as establishing or reinforcing "institutions," understood in their broad sense as relatively stable patterns of interaction. Naturally, any type of allocation of economic goods is open to challenge; what makes regulation more or less "successful" is the degree to which those who are or could be in disagreement do not openly challenge the existing order or do so only via "legitimate" means and thus do not behave in ways sharply at variance with the expectations of others with whom they interact and are interdependent.

4 Naturally, we make exception here for the general constraints which derive from the fact that we are examining democratic, capitalist economies open to the international economy.

5 Polanyi (1944) speaks of exchange, redistribution, and reciprocity as forms of social integration. Poggi (1978) discusses three modes of structuring the process of social allocation: command, exchange, and custom. Crouch (1978) refers to the three forms of social cohesion based respectively on command, system of exchange, and normative control. The discussion of Lindblom (1977) places its emphasis on politics and markets but includes as well systems based on "persuasion." This concept differs from that of custom, norms, etc., but it also reflects the existence of a category of modes of regulation that is neither authority nor exchange and that suggests an element of normative control. The same need is captured in the concept of "clan" as an institution of regulation in the economy, which Ouchi (1977) proposes for consideration alongside those of market and bureaucracy.

6 Sometimes market and community institutions are treated as a single form of social regulation contrasted to the state, as is the case in the well-known distinction between state and civil society so widespread in nineteenth-century social thought and central as well in Gramscian theory.

7 The same observation pertains to other recent attempts to expand the traditional typology of modes of regulation such as those of Crouch (1981b), who adds a fourth type based on organization, and of Hollingsworth and Lindberg (1985), who propose the following typology: markets, hierarchical organizations (which include not only the state

but also firms), clans, and associations. In both cases, the identification of institutions whose importance for regulation has grown leads to an increase in the complexity of the traditional typology, while in fact what is being observed is the incorporation of the same principles in institutional mixes that either are new or were not previously observed.

8 As will be immediately evident, our scheme is based on observation of the institutions that are most important for regulation but also takes into account that the principles of regulation considered characteristic of those institutions may predominate but are not exclusive.

9 See Streeck and Schmitter (1985). Such a delegation is granted, however, only to those organized interests that have adequate resources. Thus, the minimum of insulation from these interests implies the maximum of insulation with regard to other interests, that is, the total exclusion of the latter.

10 See Richardson (1982) for a discussion of the concept of "policy community" and Heclo (1978) for an examination of the concept of "issue" or "policy network." We are indebted to Gloria Regonini for drawing our attention to some of the detailed similarities and differences between the two concepts.

11 See Regonini (1985). From some points of view, the two outcomes that she considers likely results of a crisis of the policy network – towards a more "redistributive and conflictual" policy-making or a more "global and intersectoral" one – have features similar to the pluralistic pressure and oligopolistic contracting types we are discussing here.

12 This term should not deceive. It has heretofore been used synonymously with "concertation" among large interest organizations and government (Regini 1985). Here, however, it also includes policy-making that is dominated by large, integrative mass parties, as discussed above. One should note that oligopolistic bargaining generally involves an externalization of the costs of reaching an agreement onto actors excluded from the process. This can become a source of instability for this style of public policy-making if the excluded groups succeed in organizing and placing pressure on the decision process itself.

13 For example, it seems unlikely that bureaucrats or fragmented interests can become predominant in oligopolistic bargaining, or that large encompassing organizations can come to dominate pluralistic pressure processes.

14 Certain widely used concepts seem to suggest the opposite. "Party government," the "colonization of the state by private interests," "iron triangles," or stable alliances between a few encompassing interests sometimes are presented as characteristic of the entire public policy-making process or of its "normal" functioning. The essay by Pasquino (Chapter 1), which suggests that "party government" is the most appropriate image for the Italian political system, moves in this direction. Upon close examination, however, while this essay demonstrates the omnipresence of parties in all phases of the production of Italian public policies, it does not necessarily show the constant predominance of a logic of "partisan politics," that is, of the imposition of preferences defined by the competitive interests of the parties.

Part I

Models of regulation

1

Unregulated regulators: parties and party government

GIANFRANCO PASQUINO

No decision-making process or arena is ever monopolized by a single actor. This is especially true in competitive democracies, whatever their degree of internal competitiveness. Nonetheless, in competitive democracies, for various reasons, political parties occupy a political space and play a political role generally considered more important than those of any other actor. Moreover, various factors contribute to considerable differences between democratic regimes, including the strength of the representative institutions and of the government, the vivacity and organization of civil society, and, above all, the role of the state (and thus of political or party power). Other factors that operate in a significant manner are the stability of the dominant party or coalition, its willingness to use available instruments for maintaining power, and, finally, the sociopolitical demand for state regulation. The "boundaries of the political" can naturally change from country to country, or even from governing coalition to governing coalition (as the neo-conservative experiments have sought to demonstrate). But until now, with few exceptions, the tendency has been towards an expansion of the role of politics.

It could be that the expansion of politics has not coincided with the expansion of the power of one alone among the several political actors, that is, the parties. In fact, there are a number of authors who hold that political parties have lost their preeminence in decision-making processes (if ever they fully enjoyed it), that their political centrality is inevitably declining (Berger 1979), and that this is a positive development. Moreover, these authors argue that sociopolitical trends suggest that in the future parties will occupy less space and will play a more limited role. They even pose the question: do parties matter?

Whoever studies the Italian case, however, knows that he or she cannot ask such a question. This does not mean, however, that one can immediately assume that Italian parties are dominant to the same

29

degree in all decision-making processes and arenas. After all, in spite of their current weakness, we should not forget the attempt by the Italian unions to produce political reforms, or their later efforts, never fully successful, to implement concertation (and perhaps to create the structures appropriate to it).

However, it appears difficult to argue that the neo-corporatist experiments have marginalized parties in Italy. It is also not true that interpretive models based on "iron triangles" of interest groups, bureaucratic sectors, and parliamentary commissions, which bypass party mediation and reduce it significantly (Jordan 1981), can be applied in a satisfactory and heuristically positive way to the Italian case. It is not that party mediation has been able to act without challenges or inconveniences. But it still appears to condition and, in many cases, determine not only the results of decision-making processes but also how parties present themselves and develop.

Therefore, if we can hold that the forms of regulation of social conflict and political behavior in Italy conform neither to the models of oligopolistic bargaining nor to that of pluralistic pressure, then there are two remaining possibilities: the so-called policy networks or policy communities model and the party government model. It appears immediately that these two models are mutually exclusive. This does not mean that in all political processes and arenas regulation of social and political behavior must adhere perfectly to only one of these models. But it does imply that only one is capable of "explaining" the most important decision-making processes in a satisfactory manner, or at least better than the other.

The utility and applicability (perhaps even the explanatory superiority) of the policy networks model is advanced by Bruno Dente and Gloria Regonini (see Chapter 2, this volume). These networks of interaction among operators, experts, and possessors of strategic resources – who are all in some way capable of avoiding party control, of operating without, through, or against parties (Heclo 1978) – appear to characterize certain decision-making processes in Italy. This is particularly true of decision-making processes with greater "technical" content, or those which involve large numbers of people with knowledge and resources that are difficult for parties to acquire (e.g., health services). The proponents of this model will personally elaborate the characteristics of their model in their contribution. Here, I would like to emphasize that a convincing argument would need to identify several different areas (e.g., health and information, public agencies, and autonomous entities) and would need to demonstrate the superiority of the experts and actors, apart from their party affiliations, in the production of relevant decisions in the regulation of a range of behaviors. This thesis would be even more persuasive if one could demonstrate

that the logic of the actors in policy networks is completely unconstrained by the logic of the individual parties, of the dominant party
coalition, or of the party system.

In this chapter, instead, a completely different – in fact, the opposite
– thesis will be proposed. This thesis gives parties and the Italian party
system a more ample, diversified, and capillary control over resources
and decision-making processes. Notwithstanding the challenges and
the cracks, *partitocrazia* still holds. In order to understand why and
how this is true, to know which developments influence it and can control it, we must seek to understand the nature and identify the forms
of political regulation of socioeconomic activity in Italy.

This problem is naturally of greater importance in the Italian case. In
fact, whether or not one adheres to the thesis that the Italian case is a
significant example of *partitocrazia* or party government, there is no
doubt that common opinion assigns Italian parties a central and determining role in decision-making processes. It could be that in a hypothetical continuum that ranges from a maximum of party control (an
exemplary party government) to a minimum, the Italian case is not
exactly at the party government pole. Surely, it cannot be characterized
as a cabinet government. Nonetheless, since the various attempts to
assign it to categories of neo-corporatism have proved unconvincing
and the elaborations that might produce an Italian version of policy
networks appear embryonic, it is worth attempting to place the Italian
case within the party government model.

Towards this end it is necessary to define precisely party government. A minimal definition implies the existence of at least three conditions: (1) all the most important government decisions must be made
by people chosen in elections conducted according to party distinctions
or by people nominated by and responsible to people elected in this
way; (2) policies must be decided within the governing party or after
negotiations among the parties of the governing coalition; and (3) the
most important actors (ministers or prime ministers) must be chosen
within their own parties and must be responsible to the electorate
through their parties (Katz 1986:43). These conditions constitute party
government.

However, a high "partyness" of government does not necessarily
imply an equally high willingness or capacity to control or to regulate
the socioeconomic arenas. Still borrowing from Katz, this regulatory
capacity, defined as "party governmentness," indicates "the proportion of all the social power exercised by the parties, within the framework of the party government model" (Katz 1986:46).

The party government model is thus attentive to both formal features
(authoritative responsibilities in the political system) and substantive
aspects (the effects of these responsibilities on the decision-making

process). Because of this, it is possible to specify the components, to place them in specific arenas, and to evaluate their consequences. Naturally, all specifications and distinctions tend to analytically separate processes that empirically must be kept together. Thus, such an analytical exercise is of purely heuristic value – even while it simultaneously casts doubts on alternative or competing explanations. If we assume that decision-making processes and sociopolitical regulation can be reduced to a simple input-output-outcome-feedback cycle, the relevant questions concern the role of the individual parties and the party system in this trajectory. Let us examine it point by point, passage by passage.

1. Input: interest groups and parties

The classic political science literature on Italy, expressed at its best by Joseph LaPalombara's *Interest Groups in Italian Politics*, is clear on the matter. Not only is the process of interest articulation dominated by the parties but, also, wherever groups exercise some sort of influence in decision-making, they do so only as clients and/or patrons of political parties (especially governing parties). It has never been doubted that Italy is a textbook case of the limited autonomy of subsystems on the input side. In fact, the classic analysis of parties (the work of the Cattaneo Institute) makes this a cardinal point (Manoukian 1968).

This is not the place to analyze in detail this literature. However, no revisionist interpretation has been advanced in recent years, and one cannot help but wonder about the continuing value of interpretations advanced twenty years ago. In other words, it is legitimate to ask whether or not the explosion of 1968, socioeconomic development, the subsequent crisis, social fragmentation and diversification, and the diffusion of complexity have broken the relations between interest groups and parties and have opened the path towards an autonomous articulation of interests, unconstrained by party regulation. This question is obviously legitimate and timely. Unfortunately, research on this point is scarce (Lange 1977a).

A fertile reformulation of this problem must take into consideration two elements: (1) the possibility that interest groups exist which are capable of autonomously articulating interests, requests, and preferences in a manner not constrained by parties, i.e, neither as clients nor patrons; and (2) the ability of these types of groups to place their interests, requests, and preferences directly on the decision-making agenda, somehow overcoming party mediation (as the quasi-theory of neo-corporatism sustains), or their ability to obtain satisfaction outside of the traditional channels of party government (that is, outside of Parliament). The first case challenges the consolidated hypothesis of Italian parties as colonizers of society. The second questions the thesis that attributes to parties the role of gatekeepers, of filters of the decision-making process. It could naturally be that parties have had a weakening grip over society, but at the same time have shifted, perhaps precisely because of this, their regulatory capacity to the threshold of the decision-making processes.

Perhaps it would be too easy to evade the problem by placing the burden of proof on those who focus instead on the emergence of increased vivacity in Italian society and on the weakening of the regulatory capacity of the parties and the party system. Not that these aspects should not be explored, documented, and measured. But at the present moment, we lack even the most elementary indicators. In truth, certain macroprocesses have appeared, but their real impact on political input remains to be evaluated. In particular, it appears that organizational vivacity expressed itself less through its impact on the articulation of interests than through a multiplication, fragmentation, and even corporatization of groups.

If, instead, the essence of an eventual new input process that bypasses party mediation is expected to manifest itself above all in groups' efforts to avoid identification with the parties so as to enhance their own autonomous, potential influence and in the creation of new groups that manage to avoid such identification, then the evidence for these developments is scarce and not very convincing. It is not that intolerance for party mediation in the input phase is not widespread. Quite the contrary. For example, while the phenomenon is certainly more complex, the emergence of collective movements indicated and was a product of this intolerance. At the level of inputs, the collective movements aimed at and partially succeeded in bypassing party mediation by advancing their demands directly at the centers of decision-making. But, as we will see, at the level of outputs (and especially of outcomes), the institutions and parties regained control and the upper hand (Ergas 1985).[1]

Finally, since much has already been written on the subject (Regini 1981; Carrieri and Donolo 1986), we must touch briefly upon the issue of triangular bargaining – government/business/unions – not just as a form of input but also as a form of influence on the decision-making process in its wider sense. Although the argument is controversial, the emergence of such negotiations does not suggest in any way that party mediation is without influence. Actually, both when they succeed and when they fail, these triangular negotiations reveal that political parties, both in government and in opposition, play a significant role. Naturally, the situation could be more complex, sometimes requiring specific institutional resources and structures, or the assistance of experts. However, the decisive point is the continuing capacity of parties and their representatives to maintain control over the articulation and mediation of these interests, preferences, and demands.

2. Decision-making arenas and roles

If the above-mentioned definition by Richard Katz is adequate, it is partly because it points to the need to evaluate the weight of parties in the overall political structure. On the other hand, if *partitocrazia* has a meaning in Italy, it is to direct attention to the abnormal phenomenon of the excessive and suffocating presence of parties both at the level of interest articulation (hence within civil society) and in the decision-making (where parties expropriate state institutions).

To the extent that both operations are possible and verifiable, it appears necessary to stress the presence of party organizations and personnel embedded in society and in government institutions. The presence of parties in Italian society in all decision-making centers is enhanced by the expansion of the public sector, the existence of municipalized firms, and the vast number of politically appointed positions (from banks to tourist and exhibition agencies). While never accurately assessed, this constitutes a fact that creates a social stratum dependent on politics (and on the parties) and produces expectations and behaviors conforming to the desires of the parties. From this point of view, one can affirm with certainty that the position of Italian parties in the *Herrschaftsorganisation* (structure of power) of the political system is strong, consolidated (notwithstanding recurrent criticisms), and, above all, capable of reproducing itself.

As far as the institutions are concerned, at the cost of an overly elementary explanation, it is important to remember two facts: (1) recruitment for administrative and political positions is essentially monopolized by the parties; and (2) in formal decision-making centers, the presence of party-related personnel is not only dominant but often absolute. Of course, we know (Putnam 1976) that the positional method may induce error, that formal positions of power do not necessarily correspond to decision-making influence. To assuage these doubts, we need only advance a few precise observations.

It is inevitable that in a parliamentary system the fundamental decision-making center is Parliament or, rather, the totality of relations between the executive and the legislature. In Italy, both the executive and the legislature are composed of parties. But what counts most is that, with rare exceptions, the political class has passed through the long trajectory of administrative and party (party administration) experiences. In the recent, but rare, cases of ministerial recruitment from outside the political-parliamentary class, one cannot sustain that they represent external groups and signal the creation of a policy network. Their resource was their expertise – a rare resource for a political class formed through party experiences.

Nor is the situation very different for parliamentarians. Notwithstanding the proportional electoral system and preference votes in relatively wide districts (which favors strong and well-financed external groups), the percentage of parliamentarians who may be considered indebted to powerful external sponsors is extremely limited. Not even the shift in electoral campaigns from traditional town rallies to television debates and advertisements (with a consequent increase in costs) has produced, for individual parliamentarians, a generalized need for specific support from particular external groups. If anything, individual parliamentarians and various parties have sought to diversify their electoral support. Even in this case, parties act as filters, as gatekeepers of the old and new demands. A process of redefinition of social and economic alliances is in progress, but the role of the parties (and their parliamentarians) as filters and aggregators of demands does not appear to have diminished.

Even where parties do not directly influence political-parliamentary recruitment, they can nonetheless affect decisional processes through other paths. It is not an exaggeration to maintain that formal decision-making processes in Italy occur through triangular bargaining between party secretariats (or party political offices or departments devoted to specific issues), the executive, and the legislature, both in the Chamber and in parliamentary commissions. If this is so, as numerous studies have demonstrated (Di Palma 1977), then the next step is to show that a good part of the decisions produced in Italy occur through laws (hence, the strong demands for de-legalization and deregulation).

From what can be documented, the influence of external groups within decision-making processes both within commissions and in the Chamber is, with extremely rare exceptions, still mediated by the parties. This means that specific legislative acts, particular laws, and even simple amendments are rarely the outcome of the strength of a particular external group or actor that obtains the support of a parliamentarian or a group of parliamentarians. Even in such cases, with the possible exception of a group of parliamentarians belonging to the governing majority, these acts have little chance of being approved. Rather, legislative acts are the product of the interaction between external groups or actors and the parties. It remains *the parties* that decide what is to be transmitted to their own parliamentary groups. Any other interpretation[2] is a reductive simplification of a process with many phases and with many actors (but with the parties always in a dominant position).

The structure of political power in Italy is not concentrated or exhausted at the executive-parliamentary level. Actually, if one wants to proceed towards an identification and evaluation of the role of external pressure groups, then an important place must be given to associations of local institutions: the Association of Italian Towns, the Union of Italian Provinces. Precisely because of the extraction of the Italian political-parliamentary class, these associations are powerful pressure groups when state resources are distributed to local institutions and when legislative choices touch the structures, functions, and prerogatives of these same institutions. The parliamentary representatives of these associations are essentially people with previous, often long-standing administrative experiences; or even local administrators still active in their jobs, thanks to an accumulation of positions (still largely allowed, even if less so than in France). The truth is that a sort of transversal superparty (prevalently composed of exponents of the three major parties) develops. The emphasis, however, must be placed on "party" since this is the characteristic which aggregates interests and needs, preferences and demands.

As for local administrators, it is in part correct to emphasize the existence of recruitment channels different from those of the parties (Barberis 1973), as well as a greater turnover among them than that which takes place at the national level. Nonetheless, among exponents of local politics, only those who sooner or later acquire a precise party affiliation and position "get ahead." The most successful are those, even from the ranks of the opposition, who use their party affiliation to obtain resources (Tarrow 1977a) and, to give due recognition to the not infrequent degenerative phenomena, those who know how to place the party in an indispensable position in relation to business. (The next step in this degenerative process consists of personal gain but, significantly, always defined in party terms and through party connivance.) Finally, we must evaluate the real impact of choices by local administrators, in quantitative and qualitative terms, since it could be that many of the most important choices escape them and are "decided" elsewhere (but where?) and later ratified. The available evidence does not appear to support the thesis of irrelevance (Martinotti 1985) and thus gives parties, even local ones, a central role in social regulation.

Certainly, it is all but impossible to avoid the realization that Italian decision-making arenas are essentially formal-elective, and that within these arenas party-related personnel occupy a dominant and sometimes exclusive position. Such personnel play perhaps a variable role, but one that cannot be limited to a simple ratification of choices made, elsewhere or outside. Also, in such cases, the "elsewhere" and the "outside" could be centers where party personnel control the articulation of interests, the representation of preferences, and their transmission to decision-making centers.

3. Decision-making processes and outputs

For a long time, political science was concerned essentially with the conditions and the processes of inputs and of representation. Over the last ten years, we have seen a shift in attention, perhaps to excess, towards the area of decisions and outputs. In the Italian context, this shift, which is politically highly controversial, has only partially occurred. Nevertheless, there appears to be, even if overdramatized, greater attention to decision-making processes and to the choices that result. The dramatization derives more than anything else from the dire consequences (hence the outcomes) of poorly designed reforms: from the National Health System to rent control, to the recent pardon for abusive and illegal construction. But, viewed correctly, the problem must be sought in the modalities through which certain decisions were reached.

The perspective taken here consists in evaluating the specific role of parties in decision-making processes, in particular those concerning social and public policies (Regonini 1985). The point of departure must be the debate over the restructuring of the welfare state. The political and scientific significance of the debate and of the consequent reform acts (and in rare cases, real decisions and outputs) is not diminished by highlighting how this debate and its choices were essentially the result of a conflict among the parties (of the governing majority), between government and opposition, and between central political class and peripheral political class. Other social and institutional actors were involved only to a small degree (for the most part to defend corporate interests). Nor could it be otherwise. In fact, if I accurately understand the essence of the European (Castles 1982) and Italian (Ferrera 1984) literature on the subject, political parties and party coalitions played a central role in all these decision-making processes.

On the other hand, even where, as in the United States, one can identify complex and differentiated coalitions among policy-makers, policy-takers, and party factions, the decisions over programs (except for their perpetuation) are in the hands of the parties. In the Italian case, coalitions of this sort, while theoretically plausible, are in practice more difficult to construct, given the greater inflexibility of the administrative bureaucracies and the higher degree of conflict among the government parties. (Paradoxically, these coalitions are more likely at the local level where the Left has governed longer; but in these cases one should not exclude also the neo-corporatist decision-making model.)

Perhaps the most concrete and most convincing evidence for party control of decision-making processes and outputs can be found in its negation, that is, on the one hand, by analyzing those demands rejected by the parties, and on the other, by evaluating the resources used to contain, limit, and censor social demands. This is the essence of the history of relations between movements and institutions in Italy, with attention given within the institutions to the dominant (and often exclusive, monopolistic) presence of the parties.

As regards the first point, not even the most benevolent observer of the social movements in Italy (Melucci 1982) has ever nourished the illusion that these movements could truly force decision-making processes outside of arenas controlled by the parties. If anything, the problem for movements consisted of creating collective identities capable of producing completely renewed decision-making processes. Certainly, the social movements have exposed the incapacity of parties to articulate new interests and new demands, and they have revealed the crystallization of the entire Italian party system. But, in the meantime, the parties had already shifted the center of the movements' actions within the institutions, and from this trench they could control the processes and distribute the resources necessary for the maintenance of the minimal consensus necessary.

One cannot share, moreover, the conclusion of Ergas (1985:252):

> If the institutions thus become the medium of relations promoted by the parties, the ever more evident differentiation in some of these between "the party of administrators" and "the party-movement" reveals that the relations managed by the former acquire a proper autonomy. . . . Social policy becomes, therefore, the concrete vehicle of integration of subjects mobilized outside the institutional framework and, in the course of interactive processes, the rapport between state compartments and the protagonists of conflict is organized along modalities which do not appear reducible to *rapports* which bind political parties as specific organized forces to the emergent social interests.

It is precisely the movements and their demands that constitute the true test of party government from the perspective of decision-making processes and outputs. In fact, movements, with their anti-institutional character, constitute the strongest challenge to the dominant party feature in Italy and to the decision-making procedures based on the pre-eminence of legislative assemblies. And so, not only are the most important choices – those which absorb movement demands – in large part mediated and redefined by parties, but even more importantly, when political-parliamentary choices are questioned and brought before the electorate, the preeminence of the parties clearly emerges. From divorce to abortion, from the public financing of parties to the decree over the *scala mobile* (system of wage indexation), all referenda intended to overturn legislation have been turned down by the electorate. It would surely be too much to argue that there is absolute concordance between the views of the Italian electorate and "their" parties. But it is not at all risky to say that, in different ways and to different degrees, Italian parties maintain a secure hold over their electorates.

Naturally, one could reach a different conclusion, maintaining that the defense by parties and the party system was particularly tough towards the movements since their demands were not negotiable. On the contrary, parties are much more compliant and conciliatory when the demands of various groups entail bread and butter, material interests, which can be handled through classic mediation. This is precisely the crisis of the parties (Pasquino 1980): their incapacity to redefine the salient features of a system in deep and extensive representational and decision-making crisis; their weakness and penetrability by traditional economic interests.

We need not refer to the more or less refined analyses of the fiscal crisis of the state (O'Connor 1973) to comprehend the second point mentioned above: the distribution of resources is aimed not at accumulation but at legitimation. In Italy, the legitimation crisis and attempts at responses-solutions are tightly linked with the role of the party-state of the Christian Democrats (DC) and with the peculiar characteristics of mass clientalism. Currently, and without negating the specificity of the clientalistic link between the DC and the state, attention has shifted to seeking to understand the links between decision-making processes and the party and administrative configurations at the various levels of the system (above all local). From this perspective, parties appear as the central component of shifting equilibria between the requirements of accumulation and the needs of legitimation.[3]

None of these observations can negate the diversity of contributions in central and peripheral decision-making processes made by other actors. Each one suggests, however, that parties consciously maintain a crucial role in decision-making processes, in particular with reference to the most important challenge, that of movements. And the parties succeed at maintaining their role, with only limited difficulty, even in cases of direct challenge (abrogative referenda) or when their initial mediation has failed. The only plausible explanation, given this evi-

dence, is that of a real hold over society by parties, based both on consensus and on the extensive takeover of government institutions by a
class of political-party personnel.[4]

Of course, it could be that in doing so the parties lose touch with a
changing (and perhaps maturing) society, which becomes increasingly
demanding (and perhaps better). But only in the worst of cases do representation–decision-making crises develop. Alternative forms of representation and decision-making do not appear; solutions which
exclude or emarginate parties do not emerge.[5] To understand more, it
is necessary to shed light on the results, on the outputs of the decision-
making processes.

4. Results (outcomes)

"An output is the stone thrown in the lake and its first splash; the outcomes are the modulations of the concentric circles which increasingly
amplify and disappear" (Easton 1965:352). But in evaluating the role
of parties as agents of social regulation, is it truly necessary to push
towards the outcomes, the results? The answer is clearly affirmative, at
least for those who hold that parties (and their decisions) occupy a central place in the structure of power of the political system (in the *Herrschaftsorganisation*), in contrast to those who hold that parties are partially (or totally) irrelevant.

More specifically, in the Italian case, a respectable view shifts the
focus of analysis to the bureaucracy, the public administration in its
various branches and at various levels, not in order to arrive at a
bureaucratic decision-making model but to reformulate the role of the
parties (this is the position of Cassese [1980]). At the same time, such
a position opportunely shifts attention to implementation and the consequences of policies, not to parliamentary battles and political games.
For as much as both analytical corrections are useful and important,
they run the risk of proving a plausible but debatable thesis with inadequate facts.

In fact, it is one thing to argue that parties are not central to true and
proper decision-making processes, and, hence, to illustrate how inputs
arise from different sources and are capable of "penetrating" the parties, as well as how outputs derive from the strength of groups within
and outside the parties, to which the parties are constrained to submit.
It is entirely different to hold that, in the process of implementing political choices, the bureaucracy in the wider sense of the term enjoys
ample, and at times sweeping, discretion. This second thesis could
even be correct in describing the Italian case, at least in part. Its cor-

rectness, however, does not invalidate the central role of parties in decision-making. Rather, its validity must undergo empirical tests.

In fact, whoever sustains the central role of the bureaucracy and of bureaucrats in the Italian decision-making process could be saying several different things. In the first place, it could mean that Italian bureaucrats are capable of formulating an agenda that party politicians must later in some way use in their decisions. This point is debatable, even if in certain cases (e.g., schools) it is possible that bureaucrats play exactly this role. But then we pass to the second feature. If bureaucrats do set the agenda, do they do it against the interests of party people or because ministers, undersecretaries, or even entire parties have delegated this task to them? In the case of school legislation, it is well known that the Christian Democrats have exercised a substantial monopoly over the Ministry of Public Education. Thus, in the best of cases, for the proponents of the thesis of the prevalence of bureaucrats (or of policy networks), one can speak of substantial agreement of opinions, not of symbiosis. (If we take into account the organizational strength of Catholic teacher associations within schools, we can move towards a policy network; but does the cohesive glue of these groups derive from expertise and common interests, or rather from their relationship with a strong political party and the decision-making influence derived from this privileged rapport?)

Sticking to the question of the superior or sovereign role of the bureaucracy, one can hold that it is the decision itself that becomes "defined" by the bureaucrats. This could be partially true, at least for that which pertains to the specific interests of bureaucrats (a job, work rhythms, career, or salary – even if on all these questions it is the entire public sector that is brought under discussion). But, even if this were the case, the problem would be redefined in favor of essentially corporatist decisions, while here we are interested in more important decisions. On these, notwithstanding its weakness, Parliament always intervenes (and the government does in many cases as well). Neither one nor the other is simply "executive committees of the bureaucracy," to paraphrase Marx. In fact, parties know perfectly well what game to play and how to behave accordingly (which means that they seek as best they can to combine partisan interests with systemic interests, even if the former almost always prevail). Even supposing that a policy network does exist and manifests itself, the contribution of parties remains decisive in its affirmation.

Finally, whoever assigns major (and decisive) influence to the Italian bureaucracy in decision-making processes, at the expense of the parties (and the government), forgets certain peculiarities of the Italian case.

The first peculiarity is that the Italian bureaucracy consists essentially of party recruits, nominees, and careers. This means that, notwithstanding the system of formal public competitions, it is the parties (or their political extensions) who select bureaucrats even at the lowest levels and, naturally, much more so as one climbs up the career ladder. The spoils system (American style) is a more transparent system (and perhaps offers more guarantees for the parties) of political recruitment and loyalty, but the Italian variations are no less effective in obtaining the same goals.

A second, extremely important peculiarity of the Italian case is the enormous stability (almost immobility) of Italian government personnel. That the ministers change but the bureaucrats remain is a fact that can be found in political systems characterized by alternating coalitions. In the Italian case, the bureaucrats remain but so do the ministers in a high number of cases and often with greater tenure for the most important ministries. Even when the same ministers do not remain, other ministers of the same party (or, in the worst of cases, of the coalition of dominant interests that has governed Italy since 1947) enter to replace them. Therefore, bureaucrats cannot count on greater job tenure or, except in rare cases, on the recognition of greater quality to predominate in the decision-making process against or outside the will of the parties, nor can they even try to construct any type of policy network by themselves. Only in this perspective does the essence of the criticisms against the Italian bureaucracy become understandable.

In fact, the classic criticism against the Italian bureaucracy consists not so much in its being "politicized," but in its being "particized," that is, penetrated by the parties (obviously more by those of the government than by those of the opposition, except for the role of the unions in public employment) (Aberbach et al. 1981). Furthermore, the implementation process can be distorted by bureaucrats partially in the defense of organizational interests, partially according to the desires of their affiliated parties. That these factors count is even more true for a corps of bureaucrats with a low level of technical capacity and, hence, a high degree of political dependence.

Moreover, if the outcomes of a political choice are truly those concentric circles described by Easton (1965), it is right to doubt the technical capacity of the bureaucracy to foresee them, evaluate them, and influence them. On the other hand, it is also well known that not even legislative assemblies in Italy possess adequate instruments to rapidly and effectively evaluate laws and their impact. The instances of "reform of reforms" have recently (from the health system to local government) been so frequent that one wonders whether they are not so much examples of policy evaluation capacity as of blind experiments and reactions repeated time after time because of their repeatedly poor initial formulation.

As a result of the inadequacy of the bureaucracy and the shortcomings of the research and evaluation instruments of the legislative assemblies, it is impossible to establish that the parties are capable of comprehending and evaluating the outcomes of their policies. Nonetheless, some circumstantial evidence can be produced to sustain the hypothesis that parties are not completely lacking in these capacities. If, in fact, one does remember that parties control, through their collateral organizations and local governments, a good portion of the receivers of public policies (of course, only partially), one can hypothesize that parties know how to follow the concentric circles of outcomes for quite a distance. They can thereby intuit the impact on nearby groups, delaying the negative effects and reformulating even significant features of these policies. Naturally, in this extremely complicated process, the parties best endowed with social antenna, better embedded politically, and better supplied with resources will derive the greatest advantages. Moreover, within the governing coalition, there always exist conflictual tendencies (in the search for linakges with old and new social groups) that can have counterproductive effects for the individual parties and for the coalition as a whole.

Any further reflection would require the analytical description of appropriate case studies (from health care to schools, from territorial government to local finance).[6] Perhaps it is sufficient in this essay to question the presumed superiority of the bureaucracy over the parties in the evaluation of outcomes and in the capacity to control them both directly (through immediately profitable interpretations for potential political rallies) and more confusedly (through repeated modifications of the original provisions). Linearity and confusion characterize both this process and that of feedback, to which we now turn.

5. Feedback and social regulation

If, following Norbert Weiner, we define feedback as "the capacity to adjust future conduct on the basis of past efforts" (1954:33, cited by Easton 1965:365), this phenomenon appears to be of particular relevance for social regulation by parties in the Italian case. In fact, the immersion of parties within society and their takeover of institutions constitute the preconditions for an effective exposure to feedback. This is not to hypothesize automatic processes of information-gathering on the outcomes of policies, but to indicate only the potential which a rooted and capillary party system has at its disposal for these objectives.

Paradoxically, it is this same diffusion of the political class, in the wider sense of the term, that allows an effective mediation between policies – their impact, their capacity to achieve the ends proposed, and their ability to satisfy the needs of citizens – and the reproposition or modification of these same policies. Nonetheless, since as a whole the system does not function with the excessive satisfaction of the citizens, this indicates even that the feedback circuit may well perform its function, but some other mechanism is not doing its job. Sometimes, in fact, parties entirely ignore evidence contrary to their preferences (the latest example is the case of the Communist party of Italy on the referendum regarding the *scala mobile*). Other times, they unite in defense of situations they do not know how to change or do not want to change (e.g., the spoils system). In still other situations, the new decision-making process, while still controlled by them, appears even more confused and contradictory than the previous one in which a consistent feedback process existed (e.g., the dramatic case is the progress of the law to absolve construction abuses).

None of these examples is capable of dissolving the feedback circuit that ties parties as decision-makers to policies, and to parties as collectors of information and, eventually, of criticisms. But the effect of a feedback process that often reinforces parties in their convictions, in their positions, and in their privileges, can, over time, be counterproductive. And, at any rate, this feedback can result in important analytical consequences – although not sufficient to put into question the preeminence of parties in the decision-making process. In fact, even the social regulation that follows from the possible variations of the feedback process can be interpreted and translated not as a result of the assumption of positions of power by new groups, but rather, in the best of cases, through the acceptance of these groups (usually in subordinate positions) within traditional decision-making processes (sometimes under the form of temporary co-optation, other times as carriers of reinforcing experiences or expertise). In no case does the new process become totally or significantly disturbed.

The paradox naturally consists in the fact that this control of the feedback circuit by parties, which permits their acquisition of relevant information, is both effective and distorting, since it permits them both to eliminate unwelcome information and to avoid the influence of other actors. Thus, it reduces the competitive, contrasting, and coexisting information with high costs to the feedback process as a whole. However, in the model of party government, it is nowhere written that the "system" must function and function well. In fact, an excess of "party governmentness" translates not into better social regulation of collective behavior, but rather into the domination by parties of social mechanisms of various types (market) through which they allocate values themselves, and of institutional mechanisms (state) with which they distribute resources to themselves.

6. Conclusions: from party government to cabinet government?

Having arrived at this perhaps overly obstinate defense of the interpretive model of party government in the Italian case, it is worth emphasizing two elements that were either obscured or misunderstood. First, the fact that Italy is a case of party government, and thus an example of social regulation prevalently provided by political parties and the party system, does not mean that the phenomenon must necessarily be considered positive. Although it is true that the various functional alternatives which have emerged did not develop and do not appear either promising or convincing (from pansyndicalism to neo-corporatism, from clientalism to "movementism" and even assemblyism), party government Italian-style represents more than one inconvenience, beginning with the missing alternation between coalitions (and thus the reduced competitiveness and limited turnover of the political-party class).

Second, in the Italian case party government was installed and consolidated by default, in the absence of anything better. In an essentially weak, poorly organized, and relatively static society (like that which emerged from fascism) and in a political system characterized by weak institutions due to the fear of a "tyranny" and to choice (weak inclination to take risks of the members of the Constituent Assembly), the parties, and later party government, emerged almost unexpectedly and thus without rules. But the initial conditions have changed, in part thanks to the parties themselves. In particular, the growth of social forces and their diversification have affected the parties and the party system, fragmenting both.

One could perhaps sustain that the fragmentation of parties has almost become necessary to govern fragmentation (Dente 1985); that is, the strength of parties as regulators of social activity resides in their capacity to remain embedded in the social, without, however, succeeding (but did they ever succeed?) in faithfully and dynamically representing it. One could also argue that the parties have become loose-knit structures, more penetrable by social groups, in particular by the more cohesive and strategically placed ones; and that this alters certain characteristics of the model of party government. Nevertheless, this does not render the model inadequate.

In fact, there appears to be no doubt that parties hold together the system and control the decision-making process. Certainly, they have lost most of the propelling force. Their energies seem channeled more towards control than towards initiative, and more towards the construction of conservative coalitions rather than towards the planning of reform coalitions. Nonetheless, an immobile system does not automatically lose its party government characteristics. At the most, it makes forecasting what will follow it more difficult. And, in fact, the possible futures (Smith 1986) of the Italian case of party government are not easy to outline.

We can, however, list certain, more macroscopic, features of the Italian political system, including: an extensive social demand for decisions that outline policy directions within which actors can establish their choices with a degree of certainty; extensive dissatisfaction with the "negative" power of parties; persistent expectations of institutional reform; and the unexplored potential of an alternation between political-governing coalitions. Using these features, we can probably still explain convincingly why the model of party government permits us to analyze decision-making processes better than any other alternative.

Let us reexamine the lines of discussion, beginning with the more appropriately structural features. The model of party government is based on the existence, in the first place, of parties that are rooted, well installed, and, if not always cohesive, endowed with a strong mass following. For a series of reasons (e.g., parties create collateral organizations and distribute resources), Italian parties occupy a space between civil society and governmental and parliamentary institutions much greater than that occupied by parties in other competitive democracies (and they have also blurred the boundaries between civil society and the institutional arena). This tendency has not decreased, and the push towards occupying territory and blurring boundaries remains strong, so strong that even the Socialist party (PSI), which challenges the Christian Democrats (DC) and the Communists (PCI) on this dimension, does so by seeking to replace them, not by changing the modality of relations between civil society and governmental institutions.

In the second place, policy networks find adequate space for their presence and actions wherever they are forced to compete with fluctuating, political-governmental coalitions. Not only will policy networks be forced to structure themselves in such a way as to enable them to be effective regardless of the political-governmental coalition that emerges dominant at any one moment, but they will acquire a certain power of attraction and influence thanks precisely to these fluctuations in the political-governmental coalitions.

The Italian problem, however one defines it, is not that of ample or excessive or overly frequent fluctuations in the political-governmental coalitions. In fact, scholars, commentators, and politicians are essentially in agreement in defining the Italian problem as the lack of alternation, of a blocked political system. But often these same scholars, commentators, and politicians forget that the political system is blocked around a single dominant coalition of interests; these interests have redefined themselves over time (with the passage from the Center to the Center-Left governments and then later with the installation of five-party coalitions). Nonetheless, no matter how the interests have redefined themselves, they have not substantially changed. And the dominant coalitions have been constructed around *party* coalitions, which is the crucial point that must be emphasized.

Consequently, the same interests continue to rotate around the political parties (of the permanent majority), and the political parties of the practicing majority enjoy the resources, however limited, and have the instruments, however open to criticism, to prepare the agenda, specify the groups, proceed with the choices, and produce welcome decisions (or, in any event, to block unwelcome ones). Party government may have become more conflictual, perhaps even less pleasant; but certainly, from the point of view of the parties (and their personnel) that use it, it has not become less concrete – and is no less effective than in the golden 1950s and 1960s.

Furthermore, in the third place, these inter-institutional relations themselves are what permit party government to face challenges and reproduce itself with considerable ease. The Italian political system is characterized by one of the weakest forms of parliamentary government in Western Europe. Italian governments inevitably consist of coalitions, with a hypertrophic Parliament, lacking in autonomous and effective instruments to investigate, control, direct, and evaluate, formed by two chambers with equal powers and functions, and hence, with slow and burdensome operations. An unfinished decentralization of government, concerned more with tasks than power, contributes an element of drag rather than dynamism to the system as a whole. And, last but not least, a proportional electoral system exists that fragments coalitions and parties much more than it represents effectively new and old interests, preferences, identities, and political projects.

One might think that in a weak institutional framework, policy networks would be able to nest and operate with flexibility and effectiveness. Instead, just about everywhere, it is the parties who gain from this situation. It is they who are able to embed themselves and, in the end, are able to guarantee a little flexibility and provide a little dynamism in the system, even if only in response to social and economic demands. The parties are the dominant actors of the system.

If this diagnosis is correct, certain general and specific consequences follow. From a specific point of view, it could be that the parties (meaning the dominant coalition) decide to abandon the highly costly attempt to intervene in all possible socioeconomic arenas and instead concentrate their efforts in specific areas that are more susceptible to state regulation. Among these areas, the public sector of the economy, however restructured, and media (both press and television) undoubtedly stand out. Moreover, this development, which is foreseeable in the medium term, goes against the strategy of the Socialist party, which consists of replacing the Christian Democrats in the maximum number of functional areas. Therefore, in the short term, a push towards state regulation of many sectors and interparty conflict will increase (and as a consequence few spaces will open for policy networks). Furthermore, conflict will remain within the area of the five-party coalition and will tend to emarginate the Communist party, even while having to deal with the largest opposition party in sectors like health care. Nevertheless, neither de-legification (meaning the attribution of regulatory powers to ministers) nor deregulation (meaning the regulation of certain arenas by the actors directly involved) constitutes a hypothetical solution in the near future to the problem of moderation. In fact, both could reduce the formal power of (governing) parties and this would not further their interests.

From a general point of view, two completely opposite developments could emerge. One possibility is that society will continue to fragment and become corporatized, while parties and the party system watch this process without opening up spaces for social self-regulation. Institutions remain weak and thus are the prey of parties and the political-party class. A delayed alternation *sine die* occurs (also because of the planning incapacity of the largest opposition party). Confused, conflictual, and controversial party convergences take place at the center. Decision-making processes remain dominated by the parties.

The second possibility, surely less probable, could be represented by the emergence of a demanding and mature post-party civil society; by a real and deep self-reform of the parties, with turnovers in their personnel and renewal of their structures and methods; by a reform of the institutions that renders government transparent and efficient, the bureaucracy capable and meritocratic, with semi-federal political decentralization, characterized even by an alternation that produces competition of ideas, programs, parties, and people. In fact, in this perspective, we could hypothesize the passage of the Italian case from the model of party government by default to the model of cabinet government (in which the institutions and the government would mutually reinforce themselves). Society would obtain positive responses to its requests for stability and foreseeability in socioeconomic choices; parties would become responsible, and decision-making processes rendered more transparent; alternations would be more frequent and less traumatic.

While which model prevails is of great significance (Pasquino 1985) from the perspective of modalities of social regulation, paradoxically the actual differences that would result would be limited. In fact, there is no reason to think that the Italian political system can put itself on the road of the pluralistic model of competition-bargaining among groups, of parties reduced to equal status with any other actor; nor that it can go the way of neo-corporatism when this model is disappearing even in countries where it has been experimented with for decades, along with a decline of large union organizations. But, especially, it does not appear that policy networks can replace the parties and the model of party government in a system that has grown as a result of its parties and has structured itself around them, and in which the government and representative institutions function according to essentially party criteria.

It would be too easy (and a bit deluding) to foresee that the future of social regulation in Italy will not be much different than the past. But the transition towards a new model or towards an improved party government will be long and painful.

Notes

1 This is so even when dealing with civil rights, as in the cases of the laws on divorce and abortion in the 1970s and against sexual violence in the 1980s. Not only external groups but also the movements have needed parliamentary party sponsors, and when these have dissolved, there was no policy network that was able to produce a law in a coherent way within a decent time period.

2 Thus one can hold that certain interest groups like Coldiretti, Confcommercio, and insurance companies are sufficiently strong to directly articulate their interests. But, curiously, Coldiretti, Confcommercio, and the insurance companies have always made sure to elect one of their representatives to Parliament with the Christian Democratic lists.

3 To go to a level where the model of policy networks must apply itself and must provide an explanation, the competition within the five-party coalition between the Christian Democrats and the Socialists for control of the Presidency of the Council of Ministers is none other than a conflict over a position privileged with regard to strong socioeconomic interests, and thus able to control the outputs and the evaluation of outcomes by the respective party apparati. Only the party government model is capable of providing an explanation for this and other similar phenomena.

4 And naturally, the weakness, for various reasons, of the parliamentary institutions and of civil society (Pasquino 1985).

5 Anti-politics (Berger 1979) manifests itself, if anything, under the form of indifference towards politics or of declarations of political irrelevance.

6 From the perspective used here, it should be sufficient to raise the methodological questions relevant to each sector and area. In the case of health, for example, the relevant question concerns the nominations and composition of the directing committees of the

Local Health Districts (Unita Sanitarie Locali). Does this not represent perhaps one of the clearest, even exemplary, phenomena of capillary control by the parties, and this in an area in which, given the expertise and managerial skills which would seem called for, we would expect an effective policy network? In the case of local finance, one can argue that a transverse policy network has formed (that is, one which cuts across all the parties), that the characteristic of local administrator overrides that of elected representative of a political party. The relative cohesion of the front of local administrators would suggest that this thesis has some validity. But, once again, there is no doubt that the most important decisions concerning local finance are not the products of policy networks but of the interactions of party representatives (including those of the major party of the opposition, which is about 30 percent of local administrations and which governs in coalition with one or more of the parties of the national government, including even the Christian Democrats). And the preeminent decisions are taken within the Council of Ministers and in the parliamentary assemblies and reflect the balance of power among the parties – and little else.

2

Politics and policies in Italy

BRUNO DENTE AND GLORIA REGONINI

1. The problem

The first fact that strikes any observer who proposes to analyze Italian policy-making from a comparative perspective is the recurrent, almost pathological presence of policy-makers with party affiliations or party legitimation. They are involved at every stage of decision-making processes, in all sectors of state intervention. In this sense, Italy seems to represent an exception to the trend highlighted by many analysts in which the increase in the scope and complexity of public policies leads to a reduction in the role of political parties. These are said to be displaced by other categories of policy-makers, such as bureaucrats or technicians, who are better equipped to deal with the new responsibilities taken on by the public sector (Lehner and Schubert 1984).

The thesis that Italian political parties are by far the most important actors in the processes leading to the adoption of public policies is strengthened by the fact that it is almost unanimously accepted both by specialists (Pasquino 1986) and by public opinion. Were it confirmed, it would establish Italy as an anomaly among the western countries. This chapter, however, formulates an analytic model that is a more detailed and, in our opinion, more accurate rendering of the role Italian parties play in the processes of policy formulation and implementation.

2. A cumbersome presence

A first obvious indication of the weight of political parties in Italian policy-making is the extent of support they succeed in mobilizing. In fact, membership in Italian parties is larger than that of most parties elsewhere in Western Europe. Along with this is the correlated strength of the party organizational structures and resources (i.e., daily news-

51

papers). There is, thus, considerable evidence that the presence of the parties is extremely intrusive.

A second aspect of the thesis regarding the centrality of political parties concerns electoral data. Not only is the percentage of voters in national political elections very high in Italy, but the same is true for local elections where the vast majority of the electoral lists are more or less direct expressions of national political parties. It is significant that even where in theory the election is for category representatives, party affiliations often tend to reemerge. This is the case for local school councils, where a decrease in parental participation has apparently coincided with an increase in the party identification of those elected. However, perhaps the most outstanding example is the Consiglio Superiore della Magistratura (High Judicial Council), in which party affiliations are critical to selection despite the fact that its role is to guarantee the autonomy of the judiciary.

Related to the breadth of electoral participation is the large number of elective assemblies: from neighborhood councils to the European Parliament, by way of the town, province, region, Chamber of Deputies, and Senate. In Italy, the number of elective offices is extremely high, which also means there are a high number of elected officers, since double mandates are fairly rare as a result of legal limits.

Furthermore, the scope of intervention of the elective assemblies appears extremely wide, from both a formal and a substantive perspective. At the national level, it is widely held that the norms governing the relations between government and Parliament establish a division of power that gives the legislative branch more weight than the executive branch. And, since the agendas of both the Chamber and Senate are in fact decided by the political parties (through the creation of parliamentary groups), it seems obvious that from this perspective as well, the importance of parties is great. Descending to the regional level, it is well known that the prevalent orientation in the early 1970s (when the regional governments were empowered) assigned particular importance to the role of the regional council, which was entrusted with substantial executive power (for example, in the allocation of finances transferred to the regions) and, in turn, gave its commissions direct administrative functions.

Finally, the administrative power exercised by people nominated by political parties and members of parties appears particularly important. From the Regional Committees of Control to the boards that administer nationalized industries, the number of power centers to which access is gained through political or party nomination is very high. The local health boards, recently the subject of a heated debate, are in reality only a further application of a rule that seems to have few exceptions (one is the National Institute for Social Security [INPS], but here party nomination is replaced by union nomination). This fact is even more significant when we recall that in the Italian administrative tradition, the principle of centralizing power in the political head of the office means that high officials at all levels (national departments, regional and local administrations, etc.) have substantial "external" powers, and even the most minor details must pass through their offices.

3. The basic hypothesis

The organizational strength of the parties, the central importance of the electoral process, the great number and importance of elective assemblies, the concession of significant powers to elective or politically appointed officials: all these factors, normally implicit in the thesis that parties play a fundamental role in Italian policy-making, hardly seem open to debate. In fact, we believe that any statistical survey of which actors are most frequently found in the decision-making processes leading to the adoption and implementation of public policies, even in highly specialized sectors such as finance and energy, would confirm the intrusive presence of persons with clear allegiance to parties to which they owe their positions. As we have also indicated, in the literature on the Italian case, recognition of the numerical relevance of politically identifiable policy-makers is often linked to analyses of the consequences of this state of affairs for the characteristics of decision-making processes and outcomes. More precisely, two important areas of research can be identified.

The first proposes to assess whether or not the party credentials of a large number of policy-makers lead to a decisive preeminence of their preferences in decisional outcomes over those of other categories of actors, such as interest group representatives, bureaucrats, and specialized technicians. This type of research generally takes the concept of "party government" as a point of reference, and assesses its capacity adequately to describe Italian policy-making. For an affirmative conclusion on this issue, see Pasquino's essay in this volume (Chapter 1), which is noteworthy for its clarity as well as for its explicit use of Katz's (1986) tightly drawn definition of party government.

Here we will discuss Katz's model only to emphasize one aspect: the fact that it requires the simultaneous occurrence of four requisites – selection through election of crucial actors, their party affiliation, the autonomy of the governing coalition, and its effective control over the public administration – implies that these might also occur independently. The model further implies that the importance of political parties as recruitment agencies for policy-makers does not in itself ensure that the parties play an equally decisive role in policy-making. Thus, on the basis of these concepts, to assert that Italy represents a case of party government requires not only that most policy-makers have party affiliations but also that the policy choices made in various sectors of state intervention can be explained by the interests and positions pursued by parties in the political arena.

The second area of research proposes to establish whether or not in the Italian case a correlation can be observed between the recurrent presence of actors associated with political parties and certain characteristics – mostly negative – that appear to be peculiar to the output of Italian decision-making processes. Most scholars, in fact, share the conviction that the numerical prevalence of policy-makers with party affiliations not only gives them an advantage over other categories in the allocation of extensive public resources, but also implies precise features of the objectives pursued through public policies. These are characterized by a systematic preeminence of partial, circumscribed, and short-term interests.

In this approach, the principal analytical categories are based on the concepts of political entrepreneurship (Tarrow 1977a), clientalism (Graziano 1980), and "spoils system" (spartitorio) government (Amato 1976). We focus on this type of analysis because its proponents do not limit themselves to showing the predominance of actors with party linkages over other categories of policy-makers; they also define the specific objectives and interests these actors pursue when they exercise a decison-making role in policy arenas.

Both of the preceding approaches touch upon a series of themes that at various points are related to the subject of this chapter. Our brief presentation of them, however, is intended primarily to stress the differences – rather than the similarities – between these approaches and our own. In fact, we advance the following hypothesis: there is no logical-deductive basis and no empirical foundation for the view that the numerical dominance of policy-makers associated with parties in and of itself implies an overlap between the preferences that inspire their action at the political level – when deciding which social and political forces are allies and which opponents – and the preferences that guide their behavior in policy-making arenas where the problem is one of choosing between alternative courses of action on matters of state jurisdiction.

These statements introduce one of the most delicate and complex sets of issues in the study of policy-making. We should, therefore, define the terms of the problem we wish to focus on and the hypothesis we wish to propose very precisely. In fact, the set of questions that arises under the general rubric of "the relationship between politics and policy" is still far short of a satisfactory theoretical formulation. To avoid being drawn into the dangerous gravitational field where one risks crashing into flying fragments of the debate on "does politics matter?" or on the requisites of party government, we shall drastically limit the scope of our hypothesis in explicating its various assumptions.

The hypothesis is based on the possibility to analytically distinguish two different arenas. The first, which we will call *partisan policy decisions*, consists of processes in which the preferences of a political group – a party, faction, or clan – are directed toward other political groups. In the context of this chapter, it is irrelevant to discuss whether ideological or utilitarian motivations are at the origin of these preferences. Whatever their foundation, the choices adopted in this arena are nonetheless based on some sort of evaluation of the percentage of votes (e.g., electoral or parliamentary) controlled by those making the evaluation and those being evaluated, along with projections regarding possible winning coalitions. On the basis of the choices made in this arena, the prevalence of a more or less inclusive political coalition is determined, but this coalition is normally legitimated by some vote and endowed with the power to allocate a series of positions.

The second arena, which we will call *substantive policy decisions*, consists of processes in which the preferences of various actors – in Italy prevalently but not exclusively with party affiliations – are expressed for specific courses of action in various sectors of public intervention: for example, how many nuclear power plants should be constructed, where, and of which kind; at what level should the ceiling for publicly guaranteed pensions be established; what should be the level of taxation to be paid by self-employed workers, etc.

On the basis of the analytical distinction between these two arenas, our argument can be reformulated in the following way: the fact that representatives of the political parties are among the most active and recurrent policy-makers does not imply that the strategies, interactions, and coalitions by which they determine substantive policies coincide with the strategies, interactions, and coalitions that these same actors pursue for questions concerning relations between parties or party factions. On the contrary, in the Italian case there seems to be a marked divergence between the choices made in these two arenas, a divergence that also raises a series of issues of some theoretical importance.

Given the well-known tendency of Italian policy-making to subject even the most minute aspects of implementation to legislative approval, we can proceed to verify our thesis in "hard case" conditions, i.e., by using cases in which one finds the simultaneous presence of two conditions that individually, and even more in combination, would be expected to produce similarities rather than differences in the two types of policy arenas under discussion. We shall in fact focus on a field of decision-making defined by: (1) a type of policy, social policy, that because of its implicit redistributive content, the extent of its social impact, and ideological appeal, is a subject to which the Italian parties devote considerable space in their programs and on which they build the definition of their identities with voters; and (2) a stage in decision-making, that of legislative ratification, in which ministers and deputies are the protagonists; that is to say, the initiative rests with actors who have the same formal legitimation and are playing in the same institutional sites that characterize the politics of partisan policy.

The reconstruction of parliamentary processes leading to the approval of laws on health, education, and pensions provides a series of results that we summarize only very briefly.

4. Cooperation/competiton

The choice by political groups whether to cooperate or compete with another within one arena does not imply an analogous choice in another arena. In other words, rarely do the choices on the ally/antagonist axis made in partisan policy-making reveal the same preferences as those made in substantive policy-making. Moreover, in addition to the major differences in relations between actors in the two arenas, there is a high degree of variance in relations internal to the different areas in which substantive policy-making is undertaken. In the processes of adopting public policies, in other words, the most diverse coalitions, one for every specific issue, can exist at the same time. In fact, the frequency, scope, and consequences both of conflicts and of collaboration are quite different in the decision-making processes considered here.

First of all, let us consider competition between government allies, that is, the choice of a member of the dominant coalition to defend substantive policy preferences different from those of the other partners of the majority. Our hypothesis is that these situations are not only analytically conceivable but can also be frequently found empirically in Italy, without their having an impact on the preferences expressed in partisan policy-making. In substantive policy-making, disagreement among government allies over the course of action to be taken in a sector of public intervention can expand and become intense while still remaining circumscribed, reversible, and fully compatible with loyalty to the government coalition.

Although throughout the years there have at times been very sharp differences in the preferences of the representatives of the various parties concerning fundamental aspects of social policy, no government crisis has been caused by the failure of "the majority of the majority" to obtain the agreement of the other members of the coalition on proposals that have been formally approved by the Council of Ministers. This has, for example, occurred several times over pension and higher education reform.

As paradoxical as it may appear to an outside observer, open and explicit conflict over important public policies is absolutely compatible with participation in a winning coalition at the level of partisan policy. It is latent discontents, unrelated to particular conflicts over what specific policy to undertake, that provoke defections and are, therefore, "symptoms of discontent within the majority." Typical are the "ambushes" committed against the government by groups of parliamentarians of the coalition in secret parliamentary votes. Occasionally, these are a sign of unresolved conflicts over a specific issue. They are, however, generally inexplicable in these terms, since they lead to policy discussions that contradict decisions made elsewhere and that conclude with proposals that are impracticable at the level of substantive policy-making.

A contrary vote in Parliament is an instrument for expressing dissent that the politician interested in a specific public policy uses with much reluctance. Normally, conflict over the choice of policies results in a postponement of the decision, not in the dissolution of the coalition. For example, if we examine the parliamentary history of pension system reform, which has been on the agenda of the Chamber's Committee on Labor Problems since 1976, we see that disagreement on fundamental points like standards of equality between categories or the level of maximum pensionable earnings has provoked neither governmental crises nor attempts to resolve the disagreement by a vote. The same is true for secondary school reform, under discussion since 1972 and held up for many years now by disagreements over central points like compulsory school age or the types of possible school specializations.

This leads us to suggest that the time factor plays a very different role in the two arenas. Specifically, postponing the decision seems to have quite different consequences for politicians, depending on the nature of the decision. In the case of partisan policy, holding up decisions carries specific penalties since the inability to constitute a winning coalition leads to the dissolution of the elective assembly or to a commissionership (in subnational governments). In the case of substantive policies, no direct costs are associated with postponement of decisions. On the contrary, in certain circumstances – in fact fairly commonly – delaying tactics are the most rational choice for most policy-makers. When the distribution of preferences around a certain issue is largely polarized, with concentrations at the two extremes, leading to a sort of isolation of the median voter, the introduction of a new axis of decision-making – "immediate decision/conservation of the status quo" – can lead to the collapse of the median voter's strong position, since the two wings can converge and impose adjournments and new attempts at mediation.

This explanation seems to us the most adequate. It explains the impression of a "dirty game" that emerges from the reconstruction of a great many Italian events related to the formulation and approval of public policies, events characterized by a continuous, instrumental use of "right wing" opposition on the part of the Left, and vice versa.

A choice to postpone is more rational the more likely it is that the postponement will uncover new resources or unexpected opportunities that transform zero-sum into positive-sum games. One can think, for example, of the conclusion of a process that begins with politicians taking sharply opposing positions, such as was the case with the decision whether to direct scarce financial resources to the revaluation of public employee pensions (pushed hard by the Christian Democrats [DC], Social Democratic party [PSDI], Liberal party [PLI], and Italian Social Movement [MSI]) or the revaluation of private employee pensions (given priority by the Communist party [PCI] and sustained by the Socialist party [PSI]). In the spring of 1985, the invention of an audacious accounting trick – covering increased spending through the increased taxation on these same revalued pensions – permitted the generation, even if only in appearance, of additional resources that made possible the simultaneous approval of both provisions.

Even in cases where conflict within the majority over alternative courses of action in substantive policy-making does not result in delays, but induces the dissenters to provoke votes as a way of arriving at an outcome, the alliances made at the level of partisan policy-making can emerge unscathed by these tests of strength. Further, even when a party of the majority decides to resolve a conflict by a vote not only in Parliament but also in the nation, through the use of a referendum (as occurred over divorce, abortion, and problems of judicial administration), these initiatives are accompanied by a series of declarations and organizational devices that limit the scope of conflict and reaffirm loyalty to the coalitional choices expressed in the arena of partisan policy.

Finally, even convergence between the preferences of one part of the majority and of a part of the opposition can be repeated with great frequency at the level of substantive policy-making without generating changes in the evaluations expressed by the same actors in partisan policy. The frequent confluence of the positions of the main opposition party (PCI) with those of all or part of the majority is not limited to procedural issues, e.g., whether to vote immediately or to accept a postponement (aspects for which the considerations above hold), but also concerns the substance of policy. As has been widely demonstrated by every study on voting choices in the Italian Parliament (e.g., DiPalma 1977; Cazzola 1982), for measures of limited importance, unanimous approval in committee is very frequent. For more complex and controversial measures, for which every different party has its own proposal, joint committees composed of all the political forces are normally formed with the task of fusing all the various versions into a single text. These committees generally grant the largest and most disciplined opposition party a preeminent role in formulating not only the agenda but also the content of the single articles.

In the preceding pages we have provided examples of defections by a part of the majority in substantive policy-making in cases that of themselves do not imply a disruption of party alliances on matters of partisan policy. To explain these, we need only hypothesize that, on some specific problem, a party to the left of the DC, the PSI for example, has preferences closer to the PCI than to its allies in government. Now we propose to relate the movement of a part of the minority towards the position of all or part of the majority to a different – but not contradictory – principle. It is often the case that the positions of the legislators of the various parties on various substantive policy proposals do not reflect the same relative spatial positions (x to the left of y, who is to the left of z, etc.) that are occupied by their parties in the arena defined by partisan policy choices.

The fact that the winning coalitions at the level of partisan policy have little probability of being reproduced in substantive policy-making should not be a big surprise if one recalls that the two most popular parties (the DC and PCI) are separated by a notable space – generally occupied by many other parties – along the right-left axis. That two such vast electorates should be aligned and opposed at exactly the same intervals with respect to issues as different as the full-time hiring of substitute teachers and remission of artisans' social welfare debts appears, and in fact is, a very remote possibility, as pluralist theories have by now led us to expect. Continual agreements between the two major parties in all cases where a conflict develops between the requests of strong social groups (not only agricultural laborers or artisans but also shop owners and university professors) and other interests are in fact perfectly compatible with frontal opposition at the partisan policy level.

This is proved by the failure of the leaders of the main opposition party to get political credit for the support they have given to government proposals, even when their contribution was decisive in compensating for absenteeism or defections in the majority. In fact, in many of these cases, support for a government measure by the Communist members of Parliament cannot be considered a vote in exchange for political "rewards" since it has not required any sacrifice of their own "spontaneous" preferences. In other words, to vote against proposals of the "majority of the majority" would be counterproductive and self-damaging for the opposition representatives whenever such a vote may result in the postponement or even cancellation of measures benefiting wide social categories, within which there are members or potential members of their own electorate.

5. Comprehensiveness/segmentation

Having stressed how the politics of partisan policy-making and the politics of substantive policy-making can be characterized by very different positioning along the cooperation/competition axis, we will now seek to show that these two types of politics can occur at quite distant points even along the comprehensiveness/segmentation axis (for more on the use of this conceptual coupling, see the Introduction to this volume). The thesis that we propose can be formulated as follows: the fact that decision-making processes with an intersectoral or corporatist structure[1] prevail in particular phases of partisan policy-making does not mean that analogous tendencies will appear in substantive policy-making.

Our discussion is based on an implicit premise: the fact that the decision-makers – exclusively in the first arena, prevalently in the second – identify with political parties, that is, with groups which in the Italian case are endowed with strong organizational structures, and with centralized and highly skilled administrative officials, does not mean that intersectorality and comprehensiveness are the norm, either for partisan policy choices or, above all, for choices of substantive policy.

To better define this discussion, we would argue that a decision-making process is more "comprehensive" when it respects the following two conditions: (1) Protagonists are groups (factions, parties, government coalitions) that possess and utilize the capacity to establish an order of preferences over a wide spectrum of items. The outcome of this choice, which we can consider a type of social welfare function for the negotiating group, must respond to criteria of internal coherence, even if it is not immutable over time or unanimously agreed to. In the case of partisan policy, for example, it is well known that internal party factions differentiate themselves precisely on the basis of their preferences for ties to the other parties. (2) Since it is realistic to think that the preference orderings of various groups do not coincide, and that no single group has the power completely to impose its own preferences, decision-making processes assume the form of negotiations (among the various factions of a party, among various parties of the governing coalition, between the "social partners" and the government, etc.), where the pursuit of stable outcomes is tied to the possibility of playing on the fact that the items under discussion are diversified, as is the intensity of the preferences which the various actors have for each of these items. The attainment of some sort of equilibrium is entrusted to highly interactive procedures like the exchange of votes, lateral compensations, and logrolling among groups endowed with the capacity to impose or accept choices over a vast range of problems.

In the field of partisan policy, we can clearly identify the phases in which the preferences of different political groups for other political groups are dealt with simultaneously, that is, the phases in which a strategy of alliances, with reference to different spheres of power and to different public offices, is formulated. In party conventions, the various party factions evaluate their reciprocal preferences and advance their own choices in a series of negotiations that determine the distribution of internal positions both at the center and on the periphery. In negotiations over the constitution of a government majority, equilibria that imply specific distributions not only of ministerial chairs but also of local level or public agency positions are often established. Although specialized, single issue decision-making processes, with a very restricted agenda, occur with a certain degree of frequency even in partisan policy-making (as the phenomena of "anomalous coalitions" at the local level and of strange alliances in certain public boards demonstrate), the need for "coherence" and for comprehensiveness is nonetheless quite strong in this arena, as certain perverse features of the Italian case, like the lack of autonomy of local party offices (Graziano et al. 1984) and the "spoils system" in the state sector, confirm.

Our hypothesis is that the need for comprehensiveness is in general much less important at the level of substantive policy-making, and that, more specifically, the prevalence of tendencies towards intersectoralism in one arena does not produce a corresponding trend in another. This statement goes against important formal features of public choices in a democratic regime: established principles require, in fact, that the intersectoral negotiations in the partisan and substantive policy arenas be tightly interdependent, and that the alliances among party groups be based on, and ratified by, program documents containing proposals concerning the principal public policy decisions to be made.

In fact, both in the conclusions of party congresses as well as in negotiations over a new government or in the verification of the majority, intersectoral accords both on the level of partisan policy as well as on that of substantive policy are simultaneously reached. On the basis of what we have so far written, however, we can sustain that in this last case it is imprecise to speak of comprehensive decision-making, since both conditions listed at the beginning of this section are not respected. In these cases, instead of an intersectoral comparison of preferences, we are dealing with their simple listing on the basis of an additional criterion: that any type of demand can find a place in the program without reducing the probability that others will be satisfied. The fact that such accords rarely constitute real turning points in the history of a public policy is not due to successive accidental difficulties, but to the particular characteristics of these processes. It is, in fact, probably incorrect to define them as decision-making, since they do not result in any truly stable and constraining collective choice. Since 1978, for instance, the need for unification and rationalization of insurance plans has been included almost annually as a relevant item in party summits concluded with accords that have not survived even an initial effort at implementation.

In reality, these omni-comprehensive pacts are quite compatible with the consolidation of substantive policy-making characterized by high degrees of specialization and sectoralism: the same issues that are formally part of global programs are often simultaneously negotiated with greater effectiveness in decentralized centers of decision-making, where only those with strong preferences for the alternatives under consideration choose to participate. The segmentation of decision-making arenas along lines that reproduce those of the various areas of state intervention appears, in fact, to be a tendency which in the Italian case can coexist comfortably with the party credentials of most policy-makers. First of all, everyone who identifies with a party does not necessarily have precise opinions on all the possible options for the substantive policy problems on the agenda. Moreover, and more importantly, a party does not necessarily formulate a lot of unitary, transitive preferences endowed with internal coherence. On the contrary, all large political organizations have recently experienced increased autonomy of the committees created to direct action in determined areas (departments, offices). If we consider the party votes in Parliament on social policies, we would maintain that these normally mirror the opinions of the directors of the respective party departments without any need for coherence or convergence with the preferences that other party offices might have on the same issues.

Cases in which the political leadership of parties exercises real control over their own sectoral officers are quite rare. The types of *diktat* that at times are imposed by national party secretariats in cases of the formation of coalitions in the periphery or majoritarian and "dramatic" decisions, like those which renew alliance strategies, are quite improbable in the politics of substantive policy-making. In fact, they would risk being honored only formally while ignored in practice, as occurs each time some extraordinary circumstance (for example, an exceptional amount of attention given to an issue by the public) forces parliamentarians of a party to behave with greater internal cohesion. Since only the one responsible for a specific sector can know its precise dynamics, it is possible for this type of parliamentarian to boycott a legislative act without exposure, simply by allowing those segments of the social groups who feel themselves the losers to follow their centrifugal inclinations.

In fact, the conditions that guarantee the decision-making efficiency of specialized policy-making are exactly opposed to those which have been used to define highly global policy-making. While the latter requires the construction of some sort of complex utility function of the negotiating group, the former requires that whoever has pronounced preferences for a specific area enjoy a certain degree of isolation and be free of interference. Obtaining the necessary consensus to ensure passage of a packet of provisions in the first case is entrusted to intersectoral negotiations that depend on the existence of preferences which are diverse and, above all, which differ in intensity across issues. In the case of segmented policy-making, the consensus required to guarantee approval of sectoral provisions by Parliament or the Council of Ministers relies on the exploitation of margins of indifference, that is, on a tacit division of responsibilities accompanied by the rule of reciprocity: you decide the issues that interest you, and we will approve, so long as you approve our decisions on issues that interest us. Naturally, this does not exclude the possibility that even in substantial policy-making, phases characterized by high degrees of comprehensiveness exist. These, however, aside from being relatively rare, are structurally distinguished both from normal policy-making based on segmentation and reciprocity, and from the type of negotiations that only in appearance involve public policies and that ritually accompany highly comprehensive decisions in the partisan policy arena (commitments in leadership meetings of the majority, program documents of parties, etc.).

The circumstances in which intersectoral decision-making processes in the field of public policy develop are also quite different. They come into play when it becomes clear that not all solutions preferred within various sectors can be realized since the resources are too scarce. In these cases, accords must, among other things, withstand the test represented by the reaction of the penalized within its own ranks that each negotiating group undergoes.

6. Indifference/interest over the alternatives

In substantive policy-making, in contrast to what occurs in partisan policy-making, the participation of politicians in decision-making processes is not necessarily subordinated to the formulation of, nor tailored to, a precise preference function relative to the alternatives under discussion.

The considerations so far discussed have implicitly utilized certain "standard" assumptions that are generally taken for granted in both empirical and logical-deductive analyses. They concern the origins and the consequences of politicians' decisions to particiapte in a decision-making process, their "choice to choose," in both substantive and partisan policy-making. On the basis of this first assumption, which concerns the so-called initial reasons for deciding to participate, the interest politicians express by entering a process of public choice is normally considered a function of an interest in the issues under discussion, issues which they see as capable of influencing the pursuit of their (personal or political) "well being."

The second assumption concerns instead the final consequences of the choice to choose: the entrance of politicians into a decision-making process is usually correlated with the intention to use this role in the most effective way in every phase, from the formulation of the proposals in question to the evaluation of the impact of the subsequently victorious alternative. Whatever the final result of their effort, they will seek to highlight its importance, giving as much publicity as possible to the preferences they expressed and to the determination with which they sustained them, so that those who identify with their positions can repay their efforts through political support.

It is important to note that these assumptions – in many ways quite simple – are implied in most analyses of the choices of politicians in the two arenas considered here, even when scholars do not make explicit reference to the rational choice paradigm and to formal logical-deductive models. In fact, the assumptions we have presented are based on an elementary idea: whatever the objectives of the politicians, their participation in public decision-making processes generates certain costs, which they can recover only by informing the recipients, or at least the direct beneficiaries, of their role in decision-making.

While this is valid for all processes of partisan policy-making or substantive policy-making so far examined, whether they are characterized by conflict or cooperation, by high degrees of comprehensiveness or segmentation, it appears not to be true for another part of Italian substantive policy-making. In Italy, there are major areas of public intervention in which the relationship between the interests of political policy-makers in participating in decision-making processes – interests that are highly intense and effective – and their interests in the public "exploitation" of the choices adopted appears to be restricted and even disappearing. In other words, in certain sectors, the determination with which politicians demand a decision-making role does not correspond to an analogous commitment to the formulation of possible alternatives, to credit-taking for results, or to the effort to "sponsor" eventual discontent.

We need not dwell at length on the first part of our observation. It is universally accepted that Italian politicians insistently defend their inclusion in (or resist their exclusion from) the processes for the selection of public policies, even in highly technical sectors that in other countries are explicitly reserved to specialized bureaucracies or to self-regulation by the social partners. Evidence of this orientation exists, for example, in the exclusive power of Parliament over issues concerning the levels of contributions and allocations in the pension sector or in the right of parliamentary intervention, even if purely consultative, in issues like the four-year development plans for universities. Signs of these interests emerge also from attempts, generally concluded successfully, to politically label the candidates for technical positions that require elections (Consultative Committees of the National Research Council [CNR], etc.) or appointments (Administrative Board of the National Institute for Social Security [INPS], Executive Committees of the Local Health Districts [USL], etc.).

However, the second element of our argument – the decrease in interest in the public exploitation of decisions – does require further elaboration, since public attention is often attracted by exactly the opposite phenomenon, that is, by the skill of political policy-makers in utilizing eminently technical issues for partisan purposes, in order to capture the support of particular professional groups or to square accounts between internal factions. This type of process, while unfortunately widespread, does not present particular explanatory problems, as we will soon demonstrate.

In this section our attention is directed instead to the particular type of substantive policy-making in which no clear correlation exists between the intensity of interest politicians express in participating in decision-making processes and the concrete use they later make of this role. The choices made by political policy-makers can assume unusual characteristics when the issues involve, for example, which types of X-rays should be billed to the patient and which should be provided free of charge, or which required courses should be included in a university curriculum – all decisions which in Italy are adopted in political centers or with the use of politically nominated consultants. These characteristics are worthy of elaboration.

First of all, in these cases it becomes extremely difficult to associate the various alternatives under discussion with a particular political group; this difficulty appears to arise not only from the secrecy that surrounds these decision-making processes and from the limited attention the media give to them, but also from the existence of a tacit agreement among policy-makers with political affiliations to exclude any sort of public attribution of sponsorship of the choices being considered. In other words, the issues in question appear to be free of any articulated "social welfare function" elaborated by the statutory bodies of various political parties. It would, furthermore, prove futile to seek to identify claims to particular partisan preferences on the part of their sectoral specialists. Political policy-makers, whenever they intervene in these issues, appear to act almost individually, in total isolation from the party organizations with which they are affiliated.

The same type of prudent detachment surrounds the collective decision-making processes from which the choices that constrain the public officials arise. Contrary to what happens in the cases considered previously, policy-makers with party affiliations do not aspire to attract the attention of the public or of the final beneficiaries to the preferences they expressed or the role they played. Even when the effects of the decision begin to unfold, either positively or negatively, the party actors appear in accord in avoiding claims of merit for themselves or making recriminations over the errors of their adversaries.

The substantial indifference often manifested by politicians for the public exploitation of outcomes they have participated in producing appears less strange if one considers this fact: the widening of the sphere of state intervention in Italy places policy-makers with party affiliations directly in contact with problems for which it is practically impossible to assess the various proposed sections and their impact, whether positive or negative. If, for example, we consider decisions – even legislative decisions – in the field of welfare, we see that often these decisions have recipients who were artificially created by other legal norms (e.g., retirees before a certain date, graduates with a certain grade-point average, patients with certain illnesses, and heads of family with a certain number of children). In these cases, any assumptions about the political, social, and geographic distribution of the beneficiaries would be completely arbitrary, as would any calculation of the consequences of the policy choices adopted for the distribution of politicial resources such as electoral consensus, organizational and financial support, the likelihood of career advancement, etc.

For most substantive policy-making, the difficulties scholars have in finding the line that ties the political benefactor to the citizen-beneficiary must be sought in the contorted and underground articulation of channels which in Italy exist between policy-makers and policy-takers, passing through trade unions, associations, and even single individuals capable of playing an intermediary role (Ferrera 1984). But in the cases considered here, the problems have a more objective basis. In fact, the scholars' ignorance of the origins and consequences of the decisions is shared by the beneficiaries who receive them, who do not know to whom to attribute their paternity; and even by the politicians who promote them, who are incapable of foreseeing who will benefit from these choices.

Obviously, we do not want to exclude the possibility that some sort of limited group of users can be damaged by the decisions adopted and can blame a precise political group. However, this possibility is as obscure as its opposite, that is, that the same group is held responsible and thanked for the merits enjoyed by some particularly favored group. In either case, these hypotheses have overly fragile bases and require overly complex considerations to be the basis for some sort of organized judgment among the final users.

If these considerations have some foundation, we can deduce that the pervasive presence of actors with political affiliations does not in itself result in the elimination from Italian policy-making of a type of decision-making process, often specified by scholars who analyze other national contexts and identified by terms like technical policy-making or problem-solving (Richardson et al. 1982; Scharpf 1986). These images of the policy-making process, while they differ in detail, are recalled here since they share a precise feature: the need to find solutions to problems for which no political actor has preconstituted answers, given that the reference to party interests is weakened to the point of disappearing.

We must, nonetheless, point out that in our discussion the reference to these images implies no value judgment. In other words, affirming the existence of this specific sub-arena of Italian substantial policy-making does not, in and of itself, imply an expectation of especially rational decision-making processes or outcomes more efficient than those produced in other sub-arenas. The fact that on certain issues of substantive policy-making (1) politicians appear deprived of their own autonomous preferences and (2) traditional forms of interest organization are inactive does not imply similar indifference regarding the alternatives for all the other categories of policy-makers.

In fact, in the face of these problems, other types of actors, often defined by their professional roles and involved in the technical planning or implementation of the legislative act, can make clear evaluations and precise projections on the impact of the proposals for their own future, for example, in terms of more or less work, more or less prestige, or more or less autonomy. These better informed actors sometimes find themselves in institutional positions of authority – by election, designation, or administrative career – over specific public structures: chairs of certain departments, administrative functionaries of INPS, medical specialists, and directors of certain hospital clinics. As such, they can foresee an alteration in their situations due to politically "neutral" decisions, such as the redistribution of doctoral candidates, the establishment of the number of income brackets for family checks, or the imposition of a fee system for certain types of medical tests.

In the welfare sector, therefore, a type of paradox appears to exist. The more detailed and intrusive legislation becomes, the more politicians formally increase their power of intervention, while in fact they become mere notaries of initiatives and accords among bureaucrats, representatives of specific professional categories, and public administrators (Cassese 1983a). In the case of pension policies, for example, the large number of legislative acts (thirty to forty) concerning prevalently secondary aspects of insurance treatment can in some cases be explained on the basis of partisan interests and distributive dynamics, but in others, they are solicited by the administrators themselves, who thereby seek to place their performance under legal protection, eliminating possible interpretive ambiguities and obtaining simplifications of the procedures or authorizations for exemptions (Regonini 1987).

We must, however, specify that the existence of preferences attributable to these categories of "indirect recipients" certainly does not represent a fact peculiar to this type of policy-making. In fact, it is obvious that even for issues of great political appeal, precise evaluations by actors institutionally involved in the technical planning or in the implementation of the act can occur. Consider, for example, the negative reactions provoked among the administrative cadre of INPS by legislative acts like the revaluation of pension treatments or the insurance pardon, which entail an enormous amount of bureaucratic work, with a recalculation of millions of insured positions. Moreover, it is difficult to think of any public choice that does not provoke reactions among those concerned with its technical implementation. Functionaries of the Interior Ministry or city police certainly have precise negative preferences regarding the early dissolution of the Chamber; this, however, does not in any way prevent politicians from giving priority to their own preferred options.

If in this section we have described a type of policy-making in which the formulation of winning proposals is done not by politicians but rather by those who occupy professionally qualified roles, this does not result from the fact that the latter have their own order of preferences, but rather from the fact that the former, the politicians, are completely lacking in preferences. Actually, in these cases these same technical or administrative actors adopt ways of revealing their own interests that preclude any possible direct sponsorship by a single political group. As is well known, standard analyses of Italian policy-making generally emphasize the opposite fact, that is, the tendency of representatives of the particular administrative or institutional structures to behave as interest groups in competition with one another each of which separately negotiates protection from a specific political group.

Nonetheless, for our discussion, the fact that the interests the politicians consider in formulating their evaluations have an administrative-professional, rather than economic or territorial, basis does not represent an analytical means of distinguishing one type of substantive policy-making from another. In fact, the existence of specific options for limited categories of implementors does not exclude, but often instead enhances, the construction of preference functions by various political groups: for example, recognizing that professors of medicine or religion teachers are expecting clear benefits from a legislative act, which is being blocked by other colleagues, can simplify the evaluation process for political policy-makers, making it easier for them to become either appreciative or diffident.

What distinguishes the sub-arena we can define as "neutral" is the fact that interests with administrative-professional bases are always presented to politicians as unitary demands of an entire organizational structure. In these cases, in fact, the representatives of the sectors assume an extremely ecumenical and pragmatic style of pressure, and aim at capturing the support of all political parties, without particular concerns or proscriptions, thus eliminating the criteria on which a politician can base an evaluation. Even in the many cases in which these actors have obtained the positions they hold through precise political affiliations, they choose first to reach an accord with their colleagues and, using this, to solicit the support of all the parties. This is preferable to inducing their own party to elaborate precise priorities, thus promoting a confrontation with the directors of the sector and delegating to them the formulation of binding choices.

7. The degrees of freedom between the two arenas

The observations advanced to this point have been intended to demonstrate how the relation between the politics of substantive policy and the politics of partisan policy is much less simple and direct than current analyses suggest, even when the same people are operating in the two arenas, as occurs in the Italian case. On the basis of this discussion, it is possible to suggest some initial, tentative conclusions.

First of all, certain features normally considered responsible for the uniqueness of Italian partisan policy do not necessarily appear destined to be reproduced in substantive policy processes. The polarization of Italian politics, with the constant placement of the second largest party at the bottom of the scale of preferences expressed by all other parties, does not prevent the recurrence of much more fluctuating majorities, or even the consolidation of rules of unanimity in most substantive policy-making. And the presence of politically strong organizations, with ample and centrally organized structures and a heavy ideological baggage, appears quite compatible with the segmentation and the specialization of decision-making procedures effectively capable of controlling state intervention in a particular sector. Therefore, it is incorrect to infer the placement of decision-making processes regarding substantive policies on the conflict/cooperation or comprehensiveness/segmentation axes on the basis of extrapolations from processes and outcomes in partisan policy-making, even when the central actors in the two arenas are the same.

The second conclusion can be summed up as follows. While in partisan policy the principle that an actor who chooses to participate in a decision-making process must have some preferences regarding the alternatives under discussion is respected, in substantive policy-making one can observe cases in which politicians assume the formal responsibility for acts whose appropriateness they are unable to evaluate, even from a purely utilitarian point of view. The dimension "indifference to/interest in" possible outcomes can thus be considered as a third essential axis for mapping decision processes in which the Italian politician can be involved in the arena of substantive policy-making.

The axes of decision-making characteristics can be depicted orthogonally, since they refer to analytically different dimensions. The first axis, coinciding with the cooperation/competition dimension, concerns the degree of compatibility or incompatibility established among the preferences of politicians belonging to different political groups with regard to a single issue. The second axis, coinciding with the segmentation/comprehensiveness dimension, concerns the extent of autonomy or of interdependence among the preferences of the same political group regarding different issues. The third axis, coinciding with the indifference/interest dimension, concerns the same degree of distinctiveness among the preferences expressed by politicians on different issues and admits the possibility that their interest in an issue can decrease until it reaches values close to zero.

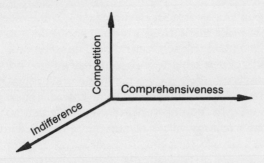

Figure 2.1. The decisional space of the politician policy-maker.

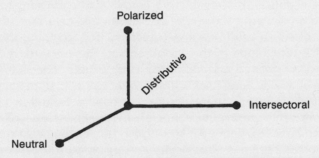

Figure 2.2. Map of types of substantive policy-making with political actors.

On the basis of these observations, the space within which the choices of political policy-makers are made assumes the configuration shown in Figure 2.1.

Both the empirical evidence employed in the previous sections of this chapter and logical consistency allow us to identify four different "pure" types of substantive policy-making, corresponding to four sub-arenas each endowed with its own internal equilibrium. These are placed at the extremes of the three axes and at the point of their intersection, and can be conventionally labeled as "polarized," "intersectoral," "neutral," and "distributive," as illustrated by Figure 2.2.

In order to identify the first three types, and to describe the conditions which determine the establishment of stable equilibrium points among the preferences of various actors, it is sufficient to recall certain observations presented above. "Polarized" policy-making is, in fact, characterized by mutually exclusive relations between interests since the issues assume a tendentially dichotomous structure. In this case, the rules of the game that permit stable outcomes are essentially founded on the exercise of political rights and respect for majority rule;

whoever captures more votes, in Parliament or in the electorate, wins. The classic democratic institutions are the central decisional loci – the parliamentary chamber, or the election box via referenda.

"Intersectoral" policy-making is based instead on the fact that the actors are able to order their preferences on a wide range of problems, such that the items on the agenda become interdependent. The rules of the game must admit some form of close interaction that permits practices like the exchange of votes, logrolling, and lateral compensations. The crucial decision-making loci are extra- or para-institutional negotiations in which the protagonists are the secretariats of parties, the secretariats of unions, and/or the government in its entirety.

"Neutral" policy-making is characterized by an extremely low degree of significance of evaluative criteria that politicians have with respect to the issues at stake. The conditions that determine the establishment of stable equilibria are, therefore, tied, on the one hand, to the explicit recognition of this "indifference" by every party aggregation, however defined and delimited, and, on the other hand, to the existence of a wide consensus among the actors with administrative or institutional credentials, permitting them both to formulate proposals and to solicit the approval of politicians. The basic centers of this type of decision have less defined institutional characteristics. At times, particular bodies designed specifically to aggregate the preferences of "institutional recipients" (for example, the National Council of Public Education [CNPI], National University Council [CUN], and at least in part, the Administrative Board of the National Institute for Social Security [INPS]) appear to assume a decisive role. In other cases, the selection of the victorious options becomes a more fluid and indefinite procedure that resembles the image of an issue network described by Heclo (1978).

8. "Distributive" policy-making

Distributive policy-making is located at the intersection of our three axes. It is characterized by: (1) relations of compatibility among interests, which lead to cooperative practices that often involve all significant political actors regardless of their position vis-à-vis the governing majority; (2) a disaggregation of competencies so that each decisional center has an agenda of items unique to it; and (3) procedures of access that guarantee the participation of those with clear and direct preferences for the issues under discussion.

Based on the fact that these conditions can be expected to produce essentially stable decision processes – even if the outcomes may be sub-optimal – a clear convergence can be established between formal, logico-deductive analyses and empirical analyses of *il caso italiano*.

With respect to the first of these two approaches, it has been explained at length how, in certain sectors of state intervention, it can be fully rational for the political policy-maker to maximize the probability of reelection by pursuing a strategy of cooperation with other politicians. For example, when the issues under discussion in a parliamentary commission deal with geographically or socially defined interests and are reciprocally compatible so that addressing the requests of one group does not necessarily hinder addressing the demands of another, the search for unanimity around a packet of benefits that gives something to everyone is the most certain way of assuring the stability of the decision-making process and avoiding cycles of adverse majorities which would occur if each proposal were put to a separate vote (Fiorina and Noll 1979; Weingast 1979). Essentially analogous arguments assume a central place in the already-cited studies on Italian policy-making, whether they are constructed around concepts of distributive government (Amato 1974), the political entrepreneur (Tarrow, 1977a), clientelism (Graziano 1980), or hidden government *(sottogoverno)* (Serrani 1978).

This last observation leads us to consider the effective descriptive power of the types we have described. Their development in fact implies the idea that the three dimensions are mutually exclusive, since the strengthening of one (for example, an increase in the degree of conflict) corresponds to a parallel weakening of the others (for example, the degree of indifference and of comprehensiveness). Now, oppositional relationship between "neutral" policy-making and the others specified above rests on the definition we gave to the former, since we tied it to the absence of precise preferences on the part of the political policy-maker. The relations of mutual exclusion between the other two variables, however, are based on a precise hypothesis regarding the frequency distribution of substantive policy-making processes in the logical space we have identified.

On the basis of data related to decision-making in the welfare sector, we can argue that, when preferences have a structure which channels them toward a zero-sum game, either tendencies toward postponement appear which draw a decision towards the distributive pole or, if the choice of confrontation has prevailed, it is up to the actors to ensure that conflict remains circumscribed and well defined. When complex preferences are at play, over a range of different policies, either the disagreements are disaggregated and treated in segmented decisional loci or maintenance of interdependence between the various issues is accompanied by the adoption of cooperative logics based on communication, negotiation, or lateral compensation.

9. The static nature of the model

A few final considerations remain before this chapter is brought to a conclusion. The first concerns the potential breadth of the application of our discussion. We have presented a static model of policy-making. The types specified are based on the recurrence of particular convergences among factors like the structure of the issues under discussion, the configuration of the actors' preferences, their organizational affiliations, and the rules that permit an equilibrium. The problem of explaining eventual shifts, which blur the boundaries between one type and another, between one sub-arena and another, remains essentially external to this approach. In other words, the problem of specifying which factor employed in constructing the various types dominates the others and can introduce dynamic elements into our framework remains completely unresolved.

Overcoming this limit is surely a research goal that should be pursued, both because shifts between sub-arenas appear particularly frequent in Italian substantive policy-making and because the character (partisan political) of the fundamental actors is such that it raises suspicions at the analytical level regarding the role this variable effectively plays. It is in fact evident that politicians, as contrasted to other categories of policy-makers, possess greater resources to influence the other factors, since they are able to play a decisive role in the conceptualization of problems, in the setting of rules of the game, and even in defining themselves as actors, that is, in the choice of which organizational level to activate.

The second consideration concerns the relationship between the politics of partisan policy-making and the politics of substantive policy-making. As we have repeated several times, this chapter is intended to demonstrate that there is sufficient evidence to consider the two arenas as distinct and relatively autonomous. Nonetheless, it is obvious that these degrees of freedom, even if greater than is commonly thought, are not unlimited since points of intersection exist between the two areas that our arguments can do little to identify. Our aim certainly was not to deny the existence of these complex relationships but rather to overcome both the excessive simplification of studies that consider the dynamics of substantive policy-making as a mere consequence of the dynamics of partisan policy-making and the circular reasoning of many self-confirming hypotheses based on the distinction between politicized and non-politicized issues.

10. Neutral policy-making

But even within a clearly static approach, a further problem remains that cannot be postponed. This concerns the clear asymmetry that exists in our typology between "neutral" policy-making and the other three types. While the latter are in some way coherent even from a logical-deductive point of view and can withstand tests based on the hypothesis of the rationality of the actors, the former appears less able to generate a self-sufficient, internal explanation of the identifiable equilibria. In particular, it appears quite difficult to explain the decision of politicians to participate in this type of decision-making process and to assume final responsibility for its outcomes, since no preference for the alternatives being considered can be identified. In fact, in the face of this type of situation, in which the links between participation in the decision and the interests of the actors weaken to the point of disappearing, explanations generally rely on psychological or anthropological variables that emphasize the cultural ties and symbolic exchanges which are established among members of a policy community (Heclo and Wildavsky 1974; Brinton Milward 1980). Alternatively, such explanations rely on systemic variables that accentuate the preeminence of institutional logics in relation to the utilitarian goals of individuals (for an up-dated review, see March and Olsen 1983).

Without rejecting the validity of these analyses, the last part of our chapter seeks to demonstrate that the interpretation of these same processes does not necessarily require the abandonment of the paradigm within which we have so far worked. In other words, we will seek to explain on the basis of the rationality of the actors the choice by politicians to participate in the selection of outcomes they are not even capable of evaluating vis-à-vis their own goals.

Our reasoning is based on a single premise: the construction of a preference ordering for the members of a political group which can be applied to the group itself is a much more costly process than that of an individual. This is so, first, because they must face complicated decision-making processes and, second, because, once formulated, the choice must be defended and advanced. Contrary to what is commonly believed, the return on these costs is not automatically guaranteed in substantive policy-making. Rather, there exist issues with obscure emotional implications or with enormous technological difficulties whose exploitation for political ends could be disastrous. One thinks, for example, of the issue of artificial insemination, the reform of higher education, or euthanasia. While current opinion holds that it is in the politicians' interests to formulate preferences and invest in the sponsorship of specific policy options, there exist many problems whose exploitation in a given cultural context would be or might be catastrophic. (For example, this occurred recently over ecological issues, and is still true today for many issues that are either intentionally kept off the agenda or are dealt with through self-regulation by the implementors.)

In light of these considerations, the participation of politicians in "neutral" policy-making can be considered a response to the same type of rationality that induces firms to participate in research projects or to cooperate in order to monitor the market (Arrow 1974). These types of activities, if, on the one hand, they are intended to identify the most promising occasions for true and proper investments, on the other hand, are designed to block initiatives in unproductive sectors.

Analogously, the "issue culture" (Heclo 1978) that politicians update by maintaining formal roles in "neutral" policy-making allows them to recognize the margins for exploitation of a problem and to withdraw when these are practically null. Actually, by observing the behavior of other policy-makers who are also affiliated with parties, politicians can assure themselves that their lack of interest in an issue does not result from ingenuousness or ignorance but is matched by an analogous indifference of their colleagues.

The politician's interest in a continued presence within this type of policy-making, and the explanation of a particular equilibrium point that guarantees stability, are in fact based on this point: the principal guarantee that an issue cannot be exploited by special interests derives from its failure to be used in this way by other politicians. When the equilibrium based on deterrence is weak, and a party manager sees the potential to exploit issues previously considered neutral – for example, through the narrow partisan sponsorship of a technical committee – the vigilance of the other partners permits them to adapt to this new situation, generally by forcing the issue towards the distributive pole.

11. The preferences of bureaucrats

The explanation we have provided for the functioning of "neutral" policy-making is based on a specific configuration of relations between the preferences of politicians and those of policy-makers endowed with other qualifications, whether as representatives of more or less extensive interests, as implementors of a provision, or because they possess technical competencies. But the fact that only in this sub-arena has the role of these actors, endowed with utility functions different from politicians', been explicitly considered does not mean that they are not important in other types of substantial policy-making. Any description, however stylized, of the decision-making process through which the public sector is managed in a particular area is, in fact, likely to resemble a network in which relations based on the most disparate preferences are superimposed.

Since this chapter analyzes the policy space open to the politician in substantial policy-making, the identification of a dimension that detaches itself from a plane defined by polarized (P), intersectoral (I), and distributive (D) policy-making is not intended to signal the presence of these different preferences as much as to indicate a particular type of relationship between these preferences and those of the politicians. In the case of issues managed on the PID plane, the interests expressed by non-political actors do not hinder, but in certain ways enhance, the constitution of the politicians' interests. In the case of "neutral" policy-making, the desire of members of a party to remain part of the flow of decisions is in some way an end in itself, while the actors with other sources of legitimation are also able to "synthesize" evaluations for the specific issues at stake. Beyond this threshold, there exists the field of public decisions that are adopted without the intervention, even formal, of politicians. These either are directly self-regulated by the relevant actors – as occurred over schoolbook policy, which developed notwithstanding ministerial passiveness – or are managed entirely by technical-bureaucratic procedures and personnel – as was the case until recently for the determination of power relations between various academic disciplines. Thus, the scope of "neutral" policy-making appears limited on the one side by processes in which politicians participate as bearers of their own specific preferences regarding the issues under discussion and on the other side by processes in which they do not even play a role because of their disinterest even in monitoring the policy area.

What we have said so far permits us to explain the structure of this particular type of policy-making, placing it in a context of decision-making types that are certainly not confined to Italy. Typically Italian, however, is the placement of the two thresholds that bound "neutral" policy-making. More precisely, issues (an example is the construction of hospitals) appear on the PID plane on which politicians act as mere observers in other countries. In Italy issues clearly not usable for partisan purposes remain in the domain of neutral policy-making, while in other countries a wide, consolidated consensus maintains such issues outside the uncertain border zone that politicians are interested in monitoring. The universally recognized fact that Italian substantive policy-making is particularly politicized can be depicted graphically as in Figure 2.3.

An explanation of the phenomenon evidently requires an analysis of the particular relations that have developed in Italy between politicians

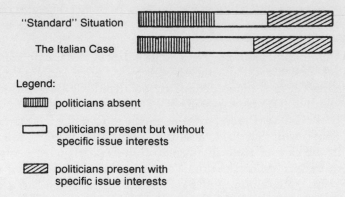

Figure 2.3. Scope of substantial policy-making with political actors.

and policy-makers with other qualifications. Nonetheless, it is commonly thought that, above all, actors with administrative responsibilities will experience a contraction of decision space within which they can undertake autonomous initiatives.

We would like to urge a reevaluation of certain widely held diagnoses. Our hypothesis is as follows: the inclusion in "neutral" policy-making of issues that elsewhere are treated as clearly of a technical or bureaucratic nature derives from the common perception – shared as much by bureaucrats as by politicians – of a fundamental imbalance in the resources available to the two types of actors for effectively pursuing their preferences. More precisely, there appear to be two disadvantages that penalize the policy-maker with administrative qualifications in Italy. The first concerns the internal difficulties the administration encounters in constituting itself as an autonomous team, given the absence of incentives that might lead bureaucrats to elaborate and to make claims for their own preference orderings, even to the point of challenging the competition of politicians. The second concerns the difficulties administrators encounter in their relations with policy-makers with other credentials, given that the procedural constraints by which they are governed under administrative law are poorly adapted to substantive policy-making.

As for the first point, analyses of the Italian bureaucracy have usually shown how a loss of executive efficiency and an incapacity to realize legislative goals have resulted from the managerial shortcomings of the bureaucracy. Here we would like to focus on another consequence of the shortcomings of public management: the absence of spokespeople for the preferences of the administration itself, who by the simple presentation of their demands could eliminate any doubt over the possibilities for political exploitation of an issue. In other words, the Italian situation appears to be characterized by the absence of a "bureaucratized market" that conditions the distribution of resources (like career promotions, salary increases, and prestige) and that the directors of an administration can use to make themselves interpreters of their own needs. There are in fact elements that block the emergence within the administration of complete and autonomous preference functions, capable of matching those of the politicians or capable of assuring the impermeability of the bureaucracy to the preferences of their adversaries. These include career patterns that are essentially determined by automatic promotions; the absence of mobility between different sectors of public employment, and between the private and public sectors; the fragility of horizontal communication networks that are essentially controlled by politicians; and organizational fragility.

The second point on which we would like to propose a reconsideration concerns the constraints placed by administrative law on decision-making processes that involve the interaction of bureaucrats with policy-makers endowed with other qualifications. Since, as we have emphasized, relations between actors differentiated by roles constitute the normal form of substantive policy-making, an eventual handicap in this type of game can seriously limit the autonomous influence of a category. Now, rules like strict hierarchical subordination, the certification of political directors, the complexity of procedures, the redundance of controls, which are in reality purely formal, impede bureaucrats from presenting themselves as autonomous and influential interlocutors at the table that brings together representatives of economic interests, organizations of consumers, experts, or those politically responsible for a department. It is their inability to propose flexible and experimental solutions, to assume binding but informal commitments, or to be the fulcrum in bipolar negotiations that condemns bureaucrats to reticence, to public inertia, or to "behind the scenes" maneuvering, even over issues which in other countries would see the bureaucrat acting as a protagonist. Instead, in Italy, bureaucrats need a politician to sponsor their goals.

Note

1 By this we mean those based on the simultaneous evaluation within the negotiation between political groups of policy issues that could otherwise be managed individually by specialized decision-making procedures.

3

Protest and regulation: the interaction of state and society in the cycle of 1965–74

SONIA STEFANIZZI AND SIDNEY TARROW[1]

As readily as Americans blame fate, technology, or the market for the ills that befall them, Italians blame their government for what goes wrong in their lives. The old aphorism *"Piove, governo ladro!"* ("It's raining; the government is a thief!") sums up this proverbial attitude well. It comes out of a political culture that has sometimes been seen as alienated, polarized, and pessimistic (LaPalombara 1965), and at other times as participatory, lively, and theatrical. For example, after decrying the alienation of Italian public life in his early work, LaPalombara (1987:Chap. 4) has come around to the view that Italian politics is a kind of *spettacolo* in which the players are found both on the stage and in the audience.

What is striking about these views is that both of them implicitly see politics as permeating – without regulating – society. In the first variant, Italians blame the state for society's ills, but their alienation from politics leaves a void in mass politics that political elites and parties are happy to fill. In the second, people from all walks of life feel that they are part of the process, of the bigger picture (LaPalombara 1987:88). Citizens, in this view, are part of a "Globe theatre" of Italian public life (pp. 91–2).

It is only with the recent successes of the Italian economy that the omnipresence of politics has been questioned and the dynamism in Italian society recognized. But with this recognition has come a rejection of the traditional emphasis on politics and a trumpeting of the virtues of social regulation (i.e., the market).[2] The reasoning is simple: if the state is as ineffective as some have seen it, but the economy is a "success story," perhaps the cause lies in successful social regulation through the market? The remedy that follows for all of Italy's ills is a familiar one – state deregulation. The advocates of this new paradigm perhaps forget the extent to which the market is permeated by the state and the degree to which the defects of the state are due to its past privatization.

81

The contributions to this volume reveal a less simple but more interesting phenomenon: in each area of policy regulation studied, a broad mix of state and social regulation has been observed. Not only that, each area has its peculiar mix of state and social regulation, determined by the institutions in place, the social interests involved, and the history of the actors' relationships. The studies seem to demonstrate the futility of classifying the boundaries between state and society holistically, as if there were a kind of "grand design" for regulation in each country (see the Introduction to this volume).

This chapter will look at state and social regulation from another angle than that of organized policy making: from that of how popular collective action intrudes between the state and society. Students of protest have often regarded collective action as "anomic," noninstitutional behavior denoting a breakdown in regulation. More recently, scholars like Gamson (1975), Tilly (1978), and one of the present writers (Tarrow 1983, 1988) have argued that protest can more fruitfully be seen as an element in political exchange. If this is so, then like more conventional politics it can studied in terms of its relation to political groups, in terms of how it translates claims into demands and how it is regulated.

In the Introduction to this volume, Lange and Regini propose three definitions of regulation:

We define as regulation the mode or form (or better, as we will see in a moment, the different modes) by which a determinate set of activities and/or relationships among actors is coordinated, the related resources allocated, and the related conflicts, whether real or potential, structured (that is, prevented or reconciled). There are, therefore, three dimensions to the concept of regulation as we use it: the coordination of activities or relationships, the allocation of resources, the structuring of conflicts.

We shall try to shed light on the three definitional aspects of regulation – coordination, allocation, and structuring – with respect to protest, by asking three questions.

1. With respect to *coordination:* when a cycle of protest occurs, what is the level of coordination between non-institutionalized protest behavior and institutional politics?
2. With respect to *allocation:* when disputes arise between groups in society and lead to publicly organized collective action, how often do these conflicts directly target the state rather than other social groups, and how frequently do private actors "cross over" from societal regulation to seek allocations from the state?

3. With respect to the *structuring of conflict:* to what extent, and in which ways, are the forms of conflict, and thus the outcomes of the protest cycle, structured by the state, by social regulation, or by a combination of the two?

We shall approach these questions by analyzing Italian collective action during a period of disorderly mass politics – 1966–73.[3] We will do so from an almost unique data archive on strikes, protests, and political violence collected from a daily reading and coding of almost 20,000 articles in Italy's main newspaper of record, *Corriere della Sera.*[4] The data were collected in order to study the more general problem of the dynamic of waves of mass mobilization, but some of the questions asked can be related to those posed above.

Skeptics may complain that a period of generalized disorder like that of the late 1960s and early 1970s in Italy is scarcely the best time in which to study state or social regulation. Our response is exactly the opposite, for it is precisely when a society is under severe pressure from many quarters that the role and limits of state regulation should most clearly emerge. We shall use these data to shed light on the ways in which protest behavior mediates between state and society.

Starting from a very different perspective than the other contributions to this volume, our findings will support the impression they produce of a complex mix of state and social regulation, one that operates even in a sphere in which ordinary conflict resolution mechanisms appear to have broken down. (We use the word "appear" because, in many cases, publicly organized collective action seems to be part of the conflict resolution process, rather than its negation.)

Our procedure will be first to examine the rise of the new wave of collective action in the late 1960s, relating it to the major issues and realignments in the political system at the outset of the cycle. Here we shall interpret Lange and Regini's first aspect of regulation – the coordination of the activities or the relations among actors – as the co-occurrence of institutional and non-institutional conflict.

Second, we will construct a typology of conflict from the data on protest, which will allow us to ask how frequently contention arose out of disputes within state or society, and how often those that organized in the private sphere "crossed over" from society to state. This will allow us to ask how frequently Lange and Regini's second aspect of regulation – the allocation of resources – is demanded of the state to resolve disputes that arise in civil society.

Third, we shall examine the forms that protest took as the cycle of protest proceeded in the second half of the 1960s and the early 1970s, to reflect on their third aspect of regulation – the structuring of conflict.

Before turning to these analyses, however, it will be useful to illustrate the possible ways in which protest and politics are coordinated, how resources are allocated, and how the repertoire of protest is structured in an archetypical industrial dispute.

1. A shipyard closes[5]

The old city of Trieste sits at the junctions of three cultures – Slav, Latin, and German – and of three political societies. With its history as the main Hapsburg outlet to the sea a distant memory and its natural hinterland closed off in Yugoslavia, the city survives as an outpost of Italian culture, more for political than for economic reasons. In the city's economy, the weight of the public sector is accordingly great – particularly in the shipping and shipyard industry that is a vestige of its former glory. As a part of the conservative Friuli-Venezia Giulia region, Trieste is politically moderate, but – as everywhere else in Italy – its maritime unions are militant.

By the mid-1960s, with shipbuilding becoming rapidly internationalized, Italian yards are suffering from overcapacity. In June 1966, in the midst of national contract negotiations, officials of the nationalized IRI (Istituto per la Ricostruzione Industriale), who control the shipbuilding firm Italcantieri, announce a plan to restructure the industry around a few key centers. As part of this plan, Trieste's Cantieri Riuniti will be merged into a larger unit with headquarters in Genoa, and the city's San Marco yard will be closed (*Corriere della Sera*, June 24, 1966, henceforth cited as *CdS*).

Two of the major union confederations, the Confederazione Generale Italiana del Lavoro (CGIL) and the Confederazione Italiana de Sindacati Libri (CISL), uniting in the name of local solidarity, call a general strike. Like most strikes called to protest plant closings, it commands local solidarity, extending from the yards to schools, shops, public transportation, and factories. A parade by the San Marco workers is followed by a public meeting in the center of town to call attention to the city's plight if the yards close down.

Their strength demonstrated, the unions meet with the president of the local Chamber of Commerce, representatives of the four governing parties, the city's parliamentary delegation, the mayor, the president of the Friuli-Venezia Giulia region, and the top officials of IRI and Italcantieri. The delegation proceeds to Rome to meet with then-Prime Minister Aldo Moro (*CdS*, June 24, 1966).

This well-orchestrated, almost ritualistic sequence of events produces assurances that a solution will be found which will trim the shipbuilding sector but take account of the needs of the city's workers. But by midsummer, nothing has been done and another general strike is called – this one led by all three union confederations and with even broader support from the local citizenry. This time, the ritual march and public meeting do not end not in a genial encounter with officials, but in a clash with police, when rocks are thrown at the offices of a local radio station for supposedly failing to give the protest sufficient coverage (*CdS*, August 2–4). The government responds with suggestions of splitting the difference – closing down the San Marco docks, but moving the Italcantieri office from Genoa to Trieste.

The governmental maneuver gives the Triestini pause. But across the peninsula in Genoa, in a far more conflictual political culture, workers, shopkeepers, and politicians react more violently. From late September to the end of the year, the Genoese unions organize a series of lightning strikes to demand the transfer of Italcantieri to their city, as well as more economic help for its decaying economy. Here too, the three union confederations collaborate and send a joint delegation to Rome to talk with the government. As in Trieste, local solidarity is the leitmotif of the agitations.

But Genoa is not Trieste: this time the union's well-run demonstrations and the citizens' expressions of solidarity trigger confrontations and violence as shopkeepers close their shutters, traffic is blocked, and young people, joining in the unions' demonstrations, clash with the police. In one mass demonstration, "maoist" university students take advantage of the unions' initiative to enter the fray, breaking windows, damaging cars, and, according to the *Corriere*, stealing books in the name of local rights. Arrests and a trial eventually follow (*CdS*, September 29–December 20, 1966).

Back on the Adriatic, the Genoa events raise the fear of the loss of Italcantieri. New strikes are held to ensure that the firm will be allocated to Trieste and that the San Marco yard will stay open. Now, as in Genoa, the conflict soon spreads beyond the shipyard and escapes the unions' control. On October 4, some of the marchers in a union-led parade spontaneously interrupt a school's inauguration to embarrass the Minister of Education, who is present. And as they pass the offices of a local newspaper, workers throw lumps of charcoal at its windows to protest its lack of coverage of the strike (*CdS*, October 5, 1966).

The uncontrolled nature of the general strike begins to worry the CISL and its local Christian Democratic allies. When, on October 9, the majority CGIL calls another strike in Trieste, the CISL hangs back, and there are clashes with police, traffic obstructions, and an attack on a Christian Democratic affiliate's offices (*CdS*, October 12, 1966). No one can now blame the CISL for the violence, but the CGIL is exposed politically by the unofficial violence carried out under its banner. As in Genoa, the reaction to the government's plan leads first to widespread enthusiasm and unity and then to divisions and to retreat by the organized actors as collective action turns to violence.

By late autumn, despite grumbling and an occasional return to collective action, the main lines of the government's compromise have been accepted by the major unions, the city administration, and the Chambers of Commerce of both cities. There have been elements of violence and elements of public theater, but a compromise solution to the conflict emerges from a mix of different forms and different types of state and social regulation.

Coordination, allocation, and structuring

The sequences of incidents in Trieste, Genoa, and Rome are not unrelated or random. They illustrate how the state in various guises can become involved in social conflicts: as the source of a grievance – since it was the state holding company, IRI, that made the decision to close the San Marco yard and touched off the conflict; as the target of the demands of groups seeking resources; and as the occasional object of protests.

The shipyard conflict also shows how Lange and Regini's three meanings of regulation can be present in the same dispute:

First, the conflicts in both cities involved the coordination of activities and relationships by trade unions, workers, management, civic groups, local governmental units, and the central state. Conventional political exchange and disruptive collective action developed in parallel, at times diverging and finally intersecting, leading to a "solution" in the form of a political compromise.

Second, the conflict was primarily about the allocation of resources, but not only to the main social actor – the port workers. Also involved were the competing claims of two cities, the needs of other social groups threatened by the shipyard closings, the political interests of local officials, and the interest of the state in maintaining social peace and public order. It was the broad mix of groups whose interests became involved that forced the state to intervene.

Third, as the conflict proceeded, it took on different forms, ranging from delegations and private meetings to peaceful public demonstrations to violence. At several points it spilled over into general political conflict (the stoning of the radio station in Trieste; the "book burning" in Genoa). Mostly, however, it kept to a well-worn "repertoire" of forms of action that the major organizational actors habitually used and that the state accepted as legitimate. The repertoire of contention was structured by mutual expectations between the social actors and the state.

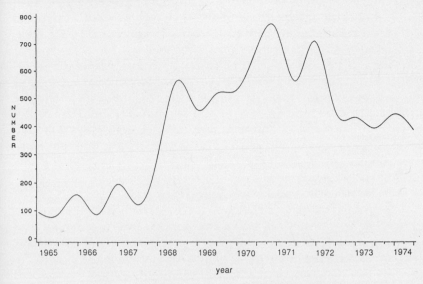

Figure 3.1. Number of events, by semester, 1965–74.

In the next section, we shall first present some of the main parameters of the wave of protest that swept over Italy in the late 1960s and early 1970s. We shall then turn to how some of key protests grew out of conflicts and realignments in the political system and how institutional and non-institutional conflicts were coordinated at different stages of the cycle.

2. The coordination of protest and politics

The period from the mid-1960s to the early-1970s in Italy divided the years of the economic miracle of "easy growth" from the economic crisis following the 1973 oil embargo. It was in this period that social and economic conflict – led first by the student movement and by industrial insurgency, but reaching very rapidly into urban and religious conflicts, public sector strikes, and protests against the social services – burst out of the largely party-run politics of the postwar decades.[6] Figure 3.1 provides us with a rough outline of the numbers of contentious collective actions we were able to study from the *Corriere della Sera* for the eight-year period 1965–1974.

The curve in Figure 3.1 includes all the strikes, marches, demonstrations, occupations, violent and symbolic events, and all other forms of contentious collective action found in the *Corriere* between 1966 and 1973 and estimates of the number of events in 1965 and 1974 based on a sample of articles from one out of every four months. We make

Table 3.1. *Sectors of protest events*

Sector	No.	%
Economic		
Industry	899	18.1
Agriculture	66	1.3
Private Services	356	7.2
Public Services	495	9.9
Social		
Education	884	17.8
Urban	157	3.2
Social services	206	4.1
Art and culture	61	1.2
Religion, women, family	79	1.6
Policy		
Regional	56	1.1
International	208	4.2
Environment	56	1.1
Justice	390	7.8
Political conflict		
Antigovernmental	16	0.3
Constitutional	21	0.4
Ideological group conflict	975	19.6
Other sectors	54	1.1
Total	4,979	100.0

no attempt to capture either the number of people who participated in the conflicts of the period or the duration or importance of the events. Nor do we have any direct means of measuring the rise and fall of movements and conflicts that were hidden from public view. The magnitude of the cycle rose through the height of the university student movements of 1967–68 and the *autunno caldo* of 1969–70 to reach its quantitative peak in 1971, before beginning a decline in 1972.

Contention, conflict, and protest were most widespread among students and in industry, and were centered in the big cities of the North. However, a significant proportion involved other policy and economic sectors and were found in regions other than the Industrial Triangle. Table 3.1 presents summary data on the distribution of conflicts in the *Corriere* dataset from 1966 through 1973 in each of the broad policy, economic, and institutional sectors to which their demands were directed.

Looking at the data presented in Table 3.1, we can classify conflict into four broad spheres – economic, social, policy issues, and political and ideological conflict. The economic sphere includes not only industrial conflicts but also agricultural ones and conflicts relating to private and public services. Alongside the high proportion of industrial conflicts – 18.1 percent of the total – we should note the high percentage of conflicts in the public services, with nearly 10 percent, recalling the importance of conflicts within the state and in the parastate sector in those years.

Although economic conflicts were the most important, with a total of 36.5 percent, we can also see that social issues – such as schools, urban problems, social services, religion, and the family – constituted 27.9 percent of the total. It was thus not just workers who protested, but also other social actors coming from other spheres, who mobilized around their own demands.

Theorists of the movements of the 1960s and 1970s have focused on the "new" social actors who appeared in these years (Offe 1985; Melucci 1980). But the actors we found were both "old" – like the working class – and "new" – like students, ecologists, advocates or opponents of divorce, and even prisoners. Another large group was characterized not by its social identity but by the fact that its conflicts were political or ideological. This group was found in fully 20 percent of the events we analyzed. Italy's was a protest cycle that was not only about people's private claims, but about the most salient issues of government: who governs, under which kind of regime, and which groups have the right to participate or exist?

The political origins of the protest cycle
Political conflicts and political realignments were at the origin of many of the issues that engaged Italians in these years. Although the movements of the late 1960s invented new forms of protest and brought a new independence and imagination to mass politics, they took many of their issues from the political debates of the early part of the decade and left behind few new interpretive frames.[7]

In the early 1960s, there was a widespread debate in Italy over the transition to mature capitalism and its costs and promises. In governmental circles this debate focused on planning, on the technical needs of a modern society, and on the defects of the existing industrial relations system. The academic tone of these debates at first disguised the fact that they bridged political subcultures and had the potential for broadening the arena of controversy. Together with the economic and social changes that had stimulated them, the debates made clear that a realignment of some kind was necessary if the Christian Democratic party was not to follow the decline of its traditional social groups. The major political result was the contested, ambiguous, and still poorly understood strategy of the Christian Democrat's "Opening to the Left" and the Center-Left coalition that it produced.

Arguments turned in part on the lack of a modern industrial relations system. Although much of management was still unwilling to reform its paternalistic and repressive labor relations, there were outcroppings of modernism in the Olivetti empire and among younger technocrats in the public sector. While the private firms represented by *Confindustria* (the General Confederation of Italian Industry) wanted to continue to rely on national-level bargaining, the public firms represented in IRI and ENI (Ente Nazionale Idrocarburi) wanted to institute articulated bargaining at the level of the firm.

At the same time, the CISL and then the CGIL were developing a parallel debate. Inspired by what they took to be American models, CISL intellectuals had sought firm-level bargaining from the early 1950s; the CGIL came around to a similar view only after its defeats in the middle of the decade. These debates had implications for the organization of the working class at the base; though the "spontaneous" worker militance of 1968–69 has often been seen as the origin of the councils of delegates that became the grass-roots expression of the unions, they were also outcomes of the earlier debates in union circles about the organs appropriate to articulated industrial relations.[8]

On the political Left, debates were more theoretical but no less portentious. The Communists (PCI), through their Gramsci Institute in Rome, held an important conference on "Tendencies in Italian Capitalism," which put them ten years ahead of their French comrades in recognizing the effects of economic change (Istituto Gramsci 1962). A strategic debate on the role of the "productive" middle class began at the same time, as – sensing the decline of its traditional rural supporters – the party looked for new electoral allies in parts of the middle class that were created by advanced capitalism.

It was in reaction to this tilt towards the center in the PCI that many young Communist intellectuals joined independent left groups like *Quaderni Rossi* and the so-called *sinistra sindacale* in advancing a modernized version of the traditional *operaismo* that was to enthrall the extraparliamentary Left for much of the next decade.[9] As for the workerism of the future extraparliamentary Left, it was always a political creation: the logical ideological symbol to use in revealing the PCI's "betrayal" of the proletariat.

As for the Socialists (PSI), they were more concerned with readying themselves for a future role in government than in understanding the future of Italian capitalism. But political opportunism has strange effects: the prospect of joining the government led the PSI to put reforms on its political agenda – education, pension reform, divorce – that would later become rallying points for mass protest. Ironically, but not for the first time in history, the themes of future protest movements were popularized by the very people who would eventually be attacked by those movements. For example, the 1967 debate over pension reform started in Parliament but soon led to widespread mobilization of the workers.

The national debate on the educational system that began in the late 1950s is a good example of how issues raised in the political establishment could provide a springboard for protest. Stimulated in part by academic initiatives and in part by industry's demand for trained cadres, the government passed a reform law in 1962 that was so quickly revealed as inadequate that it led to intensified debate on its revision. The Gui Law was opposed in Parliament by the PCI and became the target of the party's attempt to mobilize dissatisfied youth. The weapon backfired when the University Left used it to split the main party-linked student organizations, the UGI (Communist-Socialist) and Intesa Universitaria (Catholic)[10]

The debates that followed the disillusionment with the Center-Left experience were similar in many ways to debates about the New Deal in the United States; both revolved around the academic issue of whether they were progressive or conservative. But as in the New Deal, the inherent progressivism or conservatism of the Center-Left was less important than the fact that it provided political opportunities for insurgents and for people outside the political class to mobilize around. First, it placed issues on the agenda that it could not resolve; second, because of its own internal divergences, it encouraged groups outside the polity to intervene in, and radicalize, its internal discords; third, the realignment of the PSI towards the Center-Left opened political space on the Left.

There is another parallel with the New Deal that is often overlooked: that the presence of a party of the moderate left in the coalition limited the government's options for repression of dissent. Neither the old recessionary solution to wage increases nor unleashing the forces of "order" against demonstrators were possible with the PSI attempting to preserve its claim to a share of working-class votes and seeking support from the new middle class. For example, when workers were shot upon by police in Avola and Battipaglia in 1968, the PSI called for an investigation and joined the Communists in a call to disarm the police. Though the Socialists were not very effective representatives of either class, their entry into government indicated the instability of the postwar political settlement and the depth of the realignment at work in the country.

Soon after the effective start of the Center-Left experiment in 1962, realignment began to stir within the party system. Splits in the Socialist and Republican parties in 1963 and 1964 were followed by an attempted merger between the Socialists and Social Democrats and by talk of forming a unified party of labor by the moderate wing of the PCI. The Communist's youth federation, the FCGI, was in more or less open tumult throughout the late 1960s, and a Christian Democratic labor organization, the ACLI, split and produced a new secular movement under its former leader.

A deeper ferment was stirring outside the party system, where new political groups appeared and mobilization began to escape traditional channels for the first time since the 1940s. But it was never independent of the insurgency within the party system, for many of the leaders of the New Left learned their politics and their organizing skills from within either the Left or popular Catholic organizations.

In some sectors – as in the University student movement – the traditional associations were thoroughly discredited and were replaced by a new generation of New Left groups. In most others, the movements did not replace parties and unions, but stirred them to new activism and more aggressive policies. In the factories, the unions, struggling to "ride the tiger" of working-class insurgency, quickly won out over the movements of 1968–9; in the cities, movements, parties, and unions competed for the support of tenants and others; in the mass public, the wave of social movement participation was soon outstripped by an increase in PCI membership.[11]

The coordination between protest and political conflict continued throughout the cycle. A few examples will have to suffice here: the 1967 pension debate, which produced a wave of mobilization that took the unions by surprise; the killing of workers by police at Avola and Battipaglia, which triggered a wave of demonstrations; the debate over the authorship of the Piazza Fontana massacre and the political wrangling over the trial of Pietro Valprede, which prompted repeated protests; the 1972 election campaign, which was the occasion for savage conflict between extreme Left and Right; the 1970 creation of new regional governments, which led to the uprisings at Aquila and Reggio Calabria; the parliamentary debate over divorce that stretched over the early 1970s and was the occasion for a campaign of protest by both lay Left and Catholic Right; the 1972–73 prison reform debate, which was accompanied by prison riots whose leaders put forward detailed reform programs.

Protest was not simply the continuation of conventional politics by other means, for it was always expressive, often uncontrolled, and sometimes violent. But in contrast to some students of "new" social movements who are persuaded of the movements' "apolitical" vocation,[12] we found the themes of many of the movements we studied emerging out of earlier or contemporary political debates and a close coincidence between the movement's mobilization campaigns and the issues and alignments within the political system.

2. The allocation of resources

Sources, targets, objects

Protest, like politics, is an interactive process in which the objectives of protest can take several forms:

1. Those who are held responsible for the grievances of the actors or of those they claim to represent – what we shall refer to as the *sources* of people's grievances
2. Those from whom the actors demand a response to their demands – what we shall call the *targets* of their demands
3. Those who are physically acted against, either through physical attack, obstruction, or some other form of disruption – what we will refer to as the *objects* of contention

In many protest events, the source, the object, and the target of the protest will be the same. For example, industrial workers in a wages dispute will normally blame management for their grievances (the source), demand that management change its wages policy (the target), and attempt to stop the plant's production (the object). Most conflicts thus stay within the precincts in which they are generated.

But in some conflicts, source, object, and target differ as protesters go outside the boundaries within which their grievances were formed to find satisfaction. The shipyard closing in Trieste illustrates this mixture nicely: the original source of the grievance was the shipyard company that wanted to close down the San Marco yard and move Cantieri Riuniti to Genoa; the main target of the demand was the Italian government, which was asked to override IRI's decision and keep the Trieste yards open. In its course, the strikers and demonstrators attacked the objects of economic life, transport, and public order in the city. Including Genoa in the story makes the array of actors and enemies even more complex, for the Genovesi were opposing not only the shipyard management but the claim of the opposing city.

Leaving aside the physical objects of contention, what do we find about the distribution of sources and targets when we survey the almost 5,000 protest events extracted from *Corriere della Sera* from 1966 through 1973? Were the major sources and targets found in civil society, in the state, or in a combination of the two? Table 3.2 summarizes our findings in this regard. The table calculates the major groups of both specific and general, public and private actors that were

Table 3.2. *Sources of grievances and targets of demands; defining*
grievance and principal target

	Source		Target	
	No.	%	No.	%
None	—[a]	—[a]	860	18.3
A. Specific sources or targets				
Private or public firm	910	18.6	817	17.4
Union or other group	186	3.8	118	2.5
Party or movement	947	19.3	143	3.0
School or university	611	12.5	592	12.6
Local government	384	7.8	506	10.8
Police, judiciary	392	8.0	291	6.2
National agency	543	11.1	575	12.3
B. General sources or targets				
Business, capital, the economy	259	5.3	195	4.2
National government	331	6.7	435	9.3
Foreign government	190	3.9	148	3.2
Others	152	3.1	13	0.3
Missing data	75	1.5	287	5.8
Total	4,905	100.0	4,693	100.0

[a]Events were not included unless they had an identifiable source and grievance.

judged to be both the sources and the targets of the conflicts we
studied.

The most obvious finding in the "source" column of Table 3.2 relates
to the weight of political and governmental antagonists in comparison
to societal ones. When we simplify by including all schools and universities as "public" (and in Italy, the vast majority of them are) and
consider both publicly owned and private firms to be "private," then
69 percent of the sources and 57 percent of the targets are in the sphere
of the state.[13] Political parties, social movement organizations, local
governments, national governmental agencies, Parliament, the judiciary, and the national state as a whole were far more often the sources
against which protesters acted than firms, industrial associations,
unions, churches, or other collectivities in civil society.

The targets of the protests, which are found in the right-hand col-
umns of Table 3.2, were structured similarly to the sources. But there
are two important differences: first, a significant proportion of the protests – over 18 percent – were "issueless" (e.g., although there was a
source for the protest, no specific demand was made of any visible tar-

Table 3.3. *Typology of conflict, by the source of the grievance and the target of the demand*

Type	All conflicts		Strikes		Non-strikes	
	No.	%	No.	%	No.	%
Issueless	840	18.0	33	1.7	807	29.5
Society-centered	1,659	35.5	998	51.5	661	24.2
State-centered	1,853	39.3	762	39.3	1,073	39.2
"Crossover" to society	57	1.2	18	0.9	39	1.4
"Crossover" to state	192	4.1	105	5.4	87	3.2
Other	90	1.9	21	1.1	69	2.5
Total	4,691	100.0	1,937	100.0	2,736	100.0

get); and second, the various levels of government – local and national – appear slightly more often as the targets of demands than as sources of grievances.

Taken on their own, these two differences seem to have opposite implications for the character of state regulation in Italy. An "issueless" protest expresses grievances without making demands to which anybody – including the state – can easily respond.[14] In contrast, protest that arises in civil society but "crosses over" into the state sphere suggests that demands are being made for the allocation of resources from the state. To the extent that this pattern prevails, collective action may be seen as an attempt to bring in the state by actors who are not getting satisfaction from their antagonists in civil society.

Both patterns were obviously present in the period we studied. But it is only by combining the sources of the protests and the targets of the demands in individual protests that we can construct a picture of the main axes of conflict in collective action at the time. Based on these two sets of variables, we have constructed a simple typology that will allow us to ask:

How often were conflicts issueless?

How common were those in which people with a grievance against another group worked out their conflicts in civil society?

And how common were those which both began and ended in the state?

How frequently did people with a grievance against another group in civil society turn to the state for the allocation of resources and how often did the converse occur (e.g., when people with grievances against political or governmental actors turned to the private sphere for satisfaction)?

The resulting typology is presented in Table 3.3. It looks first at the protest events as a whole and then divides them into those in which strikes occurred and those in which there was no strike. The results can be quickly summarized.

Issueless protests

As we saw above, 18 percent of the protests were targetless. The division between strikes and non-strikes is particularly instructive here. There were a substantial number of such issueless protests in the non-strike events, but almost none in the strikes. Strikers know what they want and almost always know where to go to demand it. But in almost 30 percent of the non-strikes, there was no specific target for the demand and regulation would only seem to be possible through repression. We will return to these cases later.

Society-centered conflicts

Twice as many cases are found on the second line of the table – conflicts that began and ended in civil society – as on the first one. Strikes were aimed at private sources and had private targets in a majority of cases, but only in a *bare* majority. When we exclude the strikes, less than a quarter of the protests had both private sources and private targets. Nevertheless, there was a broad autonomy of conflicts in civil society from the state.

State-centered conflicts

The importance of the Italian state as the site of conflict is evident in the third line of the table, which contains almost 40 percent of the conflicts. Strikes were often lodged entirely in the state sector, and this should not surprise us, given the high proportion of public sector conflicts we saw in Table 3.1. Almost 40 percent of the strikes were of this type. More interesting, however, is the fact that an equal proportion of the non-strike events were entirely in the state sector too. In a society in which a large proportion of decisions are made politically, both strikers and other groups identify their grievances and launch their demands within the state.

"Crossover" to the state

But if the state was the target of many conflcits that began in the state sector, it was only rarely the target of conflicts that began in civil society. The relative absence of "crossover" from the private to the public sector is almost equally true for strikes and non-strike events. This is a major discovery of the research. Either the private sector had an unsuspected capacity for self-regulation, or the dismal reputation of the state for allocating resources fairly and rapidly deterred people from taking their grievances to the state through collective action.

"Crossover" to society

Finally, as expected, there were very few cases in which grievances against state actors were transferred to the private sector for solution.

Thus the Italian protest cycle had two main axes – within civil society and in the state – alongside a third route – issueless protests – that appear to lead to no outlet for state regulation short of repression. Within the conflicts we studied, "crossover" from civil society to the state was rare and the opposite route was almost nonexistent. The state was itself an enormous source of grievances which were fought out within the state sector, but so was civil society.

Two preliminary conclusions can be offered. First, the Italian protest wave owed at least part of its explosive quality to the fact that it was *neither* primarily political – as was the case in the United States, where economic conflict was muted through most of the 1960s – *nor* primarily economic – as was the case in Great Britain, where industrial relations became unusually conflictual during this period. Nor did it center around educational institutions, although these were prominent in the early phase of the cycle. Discontent was found in all these sectors of Italian society and in others, testing a capacity for decision-making that is weak even in the best of times.

Second, although the proportion of state-centered conflicts was quite high, many of these were not political conflicts, but were work-based disputes of public employees against their employer – the state. Conflicts which arose in civil society but were transferred to the state for resolution made up a small minority of the total. How then could the state affect the resolution of conflicts? The major influence appears to have been by affecting what Lange and Regini call the structuring of conflict.

3. The structuring of conflict

The first thing that people often associate with protest is violence. But as Eisinger (1973) argues, protestors with a concrete policy goal or interest seldom choose violence; they are more likely to use nonviolent disruption, or what we have called confrontation. Was this a period of uncontrolled, violent protest in Italy, as some observers today remem-

Table 3.4. *Conventional, confrontational, and violent forms of collective action as percent of total forms*

Type of forms of action	No. of occurrences	As % of total forms
Conventional forms	6,745	56.1
Confrontational and symbolic forms	1,698	18.9
Violent forms[a]	2,075	23.1
Other, unclassifiable	186	2.1
Total	10,704	100.2

[a]Includes clashes between the police and demonstrators.

ber it? Was it a period of confrontation? Or was it made up of mainly traditional protest repertoires with both violent and confrontational outcroppings?[15]

Table 3.4 presents an image that may surprise both enthusiasts and critics of *il sessantotto*. For the most part, during these years, Italians were engaging in conventional forms of collective action, and much less often in confrontation or violence. Although violence accompanied the protest wave from the beginning, it became prominent only towards the end of the period and was evident in only a minority of conflicts. Confrontational protests were most common during the intensive peak of the cycle from 1967 to 1969.

The largest category of actions were conventional strikes; next in frequency were the classical democratic forms of public marches and meetings; third in frequency were what we call "confrontational" actions – sit-ins, occupations, obstruction, forced entry, and symbolic protests. Organized violence was in no sense a major property of the peak of the cycle: it arose towards the end of the period and did not become a serious security problem until most forms of mass protest had already declined (della Porta and Tarrow 1987). Aggressive attacks on property or on other people were observed in 23 percent of the total if we include clashes with the police and in 17 percent if we do not (della Porta and Tarrow 1987).[17]

Disruptiveness reached its peak during the early peak of mobilization and declined as the number of protests rose. We can gain some sense of the disruptiveness of protest by adding the number of tactical forms used in each event and assigning a weight to each form according to its disruptiveness to others, to ongoing routines, or to public order.[18] In Figure 3.2 we present the mean level of disruptiveness for

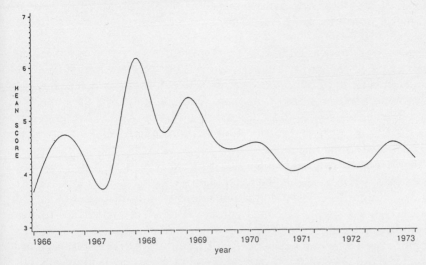

Figure 3.2. Mean disruptiveness of all protest events, by semester, 1966–73.

all the protest events. As the figure shows, disruptiveness reached its peak in 1968, long before the *amount* of participation had reached its highest level. There was a smaller peak in 1969, before a long decline through the early 1970s. Another, smaller rise can be seen in 1973, as a function of the rising spiral of violence.

The disruptiveness index shows that a qualitative change in the nature of protest began the cycle, touching off a longer and larger quantitative wave of conflict that was, for the most part, more conventional in nature. Comparing disruptiveness in Figure 3.2 with the number of protest events in Figure 3.1 confirms this impression. The confrontational mass protests of 1967–9 triggered a long, but far more institutionalized cycle of protest. Confrontation gave way to convention as the cycle continued, except for the violent events that, in any case, never involved more than a tiny minority of people (della Porta and Tarrow 1987).

Research on social movements has long focused on how protest is generated, but there has been much less research on how it is constrained. Two sets of social constraints and two political ones appear to be important. First, protest remains within the conventional repertoire because people know how to use it and opponents know how to respond (Tilly 1978). Second, movements themselves temper popular enthusiasm by adopting conventional forms of collective action that they are able to control (Piven and Cloward 1977). On the other hand, the state may limit the more disruptive, violent, and confrontational forms of protest by using repression; or it may encourage conventional forms by facilitation.

Even in Italy, where the state is supposedly "weak," it can regulate the "rules of the game" that govern conflict between private actors, even when it does not make choices between them or determine the outcome of their conflicts. The state regulates conflict and shapes its outcome, as we saw in the shipyard closing case, just by bringing private actors together and substituting less confrontational for more confrontational forms of conflict.

For example, the famous *Statuto dei lavoratori*, passed in 1969 and put into effect in 1970, helped to regulate a wave of conflict that – without it – might have reached greater intensity and magnitude. On the one hand, the *statuto* extended conflict to new sectors and to smaller factories by legitimating the use of the strike among groups that had seldom used it in the past – in small factories, in traditional regions, and in middle-class sectors. But on the other hand, by legitimating the strike, the *statuto* channeled conflict into its most institutionalized form, and away from less controllable forms of action.

Both halves of this hypothesis are supported by the data at our disposal. As is generally known, the number of strikes increased after the passage of the statute, well exceeding the strike rate of 1969, as workers began to demand local and plant-level adjustments to national contracts (Franzosi 1980, 1988). But what the official statistics fail to show is that the number of strikes in which *non*-strike forms of collective action (occupations, forced entries, obstruction, and public demonstrations and violence) were employed by strikers declined after 1969.

In Figure 3.3, we have plotted over the time the number of strikes in which more than one form of conflict – that is, in addition to the strike – were used by strikers. The proportion of strikes that were accompanied by non-strike forms, which increased from 50 percent of the total in 1966 to two-thirds in 1969, declined to about 48 percent by 1973. As the decade progressed and the strike wave continued, strikes became even more conventional, according to those who have studied that later period.[19]

What were the forms of collective action used by strikers and how did they evolve in the course of the cycle? According to Dubois (1978), they included

repeated shop-floor strikes spaced at either regular or irregular intervals, or coordinated sector-by-sector stoppages, affecting alternatively one shop or workgroup and then another, as well as acts of industrial sabotage (p. 8).

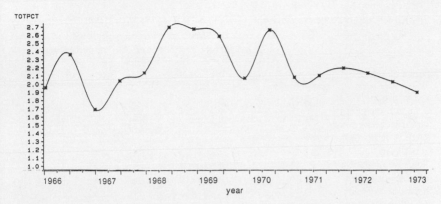

Figure 3.3. Proportion of strikes in which more than one form of conflict was used, by semester, 1966–73.

A whole new vocabulary of strike forms rapidly developed in this period, from the *sciopero bianco* (go-slow) to the *sciopero a singhiozzo* (literally, hiccup strikes), the *sciopero a scacchiera* (chessboard strikes), the *corteo interno* (marches around the factory grounds to carry along undecided workers), and the *presidio al cancello* (blocking factory gates to prevent goods from entering or leaving the plant). The logic of these innovations was to extract the maximum amount of resources through disruption with the minimum expenditure of resources (Dubois 1978:9).

In addition to these permutations within the strike repertoire, workers added distinctly different forms to their traditional repertoires, sometimes intensifying conflicts within the factory and sometimes extending it to the public sphere. Within the factory, occupations, obstructions, and forced entries challenged assembly line rhythms and the authority of foremen. This revived an old tradition in Italian factories and was an effective means of preventing plant closings and lockouts.

In the past, unions had taken the struggle into the streets only when they were too weak to prevail within the factory. But in the late 1960s, external activity was not a sign of weakness but a way of publicizing and dramatizing strikes to the public and the press. Factory workers adopted public forms of display, expressive forms of action, and traffic blockages to publicize their demands. These demonstrations often contained symbolic military elements (e.g., mechanics would frequently bang on milk cans or blow whistles as they marched), but they also contained elements of play and theater and bore a resemblance to the traditional carnival.[20]

Table 3.5. *Strike events and use of non-strike forms by strikers*

Forms of action	Aggregated protest forms by year (no. of occurrences)							
	1966	1967	1968	1969	1970	1971	1972	1973
Public display								
(march, meeting)	31	28	78	107	97	110	78	74
Workplace assembly	10	15	40	69	84	59	43	33
Routine action (e.g.,								
petition)	13	15	37	59	88	77	87	14
Confrontational forms	32	15	52	118	72	70	31	33
Violent encounter	20	5	33	18	23	34	16	15
Attack on property	12	4	13	28	19	12	3	8
Attack on persons	2	3	4	19	9	10	4	6
Total other forms	120	85	257	418	392	372	262	183
Total strike events[a]	127	117	196	306	319	416	269	224
Ratio of other forms								
to strikes	0.94	0.73	1.31	1.36	1.22	0.89	0.97	0.82

[a]Strike events include all events in which a strike was recorded.

Both the expansion in the forms of conflict within the workplace and their extension into the public sphere can be seen in Table 3.5, which analyzes the strike events in our newspaper data for the incidence within them of other forms of action. The table actually *understates* workers' use of non-strike forms, for it excludes all cases in which no strike was observed, and it does not record the myriad of ways in which the strike itself could be used (e.g., work to rule, chessboard strikes, etc.). Even so, from the data in Table 3.5 we can begin to grasp the rich panoply of forms of action of which the workers were capable.

As the table shows, in the upward phase of mobilization from 1966 through 1969, the rate of increase in the employment of collateral forms of actions was more rapid than the increase in the number of strikes as a whole. It also shows that workers were "going public" and simultaneously intensifying disruption within the workplace through the use of confrontational forms of action. The figures in Table 3.5 also show that "wild" forms of action – occupations, violence, disruption of the assembly line – began to appear in 1968, when the unions were too weak to take advantage of the potential for mobilization in the working class. They continued to be employed during 1969, when plant-level conflict was succeeded by national contract renewal strikes under union leadership. As the unions regained their grip, they integrated the "radical" forms of action into their campaigns, though at a lower level of intensity. As the cycle wound down, the use of these radical forms declined, but the more institutional public forms of action continued to be linked to the strike until the end of the period: marches and meetings, petitions, delegations and legal actions, and especially the assembly.

Assemblies in the place of work were a major acquisition of the working class during this period. The right to assemble had been rarely accorded the unions in the years before 1966, and when workers started to assemble during strikes, they did so spontaneously. But as the unions sought to recapture control of the movement, they made the legal assembly in the place of work one of their cardinal demands. The workplace assemblies, which began to appear in the newspaper data in 1968, continue into the late phase of the cycle, but now under union control (Regini 1980:54).

Was it only the growing control of the unions that filtered out the more radical forms of action that had been prominent in 1968–9, structuring participation into more organized, public forms (Regini 1980:55)? Or did the state play a role as well? Although the evidence is indirect, we would argue that state-sponsored structuring of conflict was at least partially responsible: first, because union presence in the factory was itself ratified by the *Statuto dei lavoratori;* and second, because the state provided legal and institutional structures that reduced workers' incentives to take radical action on the factory floor.

One such institution was the labor courts, to which both workers and management could have recourse in attempts to settle workplace disputes in their favor. In the atmosphere of the early 1970s, these courts were (to some people, notoriously so) inclined to settle disputes in favor of the workers; but even when they did not, their pro-labor reputation could provide incentives not to engage in strikes. In Figure 3.4, we have plotted recourse to the courts in the Milan area from judicial statistics,[21] and place them alongside our data on the number of disputes in industry (both strikes and non-strikes) in the province of Milan.

Unfortunately, our detailed data continue only up to 1972 for recourse to legal remedies and only to 1973 for industrial disputes. As far as they do go, however, they indicate a clear co-occurrence between a decline of industrial disputes and an increase in recourse to labor courts.[22] We do not have data on who initiated these legal proceedings. But given the magistracy's swing towards labor in the early 1970s, it is a good bet that workers were frequently going to court instead of going out on strike.

How important the role of the state and that of the unions were in channeling conflict into more institutional forms of collective action

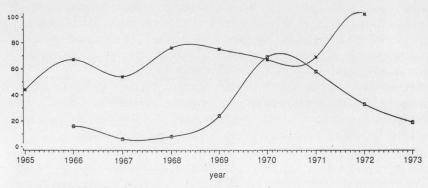

star=recourse to labor tribunals
square=industrial strike events

Figure 3.4. Workers recourse to the courts (1965–72) and industrial strike events (1966–73) in Milan, by year. Symbols: ★, recourse to labor tribunals; □, industrial strike events.

and from the shopfloor to labor courts we cannot say. What can be affirmed with confidence is that – probably more than in the coordination between politics and protest and in the allocation of resources – the repertoire of collective action was regulated in the course of the years 1966–73 by the parallel actions of the state and the unions, both of which – for different reasons – had incentives to keep protest under control.

3. Conclusions

In their historical memories of the late 1960s and early 1970s, observers of the Italian scene have emphasized violence, largely because of its bloody end in organized terrorism (LaPalombara 1987:Chap. 7). But they have underemphasized the reconstitution – or better, the reshaping – of the Italian political settlement that resulted at the end of the cycle. This is not the place to rehearse the new place that labor won as the result of the industrial strife of the period, or the fact that the movement organizations that emerged from the period were either integrated into the polity (the PDUP, Manifesto) or rapidly disappeared (Lotta Continua), or the number of new policy issues that were successfully negotiated during this period.

But the structuring of collective action that we saw in the last section left a heritage. By the end of the 1966–73 period, the "wild" forms of conflict that had marked the intensive peak of mobilization had largely disappeared, but the classical repertoire of democratic participation –

public marches, strikes, assemblies, and demonstrations – was expanded. People who had tested the boundaries of the state's tolerance with violent or confrontational action had learned, or taught others, that these could not lead to the policy results they wanted, but that less confrontational forms of action could sometimes work.

More important still – and outlasting the wave of terrorism that marked the latter part of the 1970s – grass-roots voluntary associations *not* controlled by a party but representing citizen demands expanded and would continue to expand throughout the 1980s. Parents seeking traffic signals, day care facilities, or abortion clinics; ecological and peace groups; the parents of drug addicts who were receiving little public health care: these began to sidestep the party system, creating their own associations and seeking direct contact with public officials.

During the wave of protest that we have studied, the Italian political class did not respond impressively to citizen demands, and citizens were more likely to protest against the state than to target it for solution to their problems. But at the end of the cycle, out of the welter of strikes, occupations, obstructions, marches, public meetings, and political violence, the repertoire of political participation had been incrementally expanded. This is how participation usually expands in mass politics – not by a gentle expansion of citizenship, but by the explosions of conflict, experimentation, and confrontation that we have called a cycle of protest.

A part of this expansion, it must be admitted, was made by the self-appointed advocates of armed struggle, and Italian democracy went through a period of severe testing before it emerged from the "years of lead." But less easily observed, the same years saw an expansion of conventional forms of participation, a creation of new institutions that not only regulated protest but responded to it, and a growth in new forms of representation outside the party system. From a major cycle of protest came a thin accretion of reform. For as Zolbert (1972) writes, "stepped-up participation is like a flood tide which loosens up much of the soil but leaves alluvial deposits in its wake" (p. 207).

Notes

1 This chapter is a largely rewritten version of an earlier unpublished paper, "Piove, governo ladro," Ithaca, New York, March 1987. We are grateful for the comments of Peter Hall, Carlo Trigilia, and the editors of this volume in revising that earlier paper. The research was carried out under a grant from the National Science Foundation for research on protest cycles and policy innovation, with the cooperation of the European University Institute (Stefanizzi) and Cornell University (Tarrow.)

2 It is curious, but in no way illogical, that the earlier economic "miracle" of the late 1950s was accompanied by the gloomy acceptance of the hegemony of politics. The

untenable theory of *partitocrazia* dates from the earlier economic boom. We should not be surprised that the current boom has produced an equally unsatisfactory theory of *mercatocrazia*.

3 A description of the study and its methods can be found in Tarrow (1983, 1988). For preliminary reports of the research, see della Porta and Tarrow (1987), Klandermans, Kriesi, and Tarrow (1989 [in press]:Chap. 10), and Stefanizzi (1987). The study was based on methods of direct entry, interactive data entry, and analysis of newspaper records pioneered by Charles Tilly in his work on English contention, 1758–1834. For a general description of the logic of Tilly's approach, see Tilly (1987).

4 Some may be dubious about the use of so "establishment" a source for studying protest. These fears would be well grounded were we attempting to make judgments about the deeper motives of protesters, their ideologies, or the justice of their cause. Our goal was actually much more modest: to track, via the most complete public record available, the course of a cycle of protest, the forms of action used, the publicly stated demands made, and the responses of the authorities. For evidence that *Corriere della Sera* provides a reasonably accurate impression of the rise and fall of collective action in Italy – if not of its actual magnitude – see Tarrow (1988:Appendix B). For a more elaborate and very promising approach to the content analysis of newspaper data, see Franzosi (1987).

5 This episode is treated in greater detail in Tarrow (1988:Chap. 4). The information was taken largely from reports in *Corriere della Sera*.

6 There are few general treatments of the protest cycle. The best is a doctoral dissertation, Bob Lumley's (1983) "Social Movements in Italy." Many other treatments deal almost exclusively with industrial conflict. See Pizzorno (1978), Regalia, Regini, and Reyneri (1978), and Sabel (1982). Treatments of the student movement or the extraparliamentary Left are almost invariably personal memoirs or ideological tracts. For two of the best of these, see Bobbio (1979) and Viale (1978).

7 For the concept of "interpretive frames" and their role in mobilization by social movements, see Snow et al. (1986) and Snow and Benford (1988). For the related concept of ideological "packages," see Gamson (1988). Klandermans (1988) has attempted to integrate the diffusion of new idea systems into a general approach to social movement mobilization. For a discussion of two of the central interpretive frames of the Italian protests – workerism and autonomy – see Tarrow (1988:Chap. 4).

8 See Giugni (1976) and Romagnoli (1976) for these developments. There was, of course, also a less institutionalized root of the councils of agitation that appeared in a number of northern factories in 1968 (e.g., the CUB, Comitati Unitari di Base). But the fact remains that the unions had been proposing and even experimenting with various versions of the factory council concept for years, and were thus in a position to adapt to the challenge of factory militance after 1968. For evidence to support this argument, see Tarrow (1988:Chap. 7).

9 That workerism had deep roots in intellectual circles around the PCI, as well as on the extraparliamentary Left, is shown by Magna (1978). For an assault on the PCI's "desertion" of the working class from within the party, see Accornero (1967).

10 For a more detailed discussion of this debate and of the successful splitting tactics of the New Left in the universities, see Tarrow (1988:Chaps. 6 and 9).

11 For analyses of the relationship between social movements and PCI membership gains, see Barbagli and Corbetta (1978) and Lange, Tarrow, and Ervin (1988).

12 The most articulate spokesman for this point of view in Italy is Alberto Melucci (see Melucci 1980, 1985, and especially 1988). In his most recent statement, Melucci regards the study of political protest as no more than the registering of the "objectified outcome" of the largely invisible processes of collective identity formation that give rise

to social movements. While Melucci's view of the origins of social protest in collective identity formation is intriguing, we believe that the "objectified outcomes" that he tends to discount are of great importance, not only for the political system, but also for formation of the movements on which his work centers.

13 Were we to define firms in the nationalized sector as "public," the balance would be tipped even further towards the state.

14 However, even the issueless American riots of the 1960s led to state responses in the form of government grants to the poor. For a summary of evidence on this, see Button (1978). Since there has been no equivalent of Button's multivariate analysis of protest and policy response in Italy, we cannot judge whether "issueless" protests evoke such responses.

15 We define conventional protest, with Tilly (1978), as the repertoire of forms of action that are conventionally used in the political culture. We define confrontational protest as the forms of action that physically pit protesters against authorities, elites, or the forces of order but do not aim at violence; we define violent forms of protest as those which employ purposive violence to achieve their goals. On the latter, see della Porta (1987) and della Porta and Tarrow (1987).

16 For a more thorough analysis of the forms of action found in the protest data, see Tarrow (1988:Chap. 3).

17 Students of collective action usually interpret clashes with the police as the aggressive acts of protestors, while the latter earnestly regard them as attacks by the police. Unfortunately, newspaper data do not provide an adequate empirical base to decide on who attacked whom in these clashes.

18 To construct the disruptiveness index, each form of action used in an event was assigned a base value of 1 and then weighted according to its estimated degree of disruption to others. Petitions, delegations, and assemblies were weighted only 1 (i.e., given no additional weight); strikes, public marches, and meetings were weighted as 2; occupations, obstructions and forced entry (i.e., the main confrontational forms) were weighted 3; property damage or theft was weighted 4; deliberate violent encounters were weighted 5. The level of disruptiveness rose with the number of these forms of action used in the same event, but rose higher with the addition of confrontational or violent forms of action.

19 Unfortunately, we have no systematic data on the use of these non-strike forms by strikers after 1973. The literature on the unions during that period suggests that both the autonomous role of factory councils and the workers' use of unconventional forms of collective action continued to decline through the 1970s. On the former, see Regalia (1975, 1985, 1987); on the latter, see Golden (1988).

20 See Lumley's thesis (1983), especially the description of the culture of carnival that dominated much of the disorder of the period (p. 397).

21 We are grateful to Rossella Ronchi of the IRES-CGIL of Milan for help in collecting these data.

22 Regini (1980:64) presents official data on strike volume in Italy which show an increase in strike volume in 1972 and 1973, when our newspaper data show a decline. The indicators differ in three ways: while Regini's indicator includes "the number of working hours lost per employee in all sectors of the economy," ours include only the number of disputes in industry in the province of Milan. The most important difference seems to be between the number of disputes and the number of working hours lost.

Part II

Regulation of the economy

4

Politics, institutional features, and the government of industry

MAURIZIO FERRERA

1. Analyzing industrial policy

State intervention in the industrial sector is neither a new nor an isolated phenomenon in the evolution of market democracies. In fact, given the characteristics of numerous economic "take-offs" in almost every continental West European country, state intervention originated with the actual process of industrialization. Yet, *industrial policy* is nonetheless a recent concept. Attacked by liberals and considered suspect by the reformist Left during the 1950s and 1960s, this concept gradually affirmed (legitimated) itself following the first oil crisis and assumed a central place in the public debates of the 1970s. While its notoriety has fallen a bit in recent years, nevertheless, with the exception of the United States, the prescriptive and descriptive legitimacy of industrial policy is universally accepted in all western nations (Diebold 1980; Johnson 1984; Wildavsky 1984). If the rapid rise of this concept is in part linked to the internal dynamics of academic debates (the specialization of social sciences, above all economics, and the development of policy analysis, etc.), it also has roots in a series of objective phenomena in various countries.

With the explosion of the international economic system at the beginning of the 1970s and the profound upheavals in national productive systems undergoing post-industrial transition, nations everywhere began to call for ever greater state interventions aimed at particular sectors, in order to promote "positive adjustment" of the industrial system. For about a decade, almost all nations actively pursued such policies while still respecting the limits set by various international regimes, including one as traditionally anti-interventionist as the Organization for Economic Cooperation and Development (OECD, 1979). Industrial policy was considered an organic combination of corrective measures, aimed at the reconversion and restructuring of the produc-

111

tive apparatus, and economic stimuli, aimed at the expansion of innovative sectors. As a result, industrial policy appeared as the appropriate solution to the major challenges which blocked and threatened to suffocate the processes of economic development so strenuously constructed in the 1950s and 1960s.

Removed from the invisible hand of the market (or more realistically, from the distant hand of macroeconomic policy) in order to become the object of specific recognizable public policy, structural adjustment quickly found itself at the center of the political arena. The distribution of its costs and benefits among the diverse sectors, areas, occupational categories, etc., immediately provoked a series of intense conflicts. Unable to appear simply as a "solution" to a series of economic challenges, industrial policy was immediately transformed into a first-class political *issue*. The dynamics and logics of both pressure politics and policy-making quickly complicated the issue as substantive political connotations prevailed and overshadowed industrial needs.

Even though confronted by similar economic problems and political processes, industrial policy in the last fifteen years has taken very different paths in the various nations (for a review, see Grant and McKay 1983).

The general tendency is certainly that of an increased use of financial disbursements, selectively allocated by ad hoc *specialized* agencies. Nonetheless, notable diversity exists (between and within nations) over: (1) the destination of these finances (productive "factors" versus "sectors," and within the latter, between emergent, "mature," and "declining" sectors); (2) the source of these allocations (disbursed from a general or special fund, loans, stock participation, etc.); and, finally (3) the institutional form of these transfers (according to standard, formalized procedures or rather a more flexible format based on ad hoc single decisions and contingent judgments). The variety of approaches, goals, and institutional instruments is so great that any attempt at a general and comprehensive typology would lead to a drastic simplification of the complicated national mixes. While particular mixes have shaped (or hindered, as some would argue in certain cases) the performances of different nations, some sort of ordering of this intricate panorama (aimed at isolating the specific nature of various types of industrial policies and their political and economic contexts) is necessary to explain the diversity of national trajectories and (above all) the variety of their results.

The inter-disciplinary debate over these issues is already well developed. While economists examine the problems and dynamics inherent in individual industrial systems and their congruence with the goals pursued by the state, sociologists and political scientists seek to illustrate the role various social, cultural, institutional, and political constraints play in shaping the government of the industrial system and its adjustment.

Without doubt, for instance, *industrial culture* (the public image of the firm, its role, and the state's rights and obligations in its regard) influences the capacity both to evaluate the problems that industry has developed over the last decade as well as to elaborate strategies of adjustment. Shonfield (1965) has already highlighted the importance of political-cultural traditions in explaining the different forms of state management of capitalist economies. This theme has been recently resurrected by Dyson (1983), who illustrated how sociocultural differences explain the diverse patterns of state-industry relations existent between Anglo-Saxon and continental countries (at the level of political, administrative, business, and union elites). These differences are reflected in juridical norms (legislation concerning firms, bankruptcy rights, etc.) and in the styles of industrial crisis management. Specific *political processes* promoting the formulation and implementation of industrial policy have, however, played a more direct role in shaping both the type and the results of these policies.

As stated previously, the general tendency was towards the increased use of selective distribution of public financial resources to individual firms. In certain countries (France, Italy, and in large part England) this distribution occurred within the framework of state regulation in the most "intense" sense of the term (see Introduction to this volume). In other words, the state was the fundamental pivot of the adjustment process, establishing rigid and articulate norms and using the public bureaucracy as the principal executor of policy. In other countries (for example, Austria, Germany, and Sweden), resources and state measures were instead controlled essentially by the concerted efforts of large interest groups. The regulation of industrial crises depended not so much on legislation as on somewhat "spontaneous" forms of collaboration among peak interest associations (e.g., unions, business associations, and banks). The state certainly provided resources; it did not rigidly predetermine their destination in accordance to set standards, however, but instead gave ample discretion to the social actors.

Political parties also played an important role in the new industrial regulation of the 1970s. It is clear even within the prevailing (political and associative) regulatory frameworks that the actual choices of approaches and instruments reflected the different ideological-programmatic orientations of the governing party (or coalition). One need only recall the brusque policy reversals accompanying changes in governments in Sweden, England, and France. Electoral competition among parties also influenced the rhythms and distribution of state funding (especially those linked to cases of industrial salvage).

The general "type" of regulation, whether in the form of state control, associational cooperation, or the interaction between the state and associations, and the characteristics of the party system (its ideological profiles and above all its electoral games) are not, however, the only processes that shape industrial policy. Industrial policy has gradually transformed itself into a sectorally autonomous policy arena, characterized by the frequent constitution of "secondary majorities" between the exponents of different interests and the occurrence (or recurrence) of distinctly identifiable political syndromes, in part derived from the actual features of the industrial issue and of the network of actors (public and private) that revolve around it. The presence of a "strong" demand inside this policy market, constituted by embattled social clienteles and endowed with ample financial and organizational resources, has permitted the frequent "capture" of regulatory intervention and the development of distributive "iron triangles" (among politicians, bureaucrats, and interest groups).

The intensity and frequency of these syndromes obviously depend on several contextual factors (primarily, but not exclusively, institutional factors) that vary from one country to another. In other words, if the constituent features of the policy arena have structured the politics of the specific sector, many other "external" elements have from time to time modified this structure, including the national policy style, which is linked, in turn, both to political-cultural traditions and to the rules of the market. The specification of these elements and their individual weight requires a detailed reconstruction of national industrial policy communities (of their protagonists, dynamics, etc.) and comparisons among them.

Research along these lines has just begun but has already produced several excellent studies (R. M. Grant 1983; Hayward 1984). Thus, a promising area of study lies in the identification of the specific characteristics of the industrial policy market (in both their typical forms and their concrete variants) and its connection to the external market.

An adequate understanding of all of these phenomena presupposes, nonetheless, an in-depth exploration of the institutional dimension *stricto senso*, i.e., that which pertains to the variety of organizational and procedural forms through which state action occurs. *Who* governs (in the "strong" sense of the term) industry and *how?* In other words (and to use political jargon), who is responsible, where are the headquarters, and which are the circuits that produce "sovereign collective decisions" concerning industry?

These questions are especially relevant for those nations that have chosen bureaucratic-statist forms of regulation, that is, an essentially political governing of the adjustment process. Hinging on both political representational and administrative structures, this type of regulation "naturally" tends to leave little space for economically rational criteria. This may generate hazardous effects for industrial production, an "economic" sector *par excellence*.[1] The external efficiency of this regulatory mode thus appears to be tightly linked to the presence of "intelligent" institutional features and organizational modes, that is, capable of encouraging policy-makers to also take into account economic criteria. The role of institutions and organizational features in shaping political behavior (in general, but above all in policy-making) has recently been explored by numerous authors (Dryzek 1983; Linder and Peters 1984; March and Olsen 1983; Peters 1985; Scharpf 1977, 1982, 1985).[2]

"Institutionalist" studies of industrial policy in advanced industrial nations have begun to shed light on how the degree and type of politicization of decision-making processes, or rather (its opposite) the capacity of relevant institutions to protect themselves from political pressures, are of primary importance in the "good" management of problems linked to industrial adjustment.[3] This is so because a sufficient amount of "isolation" of the decision-making process not only promotes more efficient aggregation of the numerous types of politics that collect around the policy literature, but also enhances the articulation and reasoned evaluation of the "technical-substantive" features of the decisions to be made – features especially crucial for a policy as complex as industrial policy.

This perspective appears especially useful in analyzing the Italian experience. In the European context, Italy, France, and to a lesser extent England have been the nations most inclined towards the political management of industry through the construction of an extensive regulatory apparatus run by the government. Unlike France, however, state intervention in Italy has been incapable of generating efficient and effective results. While there are many factors that explain this failure, the following paragraphs will focus on the institutional and organizational factors. My thesis is that these factors play an especially important role in all experiences of political regulation and that the Italian experience of industrial government was particularly deficient in these terms. To illustrate this point, we will first provide a synthetic overview of the French and English experiences.

2. Institutional issues and industrial policy: some foreign examples

The "institutional issue" of industrial policy has many facets. In one of the most articulated analyses of the question, Zysman (1983) sheds light on how this issue must be analyzed in terms of the relational "triangle" that links the state (or more specifically, the government and administrative apparatus), the credit system, and the firms. According to this author, the credit system and the institutions that regulate it are the most important features of this triangle, since they "condition both the market choices of firms and the administrative choices of governments" (Zysman 1983:16). Nonetheless, Zysman also recognizes that different modes of political-administrative organization and behavior play an autonomous and relevant role in industrial policy results. We will focus on this aspect of the issue.

Industrial policy deals with complex problems in continuous transformation and redefinition. Understanding these problems requires notable and specific skills, and "solutions" to this problem require rapid decisions based on a solid knowledge of markets and technology. Thus, more than for other policies, the external success of industrial policy is tightly linked to the strength and efficiency of its institutional instruments. In other words, it requires decision-making processes that quickly bring the problems to light and that promote a rapid convergence of possible solutions, while giving sufficient "voice" to industrial problems in the competition among different issues. In many countries, these technical-substantive requirements have encouraged the centralization of industrial policy-making within the executive, thus reducing the potential "flooding" of the parliamentary arena (Dyson and Wilks 1983), while increasing as well the degree of isolation from interest group pressures. International government of industrial policy spawned numerous institutional innovations (the generation or reorganization of new ministries, general programs, interministerial committees, ad hoc agencies, etc.). Yet these changes did not always produce positive results in terms of internal efficiency and, in fact, were often responsible for specific deficiencies in policy design. The comparison of the French experience (normally seen as a case of indisputable success) with the English experience (considered more or less a failure) sheds light on these issues.[4]

Even though the French industrial policy community has been traditionally very thick and fragmentary, over the course of the last decade France was able to build one of the most united, centralized, and "isolated" models of industrial policy-making (Estrin and Holmes 1983; Green 1981, 1983; Hayward 1984; Maillet 1984; Zysman 1977, 1983). This model is based on a series of interministerial committees in which the heads of the major economic ministries (Economy, Budget, Industry, Commerce and Trade, Labor, etc.) participate along with representatives of the financial institutions. In reality, however, all of these committees are formally coordinated and, in fact, directed by the extremely powerful *Direction du Tresor* of the Ministry of Economics, which acts as a true and proper center of gravity for both the entire planning system and the government of industry. The *Tresor* is the principal "interpreter" of industry's problems as well as the toughest "guardian" of the state's interests, maintaining vigilance against the pressure of various lobbies as well as against the often "particularistic" tendencies of certain components of these committees (especially of the Ministry of Industry, which could embrace particular sectoral or firm interests) (Green 1983).

This institutional design has given industrial policy-making substantial unity, stability, and continuity, especially visible when compared internationally. Surely, part of the effectiveness is due to the more general institutional features of the Fifth Republic as well as to the particular strengths of the French bureaucracy (technical preparation, efficiency, etc.). Yet these same features and strengths have not produced equally positive results for other policies (especially social policies) (Zysman 1983), which indicates that organizational-institutional features exercise a specific and autonomous role over the decisions of the French bureaucracy.

The English model of industrial policy-making is quite different, almost completely opposite to the French model (R. M. Grant 1983; Wilks 1983; Zysman 1983). First of all, because of the activism of certain Select Committees, Parliament plays a more important role in the development of industrial policy in England than in France. Second (and above all), governmental structures do not possess centers capable of exercising industrial leadership and/or of mechanisms able to generate consensus around industrial issues. Decision-making responsibilities are fragmented and distributed among numerous bodies, including the National Enterprise Development Council, the Department of Economic Affairs, and the Ministries of Industry and Technology (to cite only the most important). These bodies, over time, alternatively are responsible for policy-making. Also, unlike the French *Grandes Corps*, the characteristic features of the British Civil Service are not as congruent with the "technical-substantive" needs of industrial policy. Moreover, the institutional apparatus dealing with the decline of Britain's industrial system appears especially inadequate and certainly less "intelligent" than that of other policy areas (i.e., social policy).

In order to construct a systematic comparative framework, these examples should be developed and extended to other countries. Yet, the indications generated from these examples appear sufficiently clear. Institutional modes of policy-making at the governmental level influence decision-making outcomes in an autonomous way. What makes a difference appears to be above all the long-term presence of a clearly identifiable and sufficiently stable center of leadership and responsibility capable of defending "public" goals and institutional interests, as well as organizing the often disparate interests of the policy community along these lines.

We have already stated that the complex nature of industrial issues requires that decision-making processes in the policy area leave ample space for technical, especially economic, evaluations. This is particularly true in the area of financial incentives, above all if the goal of these incentives is to stimulate and promote the expansion of "winning" sectors. So that economic reasoning can be fully expressed in both policy and decision-making, these processes require a certain degree of know-how. It makes little difference whether this know-how is internal to the public bureaucracy (as in France) or external (as in Germany). What counts is the specific weight given to technical-economic factors in the formulation of general objectives, especially in the making of individual decisions. Even here, various sociocultural factors play a role (e.g., the type of education and culture of the policy-makers, the number of technicians within the bureaucracy, and/or the flow of information between firms and these technicians, research centers, etc.). One can also analyze these factors in a more institutional manner, focusing on the organization of decision-making paths at the micro-level.[5].

In France, the procedures followed by various interministerial committees in the selection of firms to receive funding seem to give supremacy to, and promote the greatest aggregation of, technical "voices" (Green 1983; OECD 1983). The committees usually conduct their own evaluations of the funding requests by the individual firms. Once again, the *Tresor* coordinates these evaluations, writes the final report, and oversees the implementation of the decisions by both the committees and the firm.[6] Even at the micro-level, therefore, France appears well equipped to favor the policy's economic requisites while avoiding political interference. In fact, there are very few opportunities for political distortions, since decisions are made in a context in which different preferences are aggregated and all decisional factors, implications, and costs are considered and balanced by the participants, who are held accountable for their decisions.

Even in England, selective financial assistance stemming from the Industry Act of 1972 should, in principle, depend on the economic and financial evaluation of firm projects as well as on evidence that public assistance is necessary for their realization (additionality criterion) (Grant 1983; OECD 1983). Nevertheless, decision-making procedures in England appear less effective than in France in guaranteeing respect for technical-substantive needs and in preventing the "politicization" of decisions. The Ministry of Industry evaluates requests, but it is weak both internally (since it must rely on external experts) and within the larger context in which individual decisions are made. Decisions are considered by numerous territorial and sectoral actors who lack both coordination and well-defined duties, but with formal recourse to externalize conflicts by bringing them to Parliament.[7] Thus, the high degree of politicization of assistance and salvage operations denounced by many English observers has precise (although not exclusive) origins in the decision-making procedures and mechanisms. Institutional factors matter, therefore, even at the micro-level.

The above descriptions require further detail and more systematic comparative analysis; nevertheless, the contrast between the French and English cases sheds light on at least two important "rationality conditions" (substantial and procedural) for micro-decisional processes: the existence of mechanisms that take into account, both *ex ante* and *ex post*, the presence of "internalizing" procedures which (1) insulate the decision-making process and (2) require all actors to consider and evaluate all factors and implications of the decision. This hinders "games of distinction" and, above all, the kinds of "distributive collusions" that dramatically decrease the efficiency of any public policy.

3. The Italian case

It is very difficult to outline the boundaries of Italian industrial policy and clearly identify its goals, instruments, and actors. The regulatory regime for firms is extensive and disorganized; and since World War II, numerous state initiatives (both conjunctural and structural) have had multiple and often confusing goals. A recent inventory of state action by Gobbo and Prodi (1982) indicates that the principal tendencies include: territorial re-equilibrium and the development of the South, industrial reconversion and restructuring, assistance to minor initiatives, export assistance, research and development, financial restructuring of firms, the preservation and development of industrial employment, the protection of industrial workers' salaries, and financial support of particular sectors. As one can see, state policy has set ambitious and numerous goals for itself, which over time have oscillated and overlapped with one another in a disorganized way.

An ample debate among experts has illustrated the numerous and serious defects of Italian industrial policy, shedding light on its most notable deviations from the experiences of other countries (see CER/ IRS Report 1986). The *cahier de doleances* compiled by economists and jurists is extremely long. The former have above all lamented the scarce correspondence between the strategies designed and pursued through specific instruments and the adjustment needs of the productive system. The latter have denounced the incongruencies and complexities of legislation, the high degree of juridical fragmentation, the administrative uncertainties and delays, etc. Moreover, almost all analyses have traced the low effectiveness of industrial policy to political-institutional factors. For instance, in a panoramic synthesis of the argument, Valiani (1985a) claims that "at the root of the overall ambiguous and disappointing results . . . of industrial policy lie political-institutional conditions which envelop and impede even industrial policy and which no law has been able to expel from its proper area of competence and activity" (p. 263). These conditions are political in that they reflect "the notable features of politics in our country" and their perverse "mechanisms of consensual coagulation" (p. 263), and are institutional in that they depend on the organizational factors and procedures of the state bureaucracy. But now let us examine in detail how the Italian model of political regulation of industry expresses itself in decision-making features and processes at both the micro- and macro-levels.

Macro-decision-making processes

Until the mid-1970s, Italian industrial policy did not possess a distinct and autonomous institutional profile but rather was a collection of initiatives stemming from different ministries and other state bodies that were rarely coordinated in various committees like the CICR (Comitato Interministeriale per il Credito e il Risparnio), the CIP (Comitato Interministeriale Prezzi), and above all the CIPE (Comitato Interministeriale per la Politica Economica) (Amato 1971; Grassini and Scognamiglio 1979; Palmerio and Valiani 1982).

With the governments of national solidarity of the late 1970s, a new effort at increased political control of the adjustment process sought to develop institutions to provide direction and coordinate decisions among various bodies in order to promote the restructuring/reconversion of crucial sectors and to support exports.

Law 675 of 1977 profoundly changed the rules of industrial policy-making, redesigning the responsibilities of and boundaries between Parliament, the government, and the bureaucracy (Di Gaspare 1981). Even if certain important parts of this law have now expired (i.e., the system of incentives of the Fund for Industrial Restructuring and Reconversion), the institutional framework established by the law continues to exist.

The principal innovation of Law 675 was the CIPI (Committee for the Coordination of Industrial Policy) which, by absorbing many of the responsibilities of the CIPE and acquiring new ones, was to act as the true and proper apex of the entire system of industrial government (as well as the "filter" of all financial incentives above a certain amount).

CIPI was directed by the Budget Ministry (where its headquarters were located) and included the Ministries of Industry, the South, State Participations, Labor, and the Treasury. At its meetings, the Minister of European Community Affairs, the Governor of the Bank of Italy, and the Secretary General of Planning also participated regularly.

Law 675 gave the CIPI two distinct functions: one dealing with political planning and the other, more managerial (Gallo 1983). In other words, this committee was asked to formulate industrial adjustment goals as well as implement them for single cases. The first task was given much emphasis in the original legislation since it was the greatest novelty of the law. CIPI was asked to establish both priorities among sectors and areas and a planning framework for state interventions. The Ministry of Industry was to publish a yearly *Report on the State of Industry* in which employment and productive conditions were evaluated and the effectiveness and implementation of incentives was communicated. In this way a circular system of planning was initiated in which the Plan and its directives would outline substantive and procedural goals and priorities and the annual Report would evaluate the realization of these policies.

The poor results of the CIPI have been the subject of many essays. Its major defects include: its planning deficiencies (final plans were too many, too generic, and too late); its operational sluggishness (one need only recall that the first allocation authorized from the 1977 [Law 675] Fund for Reconversion and Restructuring occurred in the summer of 1980, and that by the time the Fund's mandate had expired, only twenty-nine projects had been approved); and its proclivity toward assistance projects (above all, the use of wage maintenance for redundant workers).

Among the many reasons for this failure, we will highlight at least three related to the institutional design of Law 675: the low degree of insulation of the policy-making process and the extensive institutional involvement of other actors and other arenas, especially Parliament; the absence of a decision-making center and of incentives promoting coalescence within CIPI; and the lack of attention to the technical-substantive aspects of the policy, especially of its economic requisites, at the level of macro-decision-making.

A highly participatory model of policy-making that required CIPI to consult territorial interests (the Regions) and social actors (the unions and *Confindustria*) was imposed on CIPI by Law 675. In contrast to the French model, the Italian model of political regulation of industry foresaw the formation of "360 degree" (complete/universal) consensus, or at least the possibility for all actors to influence the decision-making process.[8] Both *Confindustria* and the unions actively exploited this possibility, with *Confindustria* repeatedly contesting the "vertical" approach to industrial policy promoted by CIPI and Parliament, and the union confederations attacking the merits of individual sectoral plans. But above all, the weight Law 675 gave to Parliament in every phase of policy-making harmfully blurred the institutional boundaries of Italian industrial policy between 1977 and 1982. The importance (and activism) of the Industrial and Commercial Commission of the Chamber of Deputies (XII) and of the Senate (X) grew dramatically after 1977.

Law 675 also created a Bicameral Commission for the Industrial Restructuring and Reconversion of State Participation Programs (not without bitter juridical disputes over the constitutionality of this commission, and notable conflicts within the Ministry of Industry) (Compagna-Marchini 1981; Vilella 1984). This commission was given notable powers in formulating industrial policy, not just at the level of control and evaluation but also (and this is the most controversial point) in the specification of goals and directions (i.e., sectoral plans), which included technical details and single decisions on particular firm proposals. Needless to say, this assemblaristic-participatory policy-making framework created ample space for and offered institutional reinforcement to the politicization of macro-decision-making processes.

At the governmental level (Council of Ministers) CIPI certainly represented a step ahead of the previous situation of decision-making fragmentation and dispersion. Nonetheless, in contrast to the analogous French committee, this body was born lacking a center and, hence, provided another arena for the expression of traditional institutional antagonisms (aside from, of course, party conflicts). As noted above, the headquarters and presidency were given to the Budget Ministry: a prestigious but institutionally weak center. (In its brief history it lost all battles waged against other ministries, especially against Treasury, over overlapping responsibilities.) The Ministries of State Participations and (above all) the South sought merely to defend their own sectoral and territorial interests and never really aspired to become protagonists in the decision-making process (even if they were important in the creation of winning coalitions, both in terms of "primary" and "secondary" majorities). Thus, the role of de facto leadership was contested among the Ministries of Industry, Treasury, and (to a lesser extent) Labor, which created many conflicts and ambiguities. This made "the specification of a public center responsible for industrial investment" extremely difficult (Cassese 1984:55), even if some analysts identify the Ministry of Industry as the "principal center of reference and propulsion of economic interaction" (Vilella 1984:121), above all with respect to the Treasury Ministry in matters of financial allocations. If we add to this institutional ambiguity the mobilization of different governmental bodies and their party composition, it is not difficult to see why CIPI failed so miserably, especially in its goals of coordinating and aggregating different governmental points of view regarding industry.

This brings us to the third problem mentioned above: the insufficient attention given to economic considerations within the decision-making process. This shortcoming is especially alarming (as we will see) at the micro-level, where a "technical" evaluation of individual cases is crucial for procedural effectiveness, but it is also quite serious at the macro-level, at the level of elaborating planning goals and formulating strategic choices. This shortcoming is due to the public administration's lack of divisions or offices specialized in planning functions and the lack of qualified personnel capable of conducting the evaluations necessary to perform these functions. Law 675 constructed an ambitious policy-making model with this concern in mind, but without taking into account the historical backwardness of Italy's bureaucracy (Compagna-Machini 1981). The use of external experts also proved to be inadequate (Vilella 1984). Aside from the lack of organizational support and specialized personnel, institutional incentives promoting rational economic behavior were also missing (or at least were too weak).

Even though Law 675 and CIPI included an ambitious "circular" form of planning, they nevertheless neglected to establish methods of updating sectoral plans and of adapting general goals according to objective analyses. The famous annual Report of the Ministry of Industry soon became a mere formality: without precise boundaries and procedural sequences, this instrument lacked any potential effectiveness. Furthermore, the Report's chapter on the implementation of industrial incentive laws (containing facts and relevant information for an evaluation of their overall success and expressly foreseen by Article Two of the law) appeared only in the first edition. Subsequent editions were incomplete and had minimal circulation (Marconi 1986a) without any protest from Parliament. In sum, the macro-institutional features specified by Law 675 reflected the well-known characteristics of the decision-making actors and areas, lacked any sense of internal responsibility or leadership, and were ill-equipped in terms of both organizational features and human resources to satisfy the technical-substantive requisites of an industrial policy.

A meaningful comparison between the Italian experience and the French and English ones is certainly premature. Nevertheless, one can note that Italy's attempt to move from a situation resembling the

English experience (dispersion of responsibilities and decision-making conflicts) to one similar to the French model (integrated, quasi-pyramidical policy-making) in the late 1970s largely failed and that this failure was in part due to institutional features and design. In fact, this design was characterized by a low degree of isolation, the preservation (if not reinforcement) of "differences" rather than cooperation, and even "distributive collusion," thanks to the many opportunities to externalize costs. The attempt to give life to a network of policy experts or to comprehensive experiments with concertation with the unions quickly died as "pluralistic pressures" immediately invaded the new "regulatory state."

Compared with the two foreign experiences outlined above, Italian state regulation was also born with certain notable incongruities in terms of banal but important infrastructural and instrumental rationality requisites. In this sense, the weaknesses are great not only compared to France but also to England, where industrial policy-making, while chaotic and burdensome, is still subject to technical competence and procedural modes much more appropriate to the issues under consideration.

Micro-decision-making processes

As stated earlier, the micro-decision-making level is where political pressures are especially able to interfere with the economic logic of policies. The stylized comparison with France and England indicated how such interference is related to policy design. The Italian debate has often focused on the perverse features of micro-decision-making procedures when denouncing the assistential character and the pervasive "political pollution" of industrial government.

The sequential procedures designed to implement industrial legislation in Italy are multiple, and it would thus be impossible in this chapter to present an exhaustive typology. A recent attempt along these lines (Abbate et al. 1985) distinguishes essentially three procedural "prototypes": a "discretional" type (which exalts the decision-making autonomy of the relevant Ministry); a "participatory" type (which instead involves numerous actors at multiple levels); and an "internal" model (even this based within a single Ministry but with more specific decision-making constraints). For our purposes we will limit ourselves to formulating some general reflections on the procedures of access to the benefits available under ex-Law 675.

The negative features expressed at the macro-decision-making level of this law were amply reproduced at the level of implementation. The procedural sequences of firm requests for financial allocations involved at least twenty different types of appraisals, deliberations, judgments, and informative notes and were extremely participatory in that they involved numerous actors: credit institutions, the Regions, Parliament, the Ministry of Industry, a Technical Committee appointed by the President of the Council of Ministers, the Treasury Ministry, and finally CIPI (Compagna-Marchini 1981; Gallo 1983). This not only affected the time required to reach decisions (for most cases, more than three years passed between the original request and the final approval) but also promoted the dispersion of responsibility for these decisions.

The procedural sequence of Law 675 set aside certain times and settings for technical considerations: appraisals by credit institutions and the opinion of the Technical Committee guaranteed, for example, an *ex ante* evaluation of the economic feasibility of firm projects. But these economic evaluations were often lost in the procedural labyrinth as a result of two factors: the lack of *ex post* controls and feedback on the *ex ante* evaluations, and the many opportunities inherent in these same procedures to circumvent or manipulate technical considerations. The first drawback was widely lamented in the debate concerning Law 675 and is considered one of the most painful aspects of the Italian system of industrial government (Marconi 1986a). *Ex post* control can be missing *tout-court* because it is not foreseen by the law, or it can be inadequate since it involves organizations that are different from those responsible for spending, or because even if it is foreseen, it is implemented either with much delay or not at all.

However, it is the second drawback that permits the true and proper privileging of "political" considerations over "economic" ones. As in other areas of state intervention in Italy, the law foresees that the political body (in this case, the CIPI) can "correct" or circumvent the conclusions of the technical investigations based on its own (often expressly defined as "socially relevant") considerations. Thus, "political" guarantees for firms that did not satisfy the financial criteria of the banks and credit institutions began to appear (Palmerio and Valliani 1981). CIPI also suspended sanctions against firms with inadequate returns on their economic allocations and conceded/extended wage guarantees to firms in crisis based on "socially relevant" considerations (Gallo 1983).

We are not saying that economic considerations *stricto sensu* should always and unconditionally determine political choices. Certainly, these criteria mix with others in appropriate dosages in all countries. The point is that given the degree of political pressures in Italy and given the significant organizational and qualitative shortcomings of Italy's public administration, the institutional spaces left open to political discretion were probably too wide. Thus, we should not be surprised by the low effectiveness of such delicate economic operations as those concerning industrial adjustment. While this analysis needs to be elaborated, one nevertheless gets the impression that institutional features in this sector permitted the formation of an "assistential market" analogous to that created around other, especially social, policies (Ferrera 1984). As discussed in the Introduction to this volume, the syndrome of "circumvention" seems to be a recurring feature of the Italian model of policy-making: a syndrome that tends rapidly to reduce any attempt at efficient regulation by public actors.

In sum, even at the micro-level, the decision-making rules adopted in Italy for the government of industry appear to lack "parsimony" in terms of actors and procedures involved and promote both a lack of responsibility and an externalization of decisions that lack congruity with the economic objectives pursued. More recently, however, laws promoting applied research and supporting innovation appear to express a new, more effective orientation (Abate et al. 1985; Marconi 1986a). However, as long as ministerial bureaucracies continue to lack organizational and qualitative effectiveness, these old deficiencies threaten to persevere (a point recently highlighted by the Rebecchini Commission [Senate of the Republic 1985]).

The path towards an organizational and procedural rationalization of industrial policy, congruent with the new objectives of "active management of the transition" formulated by the government (Ministry of Industry 1984; CEEP 1984) still appears to be quite long.

While not discussing the details of institutional issues, the recent CER/IRS Report (1986) formulated a series of very interesting suggestions regarding these concerns. Among these are: the construction of a "central headquarters" for the elaboration of strategic designs, gathering together functions dispersed among the various ministries and "insufficiently coordinated in multiple interministerial committees . . . which have often become centers of ratification or of mediation-compromise of the various ministerial requests" (p. 160); a lightening of the management load of individual interventions through the increased use of credit institutions and the financial administration; a technical upgrading of state personnel working on industry matters; and greater use of evaluation procedures and technical revisions of state intervention programs (with precise institutional constraints).

At the more general level, the indication that emerges from the CER/IRS Report (in accord with the suggestions of the Rebecchni Commission) is that of a comprehensive reorganization of Italian industrial policy, from a strategy of direct governance of industry to one of indirect governance. This is not an unconditional appeal for deregulation but rather a reasonable appeal for the adoption of a regulatory mix more respective of economic criteria and also more congruous with the (limited) possibilities of Italy's political-administrative system. The adoption of an indirect state regulation, not well adapted to Italy's policy-making traditions, would permit one to overcome the perverse links that waste public resources so typical of the Italian case.

Notes

1 We do not intend to say that the latter needs policies but rather that the dynamics of large and small political markets interfere with the development and implementation of these policies.

2 This is certainly not the place to discuss the analytic motivations behind the emergent "new institutionalism" in social science and in particular policy analysis. See Zysman (1983) for more on the importance of institutions as regulators of political issues.

3 See Dyson and Wilks (1983).

4 There is a vast debate on the success of the French model and the failure of the British experience. For an interesting discussion with ample bibliography on this issue, see Zysman (1983).

5 For more on the specific procedures followed in the allocation of financial incentives in the different countries, see OECD (1983) and R. M. Grant (1983).

6 This last point is particularly important: the *ex post* control of incentives is done by the highly efficient Inspection des Finances, which provide the committees' headquarters (i.e., the Tresor) a continuous feedback on the use and returns of public incentives.

7 If, for example, a disagreement develops between the Ministry of Industry and the Industrial Development Advisory Board (which includes businesses, banks, and the unions) the Ministry of Industry is obliged to bring the question before the local towns.

8 One must realize that this type of regulation of industrial policy has in large part been sustained even by the unions, who could have pressed for more associative (neo-corporatist) regulatory strategies. This syndrome appears to prevail also in the labor market (see Reyneri, Chapter 5 in this volume) and in industrial relations (see Cella, Chapter 7 in this volume).

5

The Italian labor market: between state control and social regulation

EMILIO REYNERI

1. Different forms of labor market regulation

A preliminary discussion of the issue of whether or not the labor market is truly only a market in which labor is allocated like other commodities would require too lengthy a digression.[1] For the purposes of this chapter we need only recall that in the labor market, the seller does not relinquish total control of the commodity to the buyer, since the social relations between the actors do not end with the exchange but continue throughout the productive process. Many aspects of this exchange cannot be understood without keeping in mind the consensus necessary for the subsequent use of labor. Thus, the labor "market" can be considered to have a dual character: as an arena in which labor power is exchanged and as one in which labor power is transformed into productive labor. In these dual arenas, groups and individuals representing both the demand and the supply of labor are brought face to face. These actors can be more or less organized, and their interactions can follow rules and procedures established by simple relations of relative scarcity, state intervention, collective bargaining, or even primary and particularistic traditions and relationships.

Individualistic market exchange, collective bargaining (i.e., organized exchange), state, and community are, in fact, the institutions that guide and organize the relations between actors in the labor market.[2] For greater clarity, we need to emphasize that the term regulation is intended here as the process of adjustment between demand and supply of labor, without necessarily implying the existence of policies consciously pursued by either or both of the actors.[3] Thus, a market is always in some way regulated, since there is always at least one institution that exists to maintain order.

Of course, the labor market can sometimes seem confused or chaotic, but this is simply because it is sometimes the "regulated" outcome of

129

institutions like the market or the community. Nor can we preclude the possibility of "regulation crises" during periods of transition or when contradictory modes of regulation are simultaneously at work. We can, however, only speak of labor markets which are more or less regulated or even unregulated if we restrict use of the term regulation to refer only to actions of collective actors with conscious strategies (the state, unions). But this threatens to obscure the importance of "diffuse" and less "strategic" modes of regulation.

Thus, the regulation of the "labor arena" can, first of all, be left to the free play of the individualistic and competitive market. Given the structural imbalance between labor supply and demand, this is a form that almost always presupposes not only the organizational and political weakness of workers, but also an oversupply of labor and a deferential attitude towards managerial authority. This does not, in fact, mean the total absence of state intervention since even the free market exists and operates thanks to legislative norms and political decisions. Rather, interventions by the political system are aimed, in this case, at eliminating obstacles and constraints on entrepreneurial freedom posed by professional and social routines, and at alleviating, a posteriori, the social consequences of this freedom.

Second, the labor market can be regulated by the state. In this case entrance into, permanence and mobility within, and exit from both employment and the wage relationship can be shaped by precise legislative norms and often controlled by part of the public administration. Moreover, to understand the most recent Italian events, a further distinction is required. In fact, state regulation can be realized primarily through universalistic and irrevocable norms, leaving to peripheral administrative bodies only the job of ensuring proper respect for these procedures, as is the case in traditional centralized bureaucratic systems. Or state action can seek to rebalance the relations between supply and demand without seeking rigidly to control all behavior and instead leaving the job of providing services and support (either financial or training) and preventing discrimination to appropriately designated agencies. This is, for example, what distinguishes Italy from France, another traditional European country characterized by significant state intervention in the labor market (Benoit 1984).

Third, the labor market can also be regulated by collective bargaining, but even this form has two variants. In the first, typical of American unionism, collective bargaining generally involves the labor market of the single firm and state actions are confined to the generic definition of the rules of the negotiating game. In the second variant, European neo-corporatism, centralized bargaining among the state, unions, and business establishes general objectives for the entire national labor market and delegates to lower levels (territorial and firm) the task of pursuing these goals. Thus, particular solutions, adapted to a diversity of situations, can be arrived at within the context of centrally set norms.

Finally, the labor market can be regulated by family, community, and clientalistic networks. This is true not only for "less developed" economic systems and various forms of "underground economy" but also for the most advanced industrial systems, in certain social and political settings characterized primarily by the presence of small firms. This "micro-social" form of regulation can be distinguished from the preceding one, in which the actors are collective subjects operating on the "macro-social" level.

This typology of regulatory processes of the labor market serves to allow us to present the characteristics of the Italian situation. Thus, its utility should be considered only with regard to this limited purpose. To elaborate the analytical categories, in fact, would require more ample comparative work. Nonetheless, other observations also inspired by the Italian case may be added.

First of all, to determine which mode of regulation prevails, we need to analyze the various forms of entry into and exit from employment rather than how the cost of labor is defined (for which the market and collective bargaining are almost always dominant, if not exclusive, regulators). Moreover, the four different modes of regulation are not entirely mutually exclusive; perhaps only regulation by the market, based on relative scarcity, can appear in exclusive form. Thus, one must view the mode of regulation as one of relative predominance or as a particular mix of different modes.

2. Traditional features and territorial differences in Italian labor market regulation

If for a moment we ignore all diachronic and territorial differences, labor market regulation can well appear "typically" Italian: at the formal level state control is pervasive and rigid, yet, in reality, the absence of efficient and competent state strategies leads to neglect of juridical norms and the prevalence of more spontaneous social modes, based on family or community micro-systems. According to our conceptualization, therefore, the Italian labor market, which traditionally is formally controlled by rigid and universalistic legislation, in practice has a notable share of micro-social regulation.

This does not mean that the existence of strong state regulation, even if largely ignored, has no real effects. In fact, it is precisely this normative framework which constrains regulation of the labor market by either the free market or collective bargaining. Instead, particularistic practices are favored, since they alone can "circumvent" rigid juridical norms thanks to the widely diffused complicity of family, community, and clientalistic networks.

Other factors also help to explain the situation. Some, as will be explained later, are the result of postwar political and union events and the legacy of the fascist corporate state. Others, however, are fundamental characteristics of Italian society. The first of these is the persistent importance of primary relations. The second is the particular juridical-formalistic "culture" linked both to the objective inefficiency of the public bureaucracy and the unlimited – in formal terms – trust in legislative norms. The absence of any form of administrative or sociological culture is especially apparent in the left-wing parties and in the union confederation – the CGIL (Confederazione General Italiana del Lavoro) – ideologically closest to them.

Perhaps the most alarming example of this confusion between the legal ideal and the actual situation concerns the hiring process. In Italy, hiring must legally take place through the State Employment Offices and, at least until a few years ago, also had to occur through a simple indication of the number of workers needed. This left the job of selecting those to be hired from among the unemployed to the Employment Offices, using criteria based on length of unemployment and family needs rather than skills or competencies.

In fact, the substance and even the form of this procedure have rarely been respected. Initially, in the 1950s, the imbalance between supply and demand in both the labor and political markets was such that this legislation was simply ignored, leaving to the firm full discretion in hiring. But with the decline of the political exclusion of the Left and anti-union discrimination, firms began to use particularistic "chains" based on church parishes and electoral clienteles. Since the late 1960s the role of micro-social systems in regulating hiring has become even more pronounced. In fact, as a result of both a change in the balance of power in favor of the unions, which try to have the laws enforced, and the increasing importance placed by firms on professional skills and personal trust, these formal procedures are circumvented through complicated legal procedures based on the extensive complicity of family and clientalistic networks.

A second example, also well known, concerns the development of irregular, part-time, and/or time-limited forms of employment. Until a few years ago, part-time and time-limited forms of employment were not foreseen by Italian legal and contractual norms. Yet, in order for the underground economy to function, it requires the complicity of family and community networks. A similar phenomenon exists for moonlighting *(doppio lavoro)*, which recent research has shown to be extremely pervasive in the public sector, that is, precisely where it is explicitly forbidden by law, but where at the same time it is enhanced by permissiveness and complicity (Gallino 1985).

Finally, we should mention various forms of exit, both temporary and permanent, from traditional forms of employment, at least in the South in the 1970s. In fact, both unemployment insurance for agricultural workers and social security payments for invalids only seem to be managed by the unions. In truth, studies on the assistential economy of the South have shown that clientalistic channels and communitarian complicity play a determining role in how these benefits are distributed (Reyneri 1979:Chap. 7).

The above summary is in reality a simplified stereotype of labor market regulation in Italy. As stated previously, both changing patterns over time and differences by location (which in Italy play a major role) have been ignored. The result is to obscure developments in the last decade. The historical approach of the second part of this chapter will seek to correct the first of these defects. As for the second, we will attempt to outline the models of labor force allocation prevalent in Italy's three major socio-cultural areas.[4] Unfortunately, the state of existent research does not permit us to take both into account simultaneously. Thus diachronic analyses often focus on only one of the three Italies, the more industrial and urban areas of the Northwest, in which evolutionary trends for the entire nation are thought to be most apparent.

In the regions of northwest Italy, until the late 1960s and thanks to the use of an "anonymous" labor force (i.e., workers uprooted from their original social context) in large industrial complexes, universalistic regulation based on the free market, administrative control by the state, or collective bargaining prevailed. These "modern" conditions were seen as hypothetically valid for the entire nation and constituted the implicit framework in debates on labor market policy.

In contrast, in the central and northeast regions, the so-called "Third Italy" of diffuse small firms, the importance of the identity of the individual worker (that is, his embeddedness in a network of social relations in which community ties are reinforced by "white" or "red" ideologies) prevails. Market regulation and micro-social regulation are not in conflict in this case but rather combine with exceptionally positive results in terms of productive and allocative efficiency. This is so because these networks of social relations guarantee the workers' acceptance of the principles of effort and subordination. This "market of trustworthy workers" is regulated as much by trust as by the price of the labor force.

The situation is again quite different in southern Italy, where micro-social regulation tends to run counter to the logic of the market, not to mention control by the state or the unions. In fact, employment is exchanged within a wider context of "social obligations"; and exchange is not concerned primarily with work effort but rather with the entire person, with all his family ties and networks of personal relationships. The term "life market" (Kammerer et al. 1983) was coined to describe this situation. Nonetheless, the reliability which is thus guaranteed cannot be translated into principles of work effort and subordination. This occurs not in large-scale factories in which hierarchies and productive goals are necessarily impersonal, but rather in the "underground economy" in which labor relations and social and community ties are all mixed together. In large firms, especially if they are somehow "assisted" by the state, workers are hired through clientalistic channels in which an exhaustive exchange of favors and deferential social (and electoral) behavior prevails. As a result, these workers see themselves as free from all deferential obligations towards firm management. In this context, therefore, micro-social regulation contrasts sharply not only with the universalistic perspective of the state and the collective and egalitarian view of collective bargaining, but also with the goals of productive efficiency.

We will now undertake an historical overview of employment policies in Italy, in which, as already stated, the territorial differences outlined above cannot be taken into account. Thus, the next section will implicitly refer to the most important labor market, that is, that of the most urban and industrial areas of northern Italy.[5]

3. Administrative control of the labor market: from anti-union device to union "utopia"

Immediately after the war, Italian unions sought to regain the control over hiring they had possessed prior to fascism. But in 1948, following the electoral defeat of the Left and with explicitly anti-union motivations, hiring became publicly controlled through the local offices of the Ministry of Labor with only token participation of the unions. However, these Employment Offices were not realistically capable of controlling a labor market dominated even at the political level by those demanding labor. Thus, they limited themselves merely to registering, a posteriori, the choices made by firms (Siniscalchi 1981:166; Arrigo 1983:14). Moreover, legislation controlling firing was liberalized and union attempts to bargain over firm employment (especially in agriculture) proved useless, especially in the liberalistic climate of the reconstruction period. During these years, market regulation prevailed.

It was enhanced by a supply of labor that exceeded demand and by the weakness of a profoundly divided union movement. Nonetheless, firms, even large ones, continued to use micro-social mechanisms of hiring in order to ensure deference and subordination.

In the early 1970s, unions gained considerable strength vis-à-vis both firms and the state. Nonetheless, instead of seeking to regain their traditional control of the labor market, the unions pressed for and obtained legislation that enforced the already existent state norms. They also increased their presence in the mixed commissions that control such procedures. This strategy did not produce great results, even on the normative front. In fact, even when strongest in the "political market," Italian unions never sought to foster a truly friendly government of the Left. Instead, they dealt with weak governments of the Center-Left, which sought to satisfy union demands without sacrificing the traditional interests of firms, and, above all, of their bureaucratic and political clients. This "pluralist stagnation" led either to paralysis in the face of vetoes by opposing forces or to administrative and financial disaster as contradictory distributive claims were accommodated. Thus, a type of "geological stratification" was formed in which the new employment policies were casually added onto the old norms. As a result, there now exist about ten different modes of hiring and five or six different forms of unemployment insurance, not to mention the eight or nine different tripartite commissions (unions, business, and state bureaucrats) that are supposed to oversee aspects of the labor market at both the national and local levels.

Thus, during the period of extensive social mobilization and equally intensive political pressure on the government, the unions pursued a strategy aimed at uniformly and rigidly controlling entrance to and maintenance of traditional full-time employment. First of all, the union sought to change all part-time, seasonal, and temporary jobs into full-time, stable positions. These demands were assisted by the courts thanks to a "guaranteeist" interpretation by the new labor court of old and seldom applied pre-industrial laws. Some firms were thus constrained to assume as full-time those workers who filled seasonal or occasional maintenance jobs. This "struggle against precarious employment," which sought to normalize even the most casual and transient forms of employment, was especially burdensome for the public sector.

Moreover, the union sought to regulate the entrance of young workers into the labor market by abolishing apprenticeships and promoting a generalized and public system of job training. The goal of this reform was noble, in that it sought to hinder the frequent exploitation of apprentices as cheap labor and to guarantee job training that was not simply subordinate to the needs of particular firms. But the risks of this "scholarization," and thus the inefficiency of the reform, became evident with the laws of 1972 and 1978.

The 1970 law on agricultural job placement and the *Statuto dei Lavoratori* rigidified the guaranteeist aspects of job placement and further reduced the firms' ability to request particular workers. The result was disappointing. The extensive participation of the unions in the tripartite commissions, which was intended to eliminate the pervasive practices of evading the laws, failed. The unions were unable to break the clientalistic power of the ministerial bureaucracy (the omni-powerful figure of the placement officer is especially visible in the South) (Bolasco et al. 1983:99–101; Arrigo 1983:22–29). Rather, when they did manage to exercise a certain amount of control, the result was often a freeze on regular placement, with "direct transfers" from one firm to another (which legally are person-specific), individual hiring in small firms, or even "black" (undeclared) employment taking its place.[6] In other words, when the union succeeded in imposing its guaranteeist model based on legislation and administrative controls, a perverse effect was generated in which the most savage forms of regulation based on family, community, or clientalistic networks were promoted at the expense of the laws. In fact, the problems with this model of job placement were no longer due to the unfavorable market conditions or balance of political power of the 1950s. Instead, they derived from the premises on which the model was founded, that is, the intermediation between the supply and demand for labor of social criteria (the needs of the workers) without any attention being paid to skills or professionalism.

During this same period two other legislative acts reinforced the micro-social regulation of the labor market, especially in the South. These concerned reform of the social security system, which made it easier to obtain a disability pension, and the treatment of agricultural unemployment. Even though the unions controlled these public functions, their effort at universalistic regulation failed. On the one hand, they were subject to too many powerful pressures (in a backward economy even an inadequate pension becomes an issue of survival) and on the other, because of their own organizational weaknesses, they could maintain and extend their organizational presence only through particularistic and assistential practices.

There are several explanations for the unions' actions. First, the rigid choice in favor of full-time and wholly secure employment can be traced to union traditions that considered the elimination of job uncertainty a principal goal, especially important in a country like Italy, which had until recently suffered from pervasive un- and under-employment (Accornero 1984:76; Berger and Piore 1980:Chap. 1). But the idea that all alternative forms of employment stemmed from employers' demands, and thus were to be refused, also is characteristic of the world of unskilled workers *(l'operaio massa)* in large industry who constituted the principal reference group for the union in these years. Moreover, it is understandable that the Italian unions, after a long period of management strength and unreliability, sought to impose set procedures regulating the demand for labor instead of creating arenas of regulation and collaboration with employers. Furthermore, the unions' pursuit of state control over job placement and job training can be explained by the "statist culture" of the Italian Left and unions. Finally, the unions were unconcerned about possible perverse effects of rigidities and constraints on the labor market (as well as on the organization of labor within firms) since they perceived themselves, until the mid-1970s, to be in a situation of economic growth and, hence, of expansion of employment (Dell'Arringa 1983:32).

This is especially true for other policies pursued by the unions in this period, especially those intended to guarantee employment in the face of economic downturns. In fact, between 1968 and 1975, the union movement obtained legislation that effectively "froze" dismissals in both large and medium-sized industries through the generalized and indeterminate application of the Cassa Integrazione Guadagni (CIG, a special state redundancy fund that covers the salaries of laid-off workers). The CIG was transformed from a temporary intervention aimed at promoting productive restructuring to a true and proper substitute for dismissals, at least in those firms which had a strong union presence or which were important in their particular socioeconomic contexts.

These are, really, macro-social forms of regulation. But since they concerned exit from employment, in the context of an overall industrial crisis, they created major problems for the unions. In fact, as long as crises of firms remained relatively isolated events, the guarantees of jobs and salaries provided by the CIG played an important role in the unions' attempt to control the labor market. Yet, with the subsequent onset of a general crisis, the CIG increasingly came to be seen as the symbol of "defensive" rigidities promoted by the union in order to protect workers organized by the union at the expense of the interests of the workforce as a whole. Moreover, as this process of particularized protection slowly increased, the formal role of the union in decisions concerning the concession and extension of the CIG grew. The particularization of control and the increase in discretionary decisions about who is to be protected are two aspects of the same phenomenon, which, on the one hand, promotes the segmentation of the labor market, strengthening the most protected segments, and, on the other hand, threatens to "corporatize" – in the traditional and pejorative sense of the term – union action.

4. From "offensive" rigidity to "defensive" and particularistic rigidity

Two sets of laws approved between 1976 and 1979 mark the beginning of the period of "defensive" rigidity, understood as the simultaneous protection of both the working class in large-scale industry and the union's own organization. The aim of the first set of laws was to extend control over employment in cases where the firm ceased to exist as a result of bankruptcy or the cessation of activity, thereby artificially creating the juridical conditions permitting use of the CIG (Reyneri 1985:109). This represented the extreme of the unions' defense of employment "job by job," primarily in firms with a high degree of unionization.

Along with this model of union-negotiated regulation, another series of laws was aimed at controlling external labor mobility in firms in crisis. The 1977 law on industrial restructuring foresaw state and union control over labor mobility so that a worker declared "redundant" would be guaranteed another job at the same skill level and in the same geographical area. The complicated mechanism of this law, the product of compromises between labor and business, should have created an alternative between dismissal and assistance (Lenti 1981:47).

In practice, the behavior of both those demanding labor and those supplying it led to the collapse of this compromise. Firms in expansion had no intention of indiscriminately hiring the "refuse" of firms in crisis, especially since the absence of any criteria in the composition of the "mobility lists" permitted firm managers to fill them with "undesirables" (elderly, disabled, absentees, union militants). But even in the face of very weak labor demand, refusals by workers "in mobility" to move were relatively numerous, for they feared a decline in skill level and pay as well as in their rights and guarantees since smaller firms were both less legally protected and less unionized.

The lack of decent unemployment compensation led the unions to insist on the principle of "job to job" mobility (i.e., the worker had to have a job to move to before leaving the previous one, often fictitiously maintained through the CIG). Nonetheless, faced with an increasingly dramatic situation, a more pragmatic policy, espoused by the more traditional guaranteeist and universalistic-statist tendencies in the unions, began to take shape. This involved the concept of collective mobility, negotiated between the union, the firm that would shed labor force, and the firm seeking workers, with the frequent participation of the central state, and in the South the local government as well. In fact, in certain cases, it was the union that directly negotiated the transfer of a group of workers from one firm to another, without any concerns for particular job placements. Successive legal decrees, "negotiated" with the union according to the prevailing practices of the period, validated this procedure a posteriori by recognizing the legitimacy of these negotiated accords for the relocation of workers in firms in crisis (Arrigo 1983:29).

According to some jurists, these procedures are illegal not only because of their retroactivity but also because they violate the principle of universalism (Lenti 1981:59–60). This criticism is part of a more general cultural and political opposition of a segment of the Italian Left to the "neo-corporatist" activities of the union. In reality, this solution could become an extension of the negotiated regulation of the labor market, thus permitting the union to break the perverse linkage of formal rigid guaranteeism with actual micro-social regulation (which, since the onset of the recession, firms sought to break in their favor by reproposing full firm discretion in the labor market). This type of "negotiated mobility," however, accentuates one of the principal forms of segmentation of the labor market: the division between "who is in" and "who is out." But the major constraint on its spread is external and conjunctural: one cannot regulate mobility in such a manner when industrial employment as a whole, and especially in large and medium-sized firms, is decreasing.

Thus, the long "war of position" between firms and unions over the issue of mobility was concluded, at least formally, at the end of the 1970s (Centre de Recherche Travail et Société 1983:235, 241–4). In a series of national category contracts, the unions won a clause guaranteeing worker reentry into the original firm. But, in fact, with the pervasiveness and continual extension of the "mobility" period, this turned into a masked form of dismissal, and the *cassa-integrati* became, in a sense, unemployed workers, even if assured their salaries (paid by the state) and protected by rehiring guarantees. In this way, the problem of mobility was further exacerbated since, in addition to the firms' process of selection, a process of self-selection among workers – resulting in the *cassa-integrati* becoming reduced to a "hard core" of unemployable workers – was added. This explains the unions' resistance, at least until the mid-1980s, to any proposal intended to limit the duration of the Cassa Integrazione Guadagni.

Also reflecting the unions' strategy of "defensive rigidity" was the legislation on youth employment that was initiated in 1977. For the first time in Italy, an active employment policy was attempted in order to enhance youth employment through a series of monetary incentives to firms and to newly formed youth cooperatives. The unions, still strong at the political level, again set out to safeguard certain general guaranteeist principles. Chief among these was the requirement for anonymous hiring practices, which was made even more rigid for youth employment than for general hiring.

This law also failed. The private sector hired very few young workers since, notwithstanding the monetary incentives, firms preferred traditional hiring channels, which they had already learned to manipulate according to their own needs. Moreover, serious errors in economic forecasting and implementation prevented the takeoff of the youth cooperatives.[7] The only "positive" result was the creation of public employment, but this was achieved in such a way that family and clientalistic networks were reinforced. In fact, in the public sector, the law foresaw only temporary positions or time-limited contracts with youth cooperatives (this last practice was especially pervasive in the South since it permitted traditional waiting lists to be circumvented and thus provided new resources for traditional political and clientalistic practices). As one can easily imagine, under pressure from the new workers (and, reluctantly, even the union) all of these jobs became converted into permanent full-time jobs through an exhaustive series of legal extensions and fictitious qualifying exams. This law, one of the last acts in a series that created "precarious" jobs, also reveals the extent to which micro-social systems of regulation in Italy can shape even national labor market policy.

Nonetheless, given the alarming extent of the problem, the successive laws on youth employment, albeit always justified as "extraordinary" and "crisis" measures, began to break the guaranteeist front. The most important innovations were the extension of the right to hire specific workers, job-training contracts that expire after fixed periods of time, the possibility of ignoring school diplomas, and regulations permitting part-time employment. It was the turning point: even more important than their promotion of labor mobility in the crucial sectors of the economy, these new youth employment laws demonstrated how inadequate and rigid contemporary legislation regulating the labor market actually had become. Building on this initial demonstration, employers became increasingly vocal and increasingly successful in seeking to abolish all constraints on their discretion. This begins the period of "rampant deregulation," to which the unions reacted defensively. Unable to develop a viable alternative, they found themselves constrained to make one concession after another.

4. Rampant deregulation of the 1980s: towards a "free" labor market?

At the end of the 1970s, an extensive debate developed between the unions and the state over reforms of the labor market, but the results were practically nil. Only in 1983, when the unemployment crisis became even more acute, were some of the earlier proposals enacted in limited and episodic legislation. These reforms sought to reduce the constraints on firms but made few concessions to the unions in terms of bargaining. Above all, the new laws did not develop the efficient public employment services foreseen in the comprehensive reform of employment practices proposed in 1979 and still being debated in Parliament today.

This reform project foresees, first of all, a "liberalization" of job placement by abolishing the anonymous hiring system. At the same time, however, constraints are imposed on "direct transfers" (a method frequently used to circumvent the system of anonymous hiring) in that a qualified job placement office sees to it that the skills of the worker and the needs of the firm correspond. In terms of mobility, the unstable equilibrium between the unions and employers negotiated in 1979 becomes translated into legislation that sets time limits on the CIG and progressively reduces the amount of salary guaranteed. In sum, "the management of the procedures continues to prevail over that of the goals" (Centre de Recherche Travail et Société 1983:263). Furthermore, "labor market regulation continues to be based on the sharing of existing employment opportunities" at the expense of an active employment policy (Arrigo 1983:34). Thus, the old notion of administrative control of the labor market (if somewhat modified) prevails, and attempts by the state to actively promote employment, as was anticipated in the political and intellectual debates over the so-called "labor agency," are few and weak.

In the early 1980s, the union, on the one hand, oscillated between declarations in favor of active employment policies and behavior which, in fact (under pressure from concerned workers), defended the assistential rigidities of the CIG and agricultural employment (Regalia 1984:77–9). On the other hand, the union remained divided over a proposal that might contribute to an offensive strategy of job development: i.e., the reduction of work hours. Nonetheless, an important result of the long debate over work hours was the discussion of full-time employment. The union began to undergo a real and proper reversal in its position on part-time work. After having long blocked this form of employment, it now began to include it in its contractual demands, at both the category and firm levels.

A real reversal of union behavior occurred with the January 22, 1983, accord among the unions, employers, and the government, which foresaw, among other things, the immediate promotion by the government of several legislative acts to be implemented immediately by decree while the more general reform of the labor market awaited parliamentary approval. These government initiatives included: (1) the establishment of employment commissions to enhance the flexibility of hiring procedures, abrogating extant norms; (2) the possibility of hiring specific workers for all youth job-training contracts (which are time limited) and for 50% of all other contracts; (3) legislative acts supporting the so-called "solidarity contracts" that sought to reduce work hours in order to promote hiring or, at least, avoid the use of the CIG. Other acts promoting part-time and time-limited employment were also foreseen in the 1983 accord, as were maxima on the use of the CIG.

A legal decree was used immediately to implement (for a one-year experimental period) those parts of the accord concerning person-specific hiring, job-training contracts, and seasonal contracts. Successive decrees promoted the solidarity contracts and the other measures, thus delaying *sine die* the possibility of a more global reform of the regulation of the labor market. This explains the unions' reservations as well as the business association's declaration that the "liberalization" was too limited (Regalia 1984:75–6). Once again, the politics of distributive bargains prevailed, but it is worth noting that the new design of the global reform included not only the particular aspects of the January 22 accord but also its "neo-corporatist" spirit. In fact, enormous value was given to this tripartite accord. It was seen as able to abolish any and all preexisting norms and as a path towards macro-social regulation of the labor market. However, it was promoted only by certain segments of the unions and of the Italian Left.

In reality, the constraints foreseen by the rigid labor legislation that prevailed until the early 1980s became progressively looser, leaving in "hibernation" the old bureaucratic apparatus without creating new, more flexible instruments able to implement the tripartite accord. Thus, the innovations could have consequences quite different from those foreseen in the more comprehensive original framework of reform. That is, they could permit development of a free labor market situation instead of regulation negotiated by the unions and business.

Thus, time-limited job-training contracts and firm-level training programs are subject to the approval of quadripartite (central state, region, employers, and unions) regional commissions which, however, do not possess the capacity to analyze and evaluate the projects. At the same time, firms use these projects to obtain a continuous flow of young workers with low or medium skill levels. The success of this measure is irrefutable in terms of numbers of youth employed,[8] but it is doubtful that additional employment was created since other forms of hiring have decreased. In reality, a "desegmentation" of the labor market has occurred.[9] And if in some partial way the barrier between traditional workers and unemployed youth has been bridged, this has taken place at the risk of institutionalizing a new form of precarious employment.

In fact, no mechanism exists to normalize the jobs of these "trained" youths once their contract expires (Abburrà 1984:37; Arrigo 1983:53).

For part-time work almost all restrictions have been overcome by collective bargaining. Here rigidity has been replaced by union-controlled flexibility, in accord with the provisions of the January 22, 1983, accord. This seems to contradict recent legislation that often "forgets" the unions, but it may provide a new alternative between rigid guaranteeism and neo-liberalism.

The majority in the unions has reacted defensively, seeking to preserve the recently won (and costly) "rigidities" throughout this entire period of rampant deregulation. The exceptions to this are certain concessions by the leadership and several firm initiatives (little known but more numerous than believed) covering above all work hours aside from, of course, obligatory bargaining over the Cassa Integrazione Guadagni. Under attack, the union refused for a long time to enter into a logic of exchange of certain rigidities (which, like the anonymous system of hiring, are more theoretical than real) for control over a more flexible management of the labor market or for increased employment and training commitments by the firms. Only with the May 1986 accord with *Confindustria* has the union conceded to a further liberalization of job-training contracts (control by regional commissions is terminated and the salary of the young workers is reduced). But the exchange is purely renumerative, as the unions gained nothing other than an end to the years-long dispute over the inflation escalator.

As is easily seen, the unions were forced to accept one concession after another. This was so not only because the unemployment crisis reinforced business but also because new demands for more flexible and variable forms of employment originated with the workers themselves and were more consistent with new production technologies.

6. The new tendencies at the end of the 1980s

For over a decade, two positions have dominated the debate over labor market policies. On the one hand, employers have called for a return to the "free market for labor." On the other hand, the unions, which declare themselves in favor of active labor market policies, have, in the face of difficulties in realizing such policies, almost always ended up defending traditional methods of universalistic and administrative regulation. As for the government, its interventions have oscillated between an attempt to promote negotiated forms of regulation between labor and business, and its frequent practices of deregulation in the face of alarming rates of unemployment and intense business pressures.

These initiatives of these actors and simultaneous changes in the characteristics of labor supply and demand have certainly modified the traditional features of labor market regulation in Italy. In fact, we have by now overcome the stereotypical characterization outlined at the beginning of this chapter. Rigid and universalistic administrative control by parts of the public administration has been progressively dismantled even at the formal level through the legal recognition of "flexible" forms of employment and the passage of numerous decrees supporting the discretion of firms or the accords of the social partners.

Even in the most traditional sectors of the union, a new perspective has taken hold. The new, more flexible forms of employment (so long as they are negotiated) are no longer snubbed, and there appears to be an intention to negotiate issues of employment with firms at all levels, in a way that does not exclude the state but rather redefines its role from the traditional one of single, authoritative, and autonomous decision-maker. Thus, the regulation of the labor market would be left neither to the free market nor to the rigid control of the state but rather to the flexible result of decentralized bargaining at the firm and territorial levels. The state's role would be to establish the rules of the game (procedures and general obligation to negotiate), to safeguard more general interests (i.e., prevent sexual, social, and political discrimination), and to develop the juridical instruments, administrative structures, and other resources necessary to enhance the accords reached between labor and management.

Nonetheless, it is still uncertain whether the result of the end of the perverse combination of state and micro-social regulation will truly be the beginning of a new form of macro-social regulation of the labor market. In the mid-1980s, there are certainly indications in this direction, above all from the unions and the state. Yet, business associations continue to express their need for full discretion if employment is to increase. And this position, expressed at every available opportunity, often wins out in a situation of high unemployment.

But this conclusion is less obvious than it initially seems, at least concerning the highly important phase of hiring. On the one hand, the Italian labor market continues to operate in a context in which vocational-training structures are not very selective and family and community networks are strong and extensive. On the other hand, in a productive system that deals with ever-increasing levels of information and communication, the need for dependable workers (not only at the technical level but also in terms of social relations) increases. Thus, characteristics of micro-social regulation could reemerge in a "free" labor market, just as they did for different reasons in the 1950s.

But at this point it is best to stop speculating on the near future. With the collapse of the traditional, stereotypical model, we are still in a transition period and thus we cannot foresee which mix of regulatory institutions will affirm themselves in a relatively stable way.

Notes

1 For a systematic discussion of this point, see Reyneri (1987a).

2 See Streeck and Schmitter (1985) for more on this typology and the recent debate on neo-corporatism.

3 The definition of regulation used here is more ample than but not in opposition to that used in the Introduction to this volume.

4 This attempt to trace the territorial models of labor market regulation draws from Cortese (1987).

5 This historical analysis draws on an earlier work (see Reyneri 1985).

6 When in Turin the union manages to impose this guaranteeist model on job placement, the degree of coverage does not exceed 25 percent, the anonymous hirings involve slightly more than 33 percent of all hirings, and they are limited to time-limited contracts for unskilled workers. See Astrologo and Ricolfi (1981) and Galante and Bogetti (1982).

7 One thinks of the absurdity of having focused on "productive" sectors, in particular on agriculture instead of the tertiary sector.

8 For more on the evolution of youth employment laws, see Reyneri (1987b).

9 Ibid.

6

The divorce of the Banca d'Italia and the Italian Treasury: a case study of central bank independence[1]

GERALD A. EPSTEIN AND JULIET B. SCHOR

In recent years, the Italian financial system has undergone a process of deregulation. The traditionally state-administered system has been transformed into a much more market-oriented one. Loan ceilings in force since 1973 have been abolished, the portfolio constraint imposed on banks has been eliminated, and financial markets in government securities are now functioning. Italy's financial sector has been "Anglo-Saxonized."

Components of the shift from an administered to a market-oriented system were essential preconditions for another major change – a structural alteration in the relationship between the Bank of Italy and the Treasury, colloquially referred to as the "divorce." The Bank has traditionally been highly integrated with the Treasury, and statutorily obligated to finance all fiscal deficits. The divorce is important because it eliminated this obligation and created a significant degree of independence for the Bank.

The degree of independence enjoyed by a central bank is, in our view, a primary determinant of its policies. Independent banks are able to exercise more restrictive monetary and credit policies, and restrain inflation more successfully. In countries that experience high levels of labor militance, shifts in the distribution of income towards wages, or social unrest, the independence of a central bank is crucial to the policy response.

The hypothesis of this paper is that the Italian monetary authority, on account of its lack of independence, largely accommodated the rise in union power that began with the Hot Autumn. Periods of restrictiveness were caused, in the main, by balance of payments crises. As a result, the monetary authority, whose aversion to inflation was salient, exhibited a growing desire for independence. By 1981, after preparing the way through the cultivation of a loyal constituency of banks and the creation of private capital markets, the Bank was able to gain its statutory independence.

1. Why does the central bank do what it does?

A complete answer to the question "Why does the central bank do what it does?" is beyond the scope of this chapter. Instead we will summarize our views, which have been discussed in detail elsewhere (see Epstein 1981, 1982; Epstein and Ferguson 1984; Epstein and Schor 1985, 1986).

Mainstream theories of the state generally assume that the central bank, like other state agencies, attempts to maximize a social welfare function, given to it by the voters. Coupled with a neo-classical vision of the economy, in which a non-inflationary full employment equilibrium is possible, the mainstream view suggests that there are no inherent conflicts of interest which render monetary policy problematic.

The mainstream view of central banking is simple, but ultimately naive. Knowledge of voter preferences is not sufficient for understanding monetary policy, and the existence of a full employment equilibrium is in fact quite implausible in a capitalist economy (see Kalecki 1971 or Schor 1985a).

An alternative is a neo-Marxian theory based on the view that the state is a locus of class and intra-class conflict and that the outcomes of that conflict are conditioned by structural constraints from the economy. The constraints relevant for an analysis of central banking are the position of the nation in the world economy and the ability of capital to withhold investment funds when policies are not to its liking. We term this theory *neo*-Marxian to emphasize that it eschews the functionalism of orthodox Marxian theories of the state. There is no presumption that the state *necessarily* acts in the interest of the dominant class, or even a fragment of it. Rather, its actions are *political* and are the outcome of political struggle. However, a dominant class or fragment is able to exercise more influence over the central bank when it is more independent – insulated, either *de jure* or *de facto* – from democratic pressures.

We define independence as *the ability to conduct an autonomous monetary policy with respect to government.* This includes, but is not limited to, the freedom not to finance a government deficit. Our research (Epstein and Schor 1986) indicates that independent central banks pursue more restrictive policies and are associated with lower rates of inflation.[2] Therefore, countries with powerful labor movements and ruling labor parties may structurally curb the independence of the central bank. This hypothesis is borne out by our statistical evidence as well as the analysis in Martin (1986).

The impact of independence is conditioned by the relation between financial and industrial capital. In cases where finance and industry are not highly integrated, and the central bank is relatively independent, the influence of industrial capital may be low, and policy will be even more restrictive. The central bank will normally turn to the financial community, to create a constituency to support its independence. If financial and industrial interests diverge, we may observe a bank pursuing restrictive policies to the detriment of industrial capital and the benefit of financial capital.

The central bank will be constrained by the position of the nation in the world economy. Small countries with few controls on capital, or high international exposure, will be able to exercise less control over monetary policy. A country with a reserve or key currency will be inhibited vis-à-vis exchange rate fluctuations.

Finally, relations between labor and capital will influence policy. As noted above, our hypothesis is that strong and organized working classes will constrain the central bank. There are a number of dimensions of working-class strength that are relevant: the degree of real wage rigidity, the amount of employment security, the level of income-replacing social welfare expenditures, and the existence of a political vehicle to express the interests of the class.[3] If a working class has a great deal of real wage protection, an inflationary strategy will not succeed in eroding real wages. Similarly, if workers have employment security, deflation will not reduce real wages.

If the state provides a high level of income replacement, or what we call the "citizen wage,"[4] the impact of unemployment on the distribution of income will be attenuated. A high citizen wage may also impair shop-floor productivity, raise wages, and undermine the effectiveness of deflation in shifting the distribution of income towards profits. Deflation will also result in a fiscal burden, incurred by the financing of the citizen wage and subsequent pressures to accommodate it. Thus, the central bank may be reluctant to deflate because it will be ineffectual. And of course, in the event of a serious electoral challenge or a labor party in office, the government may not even permit restrictive policies for political reasons. The ability of the government to block policies, however, will depend in large part on the degree of independence of the bank.

On the other hand, with a weak working class, nominal rather than real wage rigidity, and no labor party, a central bank will be free to pursue a range of policies.[5] In the United States, for example, after the

1975 recession, the central bank conducted a loose money policy that eroded real wages and increased competitiveness through dollar depreciation (see Epstein 1985). It was able to do what many European central banks thought they could not – alter the distribution of income through reflation.

2. The Bank of Italy and the Italian economy

The Bank of Italy is an integrated central bank. Contrary to common practice, we do not conceptualize banks that lack independence as "dependent" or subservient,[6] but rather as *integrated*. The Bank of Italy is an important actor within the Italian government, a power center that has often acted as a "clearing box of the conflicts of power" (Jossa and Panico 1985:8).[7] This was particularly true during the Carli governorship, when the Bank was very involved in the formulation of overall economic policy. The Bank has traditionally enjoyed a high level of prestige in Italian society. As Allum noted, "The bank has become so successful that big businessmen were claiming in 1970 that 'it is quite possible to run the economy without the government provided that the machinery for handing out funds and the Bank of Italy, one of the most modern central banks with an excellent research staff, runs the credit policy'" (Allum 1973:246).

Despite its prestige, however, the Bank has not had the power to pursue policies that are greatly at odds with those of the government. It has been obligated to finance whatever level of "needs" emanates from the Treasury, through either automatic overdrafts in the Treasury's account with the Bank or the purchase of securities.

The integration of the Bank may be due to the traditional weakness of capital in the Italian political system. As Salvati argues, "In the entire history of Italian industrial development, capitalist interests never managed to build an autonomous base of support to achieve ideological hegemony over the moderate social bloc. Capitalists were also weak within the Christian Democratic system" (Salvati 1981:340; see also Salvati 1985). The opposition of big capital to the Center-Left coalition was an impediment to its enhanced control over the Bank of Italy. However, in the 1970s the changes in *Confindustria* associated with the Agnelli presidency laid a foundation for independence.

Nevertheless, although capital did not "control" the Bank, the goal of maintaining profitability was important. Nardozzi (1981), for example, argues that at least until the end of the Carli period the protection of non-financial profitability was the Bank's primary objective.[8] This is consistent with both the integration of the Bank and the political weakness of capital. The Bank's prestige and independence from financial capital allowed it to stand above the political system and concern itself with the long-run reproduction of the economy.

But this does not mean that the Bank was unconcerned with the financial sector. Rather, relations between industrial and financial capital in Italy are close, although the relation is subtle. Most banks are publicly owned and are controlled through the party system. Historically, there has been virtually no capital market; therefore the bulk of savings has been intermediated through banks. Banks are statutorily prevented from medium- and long-term financing; in practice they have circumvented these restrictions.[9]

Italy is a medium-sized economy with a high level of international exposure. However, the ability to insulate is considerable. Because the lira is not an important international currency, there is wide scope for depreciation to enhance competitiveness. The authorities have been able to exercise a fair amount of control over capital flows and trade volumes, through capital restrictions and limitations on trade financing (see De Vivo and Pivetti 1981).

3. Class conflict and monetary policy

The Italian working class was comparatively weak throughout the 1950s and 1960s. Development was premised on abundant supplies of low-wage labor, provided through extensive internal migration.[10] Union membership was low, and the unions themselves were divided. The Bank of Italy was generally able to pursue the maximization of investment and accommodate credit demands, without risking excessive inflation or real wage increases. The Bank accommodated by pegging the interest rate on government securities until 1969, after which time it targeted monetary and credit aggregates. The exceptions to this pattern were 1963 and 1969, when wage pressures led the Bank to deflate. Thus, during the Carli period, the protection of profitability was achieved by both expansionary and deflationary policies, depending on current circumstances.

These conditions were decisively altered in 1969, when Italy experienced a wave of labor militance and political unrest that resulted in nothing less than a transformation of Italian society, and in particular labor relations. Italy was, of course, not alone, as all the major European countries witnessed an upsurge of labor militance, but the scope and intensity of conflict in Italy was unsurpassed.[11]

Italy ranked first in strike volume among the OECD (Organization for Economic Cooperation and Development) countries in this period. Work stoppages rose from a yearly average of 2,597 during 1955–68, to 4,415 in 1969–71. Days lost per thousand employees rose from

735.5 to 1,741.[12] Union membership in the two largest unions, CGIL (Confederazione Generale Italiana del Lavoro) and CISL (Confederazione Italiana da Sindacati Libri), rose 20 percent in 1969–71.

These developments were reflected in large wage increases. Product wages rose 13 and 10 percent in 1970 and 1971, respectively. Italian industry suffered its most severe postwar profit squeeze, as productivity fell off as well (see Lacci 1976).

The mobilizations of the Hot Autumn were not quickly dissipated. High levels of militance were sustained, with legislative and organizational results. The Workers' Statute institutionalized many of the new forms of shop-floor representation and workers' rights. The *scala mobile* was overhauled in 1975, and thereafter provided 90 percent of all industrial workers with an average indexation level of 100 percent. Plant-closing legislation was enacted, and firms' ability to fire workers for disciplinary reasons was virtually eliminated. Indeed, Lange et al. (1982) note that almost no workers who had been previously employed were laid off during the post-1973 economic crisis. By 1981, union density had reached an impressive 40.5 percent.

Unemployment compensation increased markedly. In 1977, the traditional flat-rate benefit of 20 percent was supplemented with a program to replace 80 percent of lost wages.

Real social welfare expenditures expanded at an annual rate of 4.6 percent from 1970 to 1981, and as a percentage of GDP (Gross Domestic Product) rose from 21 percent to 26 percent.[13] The pressures for social welfare expenditures were considerable, and must be counted as among the important effects of the Hot Autumn and its aftermath. In our view, the growth of the "citizen's wage" was an important accommodation to the social unrest and labor militance of the 1970s. This analysis is supported by Schmitter's (1981) findings that social unruliness (collective protest, internal war, and strike volume) is associated with fiscal ineffectiveness (increased expenditures and debt financing). Italy ranked third among fifteen countries in social unruliness and tied for first in fiscal ineffectiveness. Social expenditures constituted a crucial link in the cycle of labor militance/fiscal growth/monetary accommodation of the 1970s.

This suggests that the rise of government expenditures was not *primarily* a clientalistic response of the Christian Democrats to the growing power of the Communist party (PCI). Additionally, if clientalism were the fundamental cause for the growth of government, we would expect to see increases in government employment, especially in the period when the PCI posed a major threat. However, the growth of government employment in Italy was below the OECD average, and in the period 1975–82, slowed significantly (see OECD 1985).

The Bank of Italy originally responded to the Hot Autumn by continued deflation, a predictable response to labor militance and profit squeeze. However, the strength of the mobilizations forced it to expand credit by the second half of 1970.[14] Indeed, by 1973 money and credit acceleration reached record levels.

Expansionary policies were continued until a balance of payments crisis ensued, leading to an IMF (Internation Monetary Fund) standby agreement in 1974.[15] Restrictive policy was enacted in the spring of 1974. By 1975, however, policy was expansionary again. This led, in early 1976, to a second foreign exchange crisis and another round of restrictive policies, which ended in the spring of 1977.

Although controversial, our view is that the monetary authority did not have sufficient independence or political support to meet the challenges of the Hot Autumn and beyond with sustained deflation. In addition, it did not believe that deflation would aid corporate profitability. How then should we understand these intermittent periods of restrictiveness? While the external constraints carried a certain amount of force, to some extent they also provided the authorities with a means to do what they preferred in any case. They were in this sense *convenient*, and provided an alternative to structural independence. Balance of payments crises are not inevitable, particularly in the Italian case.

This view can help us make sense of the fact that in 1976–7 the authorities followed the IMF stabilization plan without actually drawing upon the Fund and were, in the words of Spaventa (1983:454), *"plus royaliste que le roi."* This view is also put forward by De Vivo and Pivetti (1981), who argue that

the government was not forced by balance of payments problems to devalue and to deflate. The devaluation and the restrictive policy, we suggest, could more easily be explained as a means of allowing a redistribution of income through the devaluation–inflation mechanism and the parallel rise in unemployment. In both cases [1973 and 1976] devaluation took place at the time of the renewals of the three-year national contracts of the main categories of industrial workers, and in both cases the devaluation was brought about by large net capital outflows. The main role of the fall in the exchange rate was to facilitate a redistribution of income in favour of profits by means of a higher rate of inflation (pp. 2, 10).

Whether inflation actually redistributed income towards profits is questionable; however, the use of unemployment is clear. Evidence that the external constraint was used to discipline domestic actors can also be found in the *Annual Reports*.[16]

By the close of 1979 the climate had changed. The impact of world recession, the eclipse of the political threat from the Left, and the cumulative effect of a decade of supply shocks and economic crisis gave the Bank more leeway to attempt deflation. Their decision to join the EMS (European Monetary System) reflects this, and contrasts sharply with Italy's earlier inability to maintain its obligations in joint pegging operations.

Nevertheless, the ability to deflate was still impeded by working-class power and fiscal policy. In 1980, social welfare expenditures rose 30 percent, on account of increased generosity in programs, and real wages remained relatively impervious to deflation. Money creation and inflation remained high.

4. The divorce of the Bank of Italy and the Treasury

In July 1981, the Bank of Italy and the Treasury concluded a "divorce" that eliminated the obligation of the Bank to act as the residual pur-chaser of Treasury securities tendered at auction.[17] The divorce was the culmination of a longstanding desire for independence, voiced as early as 1957 (see Jossa and Panico 1985:8). Two steps toward independence had already been taken by 1981. In 1969, the Bank was freed from unlimited fixed-rate financing of the Treasury, and in 1975, it gained the authority to tender Treasury bills at auction.

The 1975 decision of the CICR (Interministerial Committee on Credit and Savings) granting the bank this authority was a major step toward independence, as the creation of a private market in Treasury securities provided a mechanism for bond-financing of government deficits. However, before those markets had been created, it was considered necessary to obligate the Bank to be the residual purchaser. The divorce was the final step, and freed the Bank from the requirement to provide unlimited government financing. The Treasury can still force some monetary financing because it is legally permitted to overdraft its account with the Bank of Italy by 14 percent of that year's government expenditures, and may also request additional overdraft privileges from Parliament. Nevertheless, the amount of automatic monetary financing is greatly reduced. The Bank can now refuse to validate or accommodate public-sector deficits that do not meet its targets for monetary growth.

What was the purpose of the divorce? According to the Bank of Italy, and a great deal of professional opinion, the divorce was motivated by the desire of the monetary authorities to reduce inflation by reducing monetary growth. Under the pre-1981 arrangement, the Treasury's first recourse for revenue shortfalls was to offer securities at auction. Securities that were not placed in private hands became the statutory obligation of the Bank. These securities go directly into the monetary base, because an amount equal to their value is immediately credited to the Treasury's account. While the amount of financing the Bank was actually required to undertake varied from year to year, depending on the demands of the private sector and the level of the Public Sector Borrowing Requirement (hereafter PSBR), the obligation was constant. The link between money growth and inflation was presumed to operate in a typical monetarist fashion.[18]

In the view of the monetary authorities, the source of money creation was "excessive" public expenditures. Government expenditure as a percentage of GDP rose from 28.1 percent to 37.6 percent between 1970 and 1981. Taxation did not rise as much, resulting in large increases in government deficits and debt creation. The liabilities of the public sector, as a percentage of GDP, averaged 12.5 percent during the 1970s, compared to an average of 5.8 percent during the 1960s.[19] Italy ranked first among major OECD countries in deficit spending. In 1981, the year of the divorce, the deficit was 11.8 percent compared to an average in other major OECD countries of 2.2 percent.[20] Given the commitment of the monetary authorities to limits on total domestic credit, the PSBR was potentially a severe constraint on private borrowing. During the period 1973–81, for example, the public sector absorbed, on average, one-half of total domestic credit, and in 1978 its share rose to nearly 70 percent.[21]

The deficits were widely criticized.[22] In the Bank's *Annual Reports*, Governor Ciampi argued that government spending had grown "indiscriminately in the seventies," and that the public must abandon "the attitude that every want should be met in the first instance by the state." In this view, the sheer size of the deficits undermined the ability of government to carry out its legitimate functions.

The efficiency and controllability of expenditure have been affected by institutional changes that have divorced responsibility for decision-making from responsibility for financing the measures, increased the degree of indexation of expenditures, indiscriminately expanded the social security system and ignored demographic trends. The forms and dimensions that state aid to households and firms has acquired disregard the need for compatibility between resources and the calls upon them (Bank of Italy, *Annual Report*, 1981:180; 1980:170–1; 1982:170).

The deficits were seen to be incompatible with sound monetary policy, and greater autonomy for the Bank was proposed.

The return to a stable currency requires a real change in the monetary constitution. The first condition is that the power to create money should be completely independent from the agents that determine expenditure. This requirement should be met primarily in relation to the public sector by freeing the central bank from a situation that allows budget deficits to stimulate an abundant creation of liquidity that is inconsistent with the objectives of monetary growth.

The means by which the central bank finances the Treasury in our system – the overdraft in the Treasury account, the Bank's practice of acquiring unsold Treasury bills and the subscription of other government securities – should therefore be re-examined. In particular there is a pressing need for the Banca D'Italia to cease purchasing Treasury bills not placed at tenders.

Central bank autonomy, reinforcement of budgetary procedures and a code for collective bargaining are prerequisites for a return to monetary stability (Bank of Italy, *Annual Report*, 1980:180–3).

The Commission appointed by the Treasury to study the credit and financial system voiced similar views, contending that "The main objective . . . ought to be to make the management of monetary and credit policy as independent as possible of the need to ensure the financing of the public sector" (see Monti et al. 1983:88–9). These attitudes can be found throughout the scholarly, policy-making, and popular press.

5. Rhetoric and reality

What should we make of these claims? Without question, public deficits rose substantially in Italy. However, as a proportion of GDP they were a fairly stable 9 to 11 percent, with the exceptions of 1978 and 1982. How were these deficits financed? In the period 1970–6 the evidence is clear: the deficit was financed through monetary base creation, as the Bank's debt holdings grew on average 18.4 percent per year, in constant dollars[23] (see Spaventa 1984:121).

One result of this monetization was the 1975 decision that led to bond-financing. From 1977 to 1979, the deficits were financed through the sale of securities to the private sector. The Bank's share of public debt fell to a low of 23.9 percent in 1979, and by 1981 was still only 24.3 percent. The share held by households and banks grew rapidly. In the period 1976–82, the average annual growth of debt held by the Bank was −5.0 percent (see Spaventa 1984:121). Despite the large deficits, the monetary authorities appear to have been able to restrict total domestic credit, as they desired.

Excessive monetary growth was no longer a *necessary* result of the deficits. Why then were the authorities so opposed to the deficits? One possibility is that public expenditures "crowd out" private investment, by raising interest rates. In Italy, the private sector would be directly rationed, as a result of restrictions on total domestic credit combined with the Treasury's privileged access to funds.

Private investment does not appear to have been crowded out, however. Beginning in 1974, much of the increased expenditure that produced the deficits went to firms as investment and production subsidies, and "credits and participations." Total transfers to firms rose from an average of 18.1 percent of the PSBR in 1970-5 to 34.4 percent in 1979 (Monti and Siracusano 1979:230). By 1979, government transfers comprised over one-third of private sector investment funds. The authorities may have thought the subsidies would create allocative inefficiencies, although this concern was only occasionally voiced.

A second possibility is that debt servicing imposed an excessive burden. *Prima facie*, this claim appears to have validity. After ranging between 1 and 2 percent during the 1960s, interest payments on government debt as a percentage of GDP rose from 4.8 percent in 1976 to 8.6 percent in 1982. Remarkably enough, since 1976, the growth of revenues exceeded the growth of final expenditures net of interest payments. Interest payments can in some sense be considered to be responsible for the entire deficits (Spaventa 1984:127).

Once we account for the impact of inflation on the value of outstanding debt, however, a very different picture emerges. Although nominal interest payments were high, real interest payments to private sector bond and bill holders were *negative*, for every year between 1973 and 1981. In the two years prior to the divorce, interest payments relative to GDP stood at −1.4 and −1.8 percent (Spaventa 1984:129).

Bond-financing under conditions of negative real interest payments is conceptually equivalent to tax-financing. *What was really happening over this period was hidden taxation on holders of government securities. The view that the Italian economy was experiencing excessive levels of government expenditure is in this sense incorrect. The state was covertly taxing private wealth-holders.*

The opposition to government deficits is thus even more puzzling. The deficits did not necessarily result in monetary base creation, did not crowd out private investment, and should not even be thought of as deficits at all. Why then has there been so much "official" opinion against them?

6. Banking disintermediation and the divorce

The links between government deficits, money creation, and inflation are one part of the story. A second part is the connection to banking disintermediation.[24] Banking intermediation in Italy is unusually high. Deposits as a percentage of household financial savings rose from 27.9

percent in 1963 to a peak of 55.4 percent in 1977 (Bank of Italy, *Annual Reports*, various years), and were accompanied by growth in loans to the private sector. In large part these trends were due to the absence of financial markets to absorb the surpluses of the household sector.[25] The stock market, which made up 24 percent of household financial portfolios in 1963, collapsed after the nationalization of the electric companies, and by 1977 the share of stocks had fallen to 0.7 percent (Bank of Italy, *Annual Reports*, various years).

A second cause of growing intermediation was the attitude of the monetary authority to the ordinary banks. As Jossa and Panico (1985) have argued, during the Carli years the Bank attempted to improve its relations with the ordinary banks, in order to increase the effectiveness of monetary policy and gain their acquiescence to the goals of the Bank. It encouraged intermediation, exercised favorable prudentiary regulatory procedures, and granted ordinary banks a privileged position in the financial system. It was lenient in its interpretation of the law forbidding banks to engage in medium-term lending (see Nardozzi 1983). Competitors of ordinary banks were not permitted to develop and no new banks were chartered. Although ordinary banks fell as a percentage of all banks, their share of deposits and loans rose.[26]

The context of disintermediation was the imposition in 1973 of the ceiling on bank loans and a portfolio constraint forcing banks to hold a percentage of the increase in their deposits in fixed-rate securities, in hopes of insulating the bond market from the destabilizing events in the domestic and international economies.

The portfolio constraint reduced the interest differential between bonds and deposits, thereby encouraging households to buy bank deposits. This created a form of double intermediation. Households deposited their savings with banks, who in turn lent them to the Treasury and Special Credit Institutions, who in turn lent them to firms to finance investment. From 1972 to 1981 the banks supplied roughly 70 percent of the funds of the Special Credit Institutions (Cotula 1984:224). The ceiling on loans had a similar effect.

The result was disintermediation. The loans to deposit ratio, which stood at a peak of just under 60 percent in the late 1960s fell sharply, to a low of 46 percent in 1978. Eventually, there was a fall in the growth of deposits, due primarily to households' increased purchases of government securities. Deposit disintermediation was especially severe in 1980-1, and by 1981 bank loans as a percentage of households' financial savings had fallen to 45.9 percent, from a peak of 55.4 percent in 1977 (Bank of Italy, *Annual Reports*, various years).

The Bank of Italy, the Monti Commission, and others were concerned about disintermediation. They saw it as a usurpation by the state of the traditional functions of the banking sector. The state was considered to be "crowding out" by the banks, by competing for deposits and directly financing firms. On the other hand, the Bank worried that disintermediation would reduce its control over money and credit conditions by jeopardizing the position of the ordinary banks.

Disintermediation raises interesting questions. Why did the banks allow their deposits to fall so precipitously? They could have raised deposit rates, but did not do so, preferring instead to raise the interest margin, thereby maintaining profitability. Thus, while disintermediation was severe, it did not result in reduced profitability, at least in the short run.

Did the banks care about disintermediation? There are indications that they did. The Monti Commission argued that the banks' primary concern is the growth of deposits. And Governor Ciampi noted that the banks have focused "concern and attention on disintermediation." Furthermore, as Ciampi noted,

The shift in the public's demand from deposits to securities did not have any adverse effect on banks' profits since it occurred at a time when the size of the demand for credit and the banks' predominant role in short-term financing of firms allowed them to widen the spread between lending and deposit rates. The circumstances described above which led to a widening of the spread between bank rates might not recur, however. If they do not, the decline in intermediation will have adverse effects on banks' profits (Bank of Italy 1980:97).

A second possibility is that the decline in intermediation hurt some powerful banks, although it may not have adversely affected aggregate bank profits. The 1980 *Annual Report* noted that "The decline in intermediation affected most of all the three 'major' commercial banks and the two largest savings banks" (Bank of Italy 1980:102).

However, attitudes toward disintermediation are necessarily complex. While disintermediation and the accompanying growth of financial innovation erodes the Bank's control of credit, the banks' desires for financial innovation must also play a role in the authorities' attitudes. The Bank is caught between its desire to control the financial system and obligations to them.

In any case, the authorities were concerned about excessive levels of disintermediation, which explains the link to the divorce. The ostensible purpose of the divorce was to make it more difficult for the state to raise funds, thereby leading to expenditure reductions. This would allow a lifting of loan ceilings and help break the cycle of household/bank/special credit institution or Treasury/firm.

7. The politics of the divorce

It is difficult to reconstruct the politics of the divorce. There was virtually no public discussion about it at the time, and apparently there are virtually no memoranda or internal documents analyzing it. According to officials at the Bank, "To a lot of people . . . it seemed a technical issue. They didn't understand completely the real issue. The debate in 1981 was not so much political."[27]

From the steps in 1975 through the implementation of the divorce, there was no significant opposition to the Bank's plan. Andreatta, the Treasury Minister, was fully supportive of the divorce. According to officials at the Bank, he was above bureaucratic concerns and thought that the divorce would advance the cause of "fiscal responsibility" and the overall health of the economy.

None of the political parties opposed the divorce. It is particularly striking that the PCI (Communist Party of Italy) did not object to the creation of an independent central bank. Apparently the CPI had two main reasons for its stance. First, it has traditionally supported the Bank of Italy. Particularly during the Carli period, the Bank was open to the PCI and had PCI sympathizers among its management. The Bank has never been monetarist, but espoused a brand of Keynesianism compatible with PCI economic goals. Furthermore, the Bank has been remarkably free of clientalistic and political pressures and immune from corruption. It represents perhaps the major force in the government *against* corruption and politicization, as can be seen from its role in the Banca D'Ambrosia affair.[28] The PCI sees the Bank as a bulwark against the Christian Democratic party's use of the government to further its political strength.

The PCI's second reason for supporting the divorce is that in order to become a governing party, it believes it must make itself "respectable." Its support of the Bank is calculated to reassure its opponents that it will govern responsibly and to minimize the amount of "damage" it would be able to inflict. As the effects of the divorce began to be apparent, however, the PCI and others created a public debate on the issue.

8. The aftermath of the divorce

The divorce was clearly a statutory success for the Bank, but did it effectively decouple monetary growth and fiscal expenditure? The evidence indicates that by 1983 the authorities had achieved their aim of an independent monetary policy, although not fiscal restraint. However, in the first year, its impact was limited.

In 1982, the government deficit reached its highest level in 30 years, equaling 13.1 percent of GDP, and the new policy led to a fiscal crisis. In the fourth quarter of the year, the Treasury overdrew its account at the Bank in every month (above the allowable 14 percent overdraft). The government was therefore forced to appeal to Parliament for an Extraordinary Advance, with the consequent overshooting of the monetary targets. At the height of the Treasury overdraft crisis, the Bank did purchase securities on the secondary market.

The possibility of the parliamentary advance shows the limits to independence which still exist. "We are in fact conditioned by the fact that we know if we come to the conflict the Parliament is more likely to raise the ceiling than to cut expenditures. If Extraordinary Advances become commonplace, the Bank of Italy would have won the battle and lost the war."[29]

By 1983, however, the Bank appears to have succeeded in its immediate objectives. The share of total debt financed through monetary base creation fell drastically, to a low of 19 percent (Spaventa 1984:138). However, the history of monetary policy in Italy suggests that independence is difficult to achieve and sustain. Indeed, as Tommaso Padoa-Schioppa noted,

We should play our independence, namely our possibility not to buy Treasury bills or government securities, in connection with our ability to persuade the Treasury to conduct an interest rate policy that enables it to place the amount of securities it wants to place. So institutionally, and this is the battle we have not succeeded in winning, it would be to remove the floor price on Treasury bills because in that case, the divorce plus the fact that interest rates can go to any level . . . would bring the conflict from the Parliament where ultimately it lies today, to the market, which would be much better from the point of view of monetary policy.

The high interest rates made possible by the divorce eventually led the "question to assume political overtones. At the moment, there are mounting political pressures to remove this divorce. They come from a fairly spread set of forces – the Socialist Party itself, some sections of the PCI, and also the Republicans who want to force interest rates down."[30] As the reality of an independent monetary authority became apparent, the political actors have come to advocate what one would expect from the perspective of interests.

Assuming these political pressures do not undo the divorce, the Bank's long-run independence is still not assured. Speaking of the current situation, Ciocca argued that "the Bank of Italy is one of the most independent central banks in the world. Independent both from the government but also from private interests, industrial interests and financial interests." In the long run, however, it is unlikely that the Bank will be able to maintain its independence without support from powerful groups in society. The usual constituency is the financial community, and indeed the increasing attention paid during the Baffi and Ciampi governorships to financial-sector profitability suggests this may be occurring. Given the political control of banks in Italy, it is likely that an independent Bank of Italy will be a more politicized Bank.

9. Conclusion

In our view, there are two related "causes" of the divorce. First, there was the desire of the monetary authority to attain independence. The lack of independence throughout the 1970s left the government and the Bank of Italy vulnerable to pressures from labor and other groups desiring increases in wages and transfer payments. The integration of the Bank was a crucial precondition for monetary accommodation, wage and price inflation, and balance of payments crises.

A precondition for independence was satisfied through the privileged position granted to ordinary banks. Indeed, in contrast to the Bank's characterization, these developments have been described as "a crowding out by the banks" (Nardozzi and Onado 1980:357).

Second, the Bank sought changes in the constitution of monetary policy in order to curb the power of labor and other social groups. It aimed to reduce government expenditures and effect shifts in the distribution of income towards profits and away from wages.

In our view, the opposition to deficits may well have been opposition to government expenditures themselves, whether they are paid for by taxes, money, or bonds. There is accumulating evidence that in "classical market economies," income-replacing social welfare expenditures diminish the cyclical responsiveness of wages, contribute to productivity squeezes, and increase labor militance. The *Annual Reports* of the Bank provide evidence for this view.

The Bank also sought to reduce the power of the working class directly through abolition of wage indexation. Wages were considered to have become "impervious to growing unemployment" (Bank of Italy 1981:68). Indeed, the ability of Italian workers to protect real wages was remarkable. Real wage growth was positive virtually without exception during the 1970s, despite adverse supply shocks and high levels of unemployment. This was undoubtedly salient in the minds of the monetary authorities, who wanted to eliminate the possibility of wage and price spirals by cementing their control over money creation.

As the economic crisis of the European economies continues, the refusal of governments to enact expansionary fiscal and monetary policies should come under increasing scrutiny. In Italy, the ability of popular forces to effect this scrutiny has been weakened by the divorce between the Treasury and the Bank of Italy. We have argued that the divorce should be seen as emerging from the previous integration of the Bank, a structural factor that frustrated its attempts to engage in deflationary policies in the aftermath of the Hot Autumn and the worldwide stagnation of the 1970s and 1980s. While we have analyzed the formidable pressures for central bank independence, particularly during difficult economic times, it should be noted that democratically controlled, integrated banks that engage in sound and rational policies are possible. In our view, reforms in this direction should be a priority for labor movements or leftist parties seeking to enhance employment and economic growth.

Notes

1 Paper prepared for joint Congrip–*Stato e Mercato* conference on "The State and Social Regulation In Italy," Bellagio, Italy, April 1986. The authors would like to thank John Goodman, Stephen Marglin, Giangiacomo Nardozzi, and Carlo Panico for helpful comments and discussion. They would also like to thank Cesare Caranza, Pierluigi Ciocca, and Tommaso Padoa-Schioppa from the Banca d'Italia for valuable interviews. Carol Brown, Arik Levinson, and Joseph Gramagina provided excellent research assistance. This paper is one part of a larger project on *The Political Economy of Central Banking* conducted by the authors under the auspices of the Project on Global Macroeconomic Policies, World Institute for Development Economics Research (WIDER), United Nations University, Helsinki. The authors gratefully acknowledge the financial support of WIDER.

2 There is little comparative evidence on central bank independence. Bade and Parkin (1980) conclude that more independent banks are associated with lower rates of inflations, as do Banaian, Laney, and Willett (1983, 1987).

3 See Lange and Garrett (1985) for an interesting discussion of the relation between labor strength and political representation. See also Martin (1986).

4 We have developed this argument in detail elsewhere. See Schor and Bowles (1984) and Schor (1985b).

5 See Bruno and Sachs (1985) for a discussion of nominal and wage rigidity.

6 See Bade and Parkin (1980), for example.

7 For discussions of central banking in Italy and postwar monetary policy, see also Posner (1978), Caranza and Fazio (1983), Fazio (1979), Fazio and Lo Faso (1980), Ruini (1981), Sarcinelli (1981), Magnifico (1983), and Thygesen (1982).

8 When Carli left the bank, he became the head of *Confindustria*.

9 See Monti et al. (1983:195) for evidence.

10 For general discussions of Italian development, see Amendola and Jossa (1981),

Jossa and Vinci (1981), Graziani (1978), Rey (1982), Flanagan et al. (1983), and De Vivo and Pivetti (1981).

11 For discussions of class conflict in this period, see Soskice (1978), Regalia, Regini, and Reyneri (1978), Salvati (1981), Lange et al. (1982), and Schor (1983).

12 Data from BLS (U.S. Bureau of Labor Statistics 1983) and Walsh (1983). These data underestimate the strike waves because they exclude strikes over political issues, which the Italian government began collecting only in 1975. Political strikes increased dramatically in this period.

13 Estimates calculated from OECD (1984).

14 See Salvati (1981) for an excellent treatment of the state's response to the Hot Autumn.

15 For an account of Italy's experiences with the IMF, see Spaventa (1983).

16 See, for example, the 1975 *Report*, Governor's Remarks, p. 185.

17 There is relatively little written material on the divorce. See Salvemini (1983), Jossa and Panico (1985), Ruggeri (1984), Caranza and Fazio (1983), Magnifico (1983), Addis (1987), and the *Annual Reports* of the Bank of Italy.

18 The relation between money growth and inflation in monetarist theory ostensibly operates through expectations. Economic agents, upon observing the central bank's level of money creation, expect an exactly offsetting price rise, and in fact create that rise through their demands in labor, capital, and product markets. While the monetarist story and the money-inflation link appear to be believed by many central bankers, this is in fact quite problematic, both theoretically and empirically.

19 See Table 3 in Monti et al. (1983:222).

20 Unpublished data from Andrew Glyn and John Harrison, Oxford Institute of Statistics.

21 Table 4 in Monti et al. (1983:243).

22 Discussions of the public deficits and debt are numerous in the literature. See, for example, Spaventa (1984, 1985), Valiani (1985b), Giavazzi (1984), Ruggeri (1984), Gambale (1979), and Monti et al. (1983).

23 Interestingly, however, this rate is less than during the 1961–70 period, when holdings averaged 19.3 percent per year.

24 For a discussion of banking disintermediation, see Monti and Siracusano (1979), Nardozzi and Onado (1980), Jossa and Panico (1985), Monti et al. (1983), Cotula (1984), and Vaciago (1985).

25 Household savings in Italy ranged between one-fifth and one-fourth of gross household income over the 1970s. See Table 1 in Monti et al. (1983:221).

26 Table 14 in Monti et al. (1983:223).

27 Interview with Cesare Caranza, Research Department, Bank of Italy, April 11, 1986.

28 The Banca D'Ambrosia case concerned corruption at a major bank run by interests from the Vatican, organized crime, and the right-wing. In its regulatory role, the Bank attempted to expose illegalities. Before the incident was over, the Governor of the Banca D'Ambrosia was jailed, clearly for political reasons. The Bank emerged from the incident with an enhanced reputation as an opponent of corruption.

29 Interview with Tommaso Padoa-Schioppa, Vice-Director General, Bank of Italy, April 1986.

30 Interview with Pierluigi Ciocca, Direttore Centrale per le Attivita Operative, Bank of Italy, April 11, 1986.

Part III

Industrial relations and its actors

7

Criteria of regulation in Italian industrial relations: a case of weak institutions

GIANPRIMO CELLA

1. The regulation of industrial relations

This chapter seeks to analyze the changes in the regulation of demands, protests, and conflicts in Italian industrial relations over the last decade. It will examine the uncertain and contradictory extension of political regulation, as well as the difficulties in establishing "associative" or cooperative criteria, which resulted from the failure to extend their scope to related issues, such as industrial and employment policies.

The theoretical framework of this chapter relies on two basic schools of explanation. On the one hand, it rests on models of economic and social regulation and on types of integration between the economy and society. On the other hand, it borrows from the pluralist model of interest regulation, that is, the model that accompanied the birth and spread of institutionalized industrial relations and whose crisis has provoked change in established industrial relations systems.

The work of Polanyi (1944) is the source of the first explanation since all contemporary reflections on this issue, admittedly or not, begin from his typology of forms of integration between the economy and society, and, indirectly, from his principles of resource allocation. Allowing for terminological differences, Polanyi's identification of three types of integration and their related criteria of regulation – reciprocity or tradition, market or exchange, redistribution or politics – is evident in most contemporary analyses.

This "trinitarian" formula has been extended by those who, on the wave of the neo-corporatist literature, have identified a fourth possible criterion of regulation. Streeck and Schmitter (1985), for example, speak of "associative" regulation. This is defined on the basis of its "guiding principle of interaction and of resource allocation" as "organizational concertation, as opposed to solidarity, extensive competition, and hierarchical organization" (p. 49). The authors are certain of the theoretical status of this fourth type, even if they reject the "idea of a global corporative-associative social and political system" (p. 82). Personally, I believe that this fourth type is not sufficiently distinguished from, or independent of, politics, which is an immediately adjacent type (see also the Introduction to this volume). Moreover, even Streeck and Schmitter (1985) admit that the "public use of organized private interests requires a stronger rather than weaker state," and that the delegation of state functions "must be accompanied by a simultaneous acquisition by the state of the capacity to design, guide, and control these new systems of self-regulation" (p. 79). Nevertheless, the idea of using sectoral interests in order to promote a social order more extensive than these sectors, or rather the idea that associations, which are generally treated as sources of political disorder in models of liberal individualism, can become the source of political and social order establishes substantial plausibility for this supposed conceptual autonomy. Thus, with some caution, this chapter will also use the expression "associative criteria."

In recent years, other contributions have also pushed towards the identification of some form of "cooperative-associative" order, which is separate from the three classic types (Crouch 1981b; Salvati 1982). Salvati, for example, has placed special emphasis on the need to distinguish between regulation based on "decree" and that based on "accord."

What is still missing in these contributions are theoretical explanations of the transition from one criterion of regulation to another. One explanation, based on historical-descriptive changes, has already been mentioned. Streeck and Schmitter (1985:57) point to the "dysfunctional interdependence" of the three classic orders, which have always been interdependent and have each been influenced by "unresolved problems or problems exported from the others." These are seen as a possible source of the emergence of the fourth, associative order. Nonetheless, pragmatism is emphasized in this account: the need to respond pragmatically to particular conflicts and dysfunctions – conflicts and threats, generally arising exogenously, which damage the efficency and the legitimacy of the orders.

The theoretical problems remain unsolved, and certainly this is not the place to address them. Nevertheless, if historical-descriptive changes can account for the passage from one dominant order to another (for example, from the communitarian order to one guided by market criteria), they cannot explain how and why a particular issue moves from regulation by one criterion to another, in a situation in which three or four different orders exist concurrently and in competition.

One possible path towards such an explanation relies on "transaction costs," which are costs of information related to the definition of property rights, or the costs to render these rights effective. This is the approach proposed by North (1977, 1981): "Transaction cost analyses represent a promising analytical framework with which to explore non-market forms of economic organization" (1977:709). A new type of regulation establishes itself when it can resolve a problem of transaction or allocation with lower "transaction" costs than the preceding or alternative types. With specific reference to the market, this means that market criteria become established when a decrease in costs makes their use possible.[1]

This is the approach Paci (1982b) used to explain the transition from one form of allocation of welfare goods to another. But this could also be successfully used to explain the passage from one regulatory criterion to another in industrial relations. Take, for example, the issue of work loads and rhythms, which is a problem of defining and applying a property right like the right to work. In a situation of high skill-levels and pre-tayloristic organization, it is practically impossible, or rather would entail extremely high transaction costs, to bargain over work loads using market criteria. Regulation is entrusted to craft leagues in the context of self-regulating criteria, which are based on the traditions of the community of skilled workers. With mechanization, mass production, and its related tayloristic organization, these obligations and rights can be defined. Thus, collective bargaining based on market principles develops, even though no longer in a market of atomistic competition but, rather, in a market of organized competition. When new information technologies requiring highly flexible use of labor are introduced in the workplace, this same highly defined and rigidly normative bargaining becomes costly and inefficient. As a result, associative forms of regulatory criteria may develop through bargaining based on cooperation, collaboration, and concertation. This type of bargaining favors the management of the process rather than the definition of the institutions.[2]

A second important theoretical reference point is the pluralist model of interest regulation, a model essential for understanding the characteristic dynamics of industrial relations. The features of this model and its variants are well known, and I have already discussed them elsewhere (Cella 1981). With reference to this model, one must keep in mind, on the one hand, the role it plays in the industrial relations system in decreasing conflicts and in the joint regulation of wage labor and its related problems (see Fox and Flanders 1969). On the other hand, one must remember the regulatory criteria that this model allows. In pluralist industrial relations, collective bargaining is the typical instrument of regulation, and, thus, the various forms of regulation are always based on an agreement between the different actors. Nonetheless, this bargaining is primarily concerned with relatively narrow, particular sectoral issues. Only when it is extended to more general issues, or when it explicitly addresses issues of management and co-management, can it be properly called the associative type described above.

The criterion of reciprocity or tradition plays a small role in the pure form of pluralist industrial relations. It appears where a tradition of craft unionism exists. Political criteria also normally play a role only in guaranteeing the rules of the game and do not tend to displace other criteria. Variants of market regulation are, in contrast, pervasive.[3] In recent decades, however, the exclusive regulation of demands through market criteria has occurred only in North America. In European pluralist experiences, various forms of political regulation and the balanced use of organizational, financial, and conflictual resources by centralized labor confederations have frequently managed to block exclusive reliance on forms of market regulation.

To this theoretical discussion of regulatory types and criteria and of the features of the pure pluralist model, we must add a few considerations regarding the degree of institutionalization of these types and this model.

Institutional issues are often undervalued in analyses of these issues, leading to an analytical void between abstract models of regulation and the real dynamics of interest group conflict and cooperation. This is not to suggest that we must repeat analyses à la Huntington (1968), who tends to include within institutions the entire political process and who attributes to institutions in modern political systems an excessive degree of autonomy. In the end, this merely reduces all theories of democracy to a theory of institutionalization. It is also important to avoid the often implicit view of many political scientists who perceive institutionalization as an almost exclusive dimension of the political process.

With these two premises, we can return to an extensive tradition of social theory from Blau (1964) to Polanyi (1978), which uses the concept of institutionalization to refer to the processes through which different types of regulation – social, economic, and political – acquire unity, coherence, stability, and the possibility, even if uncertain and contested, of perpetuation. According to this theoretical tradition, institutions create the frameworks within which interest groups measure themselves, compete, and are regulated. These frameworks are certainly more rigid and tight in political forms of regulation, but they are also present in other forms of regulation, especially in the market.

In industrial relations systems, institutionalization involves that amalgam of norms which tend to regulate not only the bargaining process but also the conflicting interests involved in the bargaining. It does not matter whether these norms are legislated or negotiated even if their consequences are quite different in terms of the autonomy of the system. They influence the composition of conflicts as well as their prevention; they constitute, forestall, and regulate the manifestations of industrial conflict. Considering the double dimension – vertical and horizontal – of the structure of bargaining relations, institutionalization pertains not only to the bargaining process but also to the internal relations of the actors. Lehmbruch (1984) has recently stressed this point by insisting on the importance of vertical institutionalization (i.e., within organized interest groups) in encouraging the development of solid concertative relationships.

The reasons for the loss of vitality of the pluralist model, whether in more or less institutionalized form, can be traced to its difficulty in controlling the economic crisis of the 1970s and 1980s, in resolving the main problems – inflation, unemployment, and public deficits – provoked by the crisis, and in regulating the processes of industrial restructuring and reconversion. These difficulties primarily derive from the model's incapacity to promote the pursuit of "common goals" (for instance, reducing the effects of the crisis) or the selection of demands. These problems of pluralism were addressed either by strengthening the regulatory and distributive role of politics, sometimes in the form of an "associative" model rather than a strictly political one (as in several North and Central European countries) or by attempting to relaunch the allocative and regulatory role of the market, with all that this implies for the breakdown of organizational structures central to the pluralist model (as in Britain and North America). In other words, countries sought to escape these problems by increasing the hierarchical coordination of demands, by proceeding towards collaborative-participatory solutions, or by returning to typical features of liberal individualism. Let us see what happened in Italy.

2. Trends in Italian industrial relations over the last decade

Beginning in the late 1970s, state intervention increased not only in industrial relations but also in the area of industrial policy. Nonetheless, the weak institutionalization of the Italian industrial relations system remained essentially unchanged. This situation was accompanied by a shortage of state intervention explicitly promoting bargaining relations and by the low capacity of state institutions to implement reforms. Perhaps the sole exception to this trend was the law *(legge quadro)* on public employment (no. 93, March 1983), which sought to rationalize industrial relations, to identify and assign prerogatives to "labor" and "management," and to promote a well-defined, if not easily realizable, bargaining structure between the different actors in this sector.

During the years of the governments of national unity (1976–8), experiments were undertaken that involved bargaining moderation and relative consensus over the government's economic policies, in exchange for somewhat successful state intervention protecting employment.[4] Beginning with this period, we can identify significant indicators of the growing centralization of Italian industrial relations. These include:

1. The full return of a joint, peak level, inter-confederal bargaining unit of the CGIL (Confederazione Generale Italiana del Lavoro), CISL (Confederazione Italiana de Sindacati Libri), and UIL (Unione Italiana del Lavoro) in wage negotiations and wage controls. This began with the agreement over the *scala mobile* (escalator clause) in 1975.
2. The use of this level of bargaining for other issues (work hours, labor market, etc.).
3. Organizational centralization promoted by the unions through the creation of regional structures and the amalgamation of numerous categories; and, to some extent, similar reform efforts by *Confindustria* (all of which tended to enhance the powers of control and coordination of the peak organizations).
4. Transformations in the forms of conflict as strikes became less numerous, less serious, and less decentralized.
5. Bargaining control by higher levels in the organizations over lower ones (i.e., the reduction of "internal" autonomy of bargaining units).
6. Experimentation with industrial policies (i.e., Law 675 of 1977), which favored the centralization of proposals and a coordination of requests at the sectoral level. It is not by chance that these policies were accompanied by the introduction of "information rights" in national contracts.

However, other conditions, such as greater centralization of interest group organizations, representational monopoly, and explicitly pro-labor governments, were missing in Italian industrial relations. This hindered the development and entrenchment of collaborative-participatory features that had already been successful in other European countries in the 1970s (see Bordogna and Provasi 1984).

At the beginning of the 1980s, there were many issues that favored centralized and tripartite bargaining solutions. These included: wage dynamics and inflation controls, the role of tax policy, the governing of the labor market, industrial restructuring, policies aimed at reducing work hours, and the structure and functioning of industrial relations. The role of government also evolved from that of spectator-mediator to that of direct participant in industrial relations, a transformation linked above all to non-Christian Democratic premiers (see Benedizione 1984; Veneziani 1985). Even in the absence of conditions generally deemed necessary for the realization of tripartite agreements such as a pro-labor government, the urgency of the policy issues pushed the various actors towards these agreements, which entailed criteria and forms resembling associative regulation and which were aimed at reducing the transaction costs of many bargains.

The features of the January 22, 1983, accord between the government and the social partners are by now well known: the explicit triangularity (union confederations, *Confindustria*, and the government) of the accord, the link established between collective bargaining outcomes and compatible macro-economic conditions, the emphasis on centralized bargaining, and the beginning, if uncertain, of a phase of greater procedural regularity in industrial relations. The shortcomings in the application of the procedures and contents of the January accord assumed an important role in the subsequent unsuccessful pursuit of concertative politics. It is also important that no significant and stable institutional innovation in Italian industrial relations developed out of the 1983 accord (see Treu [1984] and essays on the Italian case in Jacobi et al. [1986]).

The bargaining experience of February 1984 repeated only in part the experience of the previous year. The negotiation was formally tripartite, but it did not end with the consent of all the participants because the CGIL refused to sign the accord. The reasons for this must be sought in that same amalgam of factors, which were, in part, overcome during the 1983 negotiations as a result of the efforts of all actors. These factors include: the weak institutionalization of industrial relations; the incomplete centralization and vertical integration of interest group organizations; the absence of a representational monopoly for labor; the precarious autonomy of certain confederations, in particular the CGIL, vis-à-vis political parties; and the exclusion from the governing coalition of the largest party representing labor interests.

Elsewhere I have stressed an interpretation of the failed unitary accord, which emphasizes the prevalence of political factors external to industrial relations in hindering the formation of a collaborative-participatory coalition between parties and interest group organizations in interpreting the failed unitary accord. Three years later I remain convinced of this interpretation.[5] The thesis can be outlined as follows: In a situation in which the governmental leadership had changed from 1983 and in which the unions were faced with an agreement that called for trust in future government policies and required certain immediate sacrifices in exchange for uncertain future benefits, the asymmetry between political representation and union representation became explicit and hindered the formation of a union-party coalition. It is all here: the governmental leadership had changed to a Socialist leadership of a Center-Left cabinet, which increased frictions and divisions within the Left; the present agreement required the freezing of the *scala mobile* in exchange for a future reduction of inflation; and, as a result, the asymmetry between political representation (marked by divisions between the Communist and Socialist parties and the exclusion of the communists from government) and union representation (marked by Communist domination of the CGIL) became evident. But, as we can see, we are dealing with causes more complex than simply union dependence on political parties. (On these points, see Rusconi [1985].)

Keeping in mind inevitable simplifications, we can identify the essential changes in the types and criteria of regulation that have accompanied the crisis of Italy's pluralist industrial relations system over the last decade. This will be the core of our analysis, and I will stress this theme at the expense of other, related issues.

There has not been an extension of individualistic market criteria in this period, at least if this extension is understood as a decline in the extent of coverage of collective bargaining or the growth of sectors outside the collective bargaining system, rather than as an increase in the production of neo-liberal ideology. Certainly, the most skilled sectors of the labor force have increasingly freed themselves from union and contractual controls, and the increase in employment in many fragmented areas of the tertiary sector has posed serious problems for bargaining. Nonetheless, these do not represent a significant or massive return of market criteria. In other words, no relevant institutional change has permitted the explicit enlargement of market regulation, as might have occurred with legislation limiting union rights.[6]

A modest deregulation did occur in the labor market as illustrated by the reduction of constraints on public job placement, increased possibilities for name-specific (nominal) hiring, and increased flexibility in the use of youth employment. Such changes were partially anticipated by provisions of the 1983 accord, in part as a response to the failures of the 1977 attempt at deregulation. Their effective implementation, however, required passage of new legislation (Law 863 of December 1984), which established a revised regulatory framework. Even so, this tendency toward deregulation was countered by a new, more open attitude on the part of unions toward the negotiation of more flexible forms of labor control. We are dealing, therefore, primarily with bargained forms of deregulation, which significantly moderated the destructuring nature of the latter (see Garonna 1986). One also does not see an increased role of market criteria in the regulation of conflict. Certainly, the increases in unemployment account for part of the decline in conflict over the last few years, but political factors, including the centralization of bargaining and other general changes in the industrial relations system, are even more important in explaining the changes in the forms and levels of conflict (Cella 1985; Bordogna 1985).

By contrast, there has been a noteworthy increase in the role of political criteria in regulation, as indicated by a growth in direct state intervention in the characteristic features of collective bargaining. These features include: legislation on ceilings on wage indexation increases, the systematic participation of governments in negotiations between labor and capital, and the extension of mediation by state agencies, including some not related to the Ministry of Labor. Rarely, however, has the increase in state intervention and the growing use of political criteria of regulation deprived the organized interest groups of their bargaining autonomy. Attempts along these lines occurred mainly during the period of national unity governments, especially during 1977. However, even though injunctions were occasionally issued against workers in certain public services, no real regulation of strikes was achieved during the decade. During 1986, there was once again talk of a law on strikes, but this proposal was viewed as a necessary consequence of the self-regulatory codes on strike behavior, which were underwritten by the central union confederations and by the major autonomous unions in certain public employment sectors. These codes implemented criteria included in the 1983 law and 1985 global accord *(accordo quadro)*. Thus, for the moment, strike regulation remains primarily regulated under associative criteria.

The acceptance of the most representative principle of union organization in the law on public employment can be considered a form of regulation of organizational autonomy within the sector, but also as the continuation of a principle already consolidated in the private sector, beginning with the *Statuto dei Lavoratori* (1970). The extension by governmental decree of the partial accord of February 1984 certainly constitutes the most clamorous act of political intervention in industrial relations of the decade. Moreover, one must recognize that this inter-

vention enforced an accord that failed to be accepted by only one of
the major union confederations, albeit the largest, the CGIL.

The extension of *political criteria* of regulation was almost always
accompanied, in complementary ways, by the use of *associative criteria*,
that is, of those criteria that are based on the strategic interdependence
of the organized actors and the delegation of responsibilities by political authorities in order to resolve problems, which extended beyond
the immediate interests of the actors involved. The extension of these
criteria occurred through forms of regulation that Lehmbruch
(1984:62) calls "corporatist concertation," thus distinguishing them
from forms of "sectoral corporatism," which specify corporatist representation of single interests organized in specific sectors of the economy. These associative criteria and forms of "corporatist concertation"
surfaced informally over the course of the last decade, but were fully
realized only with the concertative accord of 1983, which was successful, and the accord of 1984, which was only partially successful. Nevertheless, one condition appears necessary in the Italian case for the
realization of associative forms of regulation and the adoption of their
corresponding criteria: the participation of the state within a more or
less formally tripartite negotiation. When the peak interest associations
decided in the fall and winter of 1985 to proceed with a bilateral negotiation, they were unable to conclude a single agreement. A notable
diffusion of associative criteria is evident at the territorial level as illustrated by the creation of labor market management organizations and
the joint definition of particular procedures for labor mobility (see
Kemeny and Napoli 1986).

The most striking feature of the Italian experience is the scarce institutionalization of both the political and associative criteria, which is a
result of the low institutionalization of the entire system of industrial
relations. Increased institutionalization appears necessary not only if
associative criteria are to be consolidated and prevail over political
ones, but even for the increased efficiency and rationalization of political criteria themselves (for example, in the field of conflict and mediation). In addition to the increased institutionalization of industrial
relations, a strengthening of the decision-making capacities of public
institutions (and, in the first place, government authorities) would
seem necessary in order to move toward the goal of reinforcing concertative politics.

One of the most famous scholars and interpreters of Italian industrial
relations agrees with this point: "It is these improvements in the institutional context which could make concertative politics more stable
and more autonomous from political-parliamentary events" (Giugni
1985:67). Moreover, as Treu (1985:33) has observed, Italian industrial

relations need to be reformed, but this above all must be an internal reform or, if one prefers, a "self-reform." It does not appear necessary to return to the old problems concerning the implementation of the constitutional mandate legally recognizing unions. On the basis of a comparative analysis of European experiences, it is not such legal, institutional modifications that appear particularly useful for the stability and functioning of industrial relations.

If we once again follow Lehmbruch's (1984:68) analysis of concertative politics, we must distinguish between two different dimensions of institutionalization: first, the vertical dimension, which identifies the models of participation of organizational leaders in policy-making and in its related implementation as well as the corresponding integration of the lower organizational levels in concertative features; and, second, the horizontal dimension, which refers to models of concertation between different organizational leaders and the government. The institutionalization of vertical participation is an important aspect of sectoral corporatism, but it is also an essential component for the consolidation of concertative practices. In contrast, the horizontal dimension can remain informal as it does in countries with even the most solid concertative features, such as Austria and Sweden. In the Italian case, however, both dimensions remain informal and the informality of one reinforces that of the other.

On the vertical dimension, the institutionalization of associational participation in policy-making does not exist (as we will see when analyzing the evolution of industrial policies). Participation remains purely consultative as well as informal and occasional. Institutionalized forms of participation that reproduce the concertative policies of the leadership do not exist at the decentralized organizational levels (for example, at the firm level). Union representation at the base continues to be constructed on the single union channel principle. And it needs to be stressed that in all European countries where associative criteria have developed, whether in their "weak" or "strong" variants, forms of participation at the firm level exist which reproduce in substance those in operation at the peak levels. In the last two years something has occurred among firms with state participation through the so-called "Union-IRI Protocol," which introduced new forms of participation. This has not, however, replaced the "single channel," which perhaps is still necessary in Italy (Carinci 1985).

The entire structure of representational democracy within union organizations has also remained informal, a situation that labor lawyers have defined as the absence of an "internal union law." This informality makes the exercise of democratic procedures and control over the leadership group, as well as the evaluation and approval of policies and accords, uncertain and troublesome. Above all, the efficient functioning of representational democracy is seen as an essential condition for the experimentation with regulatory accords, especially wage agreements. (See Lange [1983] and, for the Swedish case, Lewin [1980].)

At the horizontal level, a high degree of informality continues to exist. Even the important episodes of tripartite concertation in 1983 and 1984 did not give rise to any stable institutions for the associative government of industrial relations and its related problem areas, which include industrial and labor market policies. No institutions were developed that were capable of providing a shared interpretation of the accords, or of mediating the controversies related to their application. One need only think of the question of the *scala mobile* decimal points,[7] which dragged on for three years, for evidence of the extremely modest degree of efficiency in bargaining relations.

Excessive institutional latency renders Italian industrial relations unstable and highly unpredictable, even at the central levels of interconfederal bargaining or tripartite concertation. It is certainly not a good sign for the stability and efficiency of Italian industrial relations that between 1982 and 1985 different approaches were taken each year to confront essentially the same problems, namely, the reduction and control of inflation, compensatory forms of wage moderation, and government intervention in the labor market. These approaches included: multiple bilateral quasi-negotiations with the government, which failed to end in an accord in 1982; informal trilateral negotiations with the semi-arbitrational intervention of the government, which resulted in the unitary accord of 1983; trilateral negotiations, which concluded in a non-unitary way and with a "decree-accord" in 1984; and unfinished and informally open bilateral negotiations in 1985. Even the solution later discovered in the spring of 1986 is quite unique. Bilateral negotiations between the union confederations and *Confindustria* resulted in the adoption of the same provisions on the *scala mobile* that had been signed by the unions and the government for the public sector the preceding winter and that public officials had threatened to extend to all of wage labor by law. On other issues, such as labor market procedures, the 1986 agreement relied heavily on state intervention. This almost annual shift in approaches might perhaps be taken as a sign of institutional imagination, but if this is indeed an asset, it is certainly one that also delays serious efforts at reform.

The institutional latency of industrial relations exposes it to the influence of events in the political system. It also makes procedures and outcomes truly indeterminate. The loss of transparence, lack of control, and eventual collapse of procedures during the interconfederal bargaining rounds in the fall of 1985 were calamitous, and peak-level bargaining fell into dangerous informality. One indicator of this was the quasi-official practice of the "reserved" or "off-the-record" meeting.

What are the reasons for this institutional latency, for this low degree of institutionalization of Italian industrial relations? Before attempting a response to this question, we must remember, once again, that the term institutionalization is not intended to imply exclusively the intervention of the law; it can also occur through negotiated regulation by the leadership. In this case, the overall autonomy of the industrial relations system would be preserved. And this autonomy, in turn, could constitute a precious resource in protecting the system from excessive intervention by the political system.

One can list a number of plausible reasons for this institutional latency: a tradition of weak institutionalization, which is the result of decades of union weakness in the postwar period and of interest group organizational pluralism in both business and labor; the weak reform capacity of state institutions; and the persistent dualisms of the Italian productive system. Among these reasons, one appears particularly relevant in explaining the poor institutional development of associative or collaborative forms of regulation, which for several areas (for example, the labor market) would otherwise appear to entail decisively lower transaction costs than other forms of regulation. This reason concerns the relations between political parties and interest group organizations, most importantly, the unions.

The institutionalization of associative criteria, and of a solid corporatist framework, is facilitated when political parties tend to de-politicize the issues that fall under the jurisdiction of corporatist relations. This is an important observation by Lehmbruch (1984:77), who claims that: "the formation of a neo-corporatist consensus on economic and social policies is not compatible with inter-party conflict over these same issues." If we consider the reactions by the political parties to the contents of the February 1984 accord, this observation is fully confirmed in the Italian case. The referendum promoted by the Communist party on the freezing of the points of the *scala mobile* is a case in point. It is difficult to imagine a more blatant form of re-politicization of the accord's contents, especially if one considers that the referendum followed several months of parliamentary filibustering. But the reaction of almost all the parties to the proposed tax reform contained in the same accord, and later embodied in the so-called Visentini law, also had a similar effect. To discover the most important reasons for the institutional weakness of associative forms of regulation in Italian industrial relations, we need to reflect on the totality of relations between political parties and organized interest groups. These relations are always *formally* independent, but in some cases there is substantial dependence of one on the other, and in no case is their relationship on an equal footing.

In certain ways the weak institutional autonomy of industrial relations is due to the situation of party government that characterizes the Italian political system (see Chapter 1). In such a situation, the institutional weakness of industrial relations becomes a "resource" for all parties, both in government and in opposition. This resource, which accentuates their ability to mediate and control conflicts in civil society, became increasingly available after the mid-1970s when, with the aggravation of the economic crisis, the bargaining autonomy of organized interest groups decreased. A small indication of this weakness and of its use by political parties is illustrated by the small or nonexistent role played by experts on both sides in the settlement of controversies.

If this weakness is a resource available for all parties, it is especially useful for the opposition parties, which have fewer opportunities than the government parties to mediate or intervene. This is above all true for the Communist party, which not only plays a mediation role (and in this it is no different than other parties), but which also has a direct role in industrial relations. One need only remember the famous Fiat strike of 1980 and the role the party played both in determining the demands and the forms of struggle of the strike and in its subsequent mediation. To this one can add that Communist leadership groups, both in the party and in the union, do not seem culturally or politically open to accepting forms of direct, autonomous involvement by the union in economic and social policies that do not enhance possibilities for the party's entrance into the government arena. As evidence, one can recall the bitter initial opposition by the Communist party to the proposed creation of investment funds managed by unions, and to the plan for democratization of the firm, called the "Firm Plan," which was proposed several years ago by the CGIL and which would have given a greater role to state institutions than to interest group or party organizations.

At this point one might well ask whether this institutional weakness of industrial relations is mirrored in other related fields of regulation, thus adding to an overall framework of interest representation and mediation only partially capable of addressing the problems of the pluralist model. The next several pages of this chapter will seek to answer this question.

3. Industrial policies

One way of analyzing the composition of regulatory criteria of industrial relations and the extent of their changes is to examine the criteria and changes that operate in related areas of regulation. The models of regulation in industrial relations manage interests that also compete and cooperate in the formation of industrial and labor market policies. In the pluralist model, interests and demands are counterposed against one another in a more or less organized market so that nobody prevails regularly over the others. In this model, the state does not tend to act directly, at least from an institutional point of view. In the participatory (or collaborative or associative) model, different interests are harmonized and coordinated by various, often tripartite institutions, to which the state delegates the job of regulation. In the political model of regulation (or by decree, if we wish to use Salvati's [1982] terminology), certain interest groups are weakened in relation to others, demands are hierarchically ordered, and a fraction of these are repressed.

Even in industrial policy, institutional features assume central importance (see Chapter 4). This was demonstrated by the industrial crisis that all the advanced economic systems experienced beginning in the mid-1970s. The extent of the crisis in each country reflects its productive structure, the health and composition of the national economic system, the government's political goals, and the expectations of organized social groups (Dyson and Wilks 1983:8, 12). The typical institutional features of different nations influence the various responses to the crisis.

An interesting question from our point of view is whether or not the different models of regulation for industrial relations described above are also typical of industrial policy, thus representing more general "institutional styles." In perhaps the most complete comparative analysis of these issues during this period, Dyson and Wilks (1983:2) indicate that they *do*, in fact, exist: "While a 'typical' industrial crisis may not exist, typical national reactions to the crisis do exist." And again: "The management of industrial crises, for instance the type of political instruments utilized, will depend above all on national political factors rooted in the ideologies, institutions, and character of capitalist development. National political factors mediate relations with the international economy" (p. 17).

Wilks and Dyson's use of the French and German cases to illustrate their points is convincing. The industrial policy experiences of both cases are selective and even "collaborative" (in the sense, at least, of collaboration among different institutions). But in France, unions are marginal and excluded from the governance of the industrial crisis, and in Germany the incorporation of the unions has meant giving priority to the interests of the central nucleus of the working class, namely, the highly skilled workers. In both cases, policy-makers are isolated and protected from the pressures of particular and fragmented interests. This can favor a "collaborative" style of crisis management, but within very different institutional frameworks. In one case, political criteria of regulation prevail; in the other case, associative criteria have ample space.

If the above-mentioned models of interest regulation identify different styles of industrial policy, then relations of reciprocal influence exist between these and industrial relations in the narrow sense of the term. Changes in the selection processes of interests in industrial relations should spawn analogous changes in industrial policy. Alternatively, the more or less stable institutional changes in the structure and management of industrial relations could favor institutionalized changes even in the sphere of industrial policies.

I would like, therefore, to attempt an answer to the following question: Have changes in industrial relations over the last decade provoked, or been accompanied by, similar changes in industrial policy? Or has industrial policy continued to proceed along the lines of a tradition well consolidated before the crisis of the mid-1970s?

The best and most recent analyses [for example, CER-IRS (1986)] agree on the persistence of certain traditional features of Italian industrial policy. Here we can only list these features:

1. The absence of a long-term strategy (or, put another way, shortcomings in planning).
2. The prevalence of indirect interventions, "with the effect of preserving, more than renewing, Italian industry" (Gobbo 1984), and direct intervention only for salvage operations.
3. The prevalence of credit assistance and, more generally, a predominance of monetary transfers in policies: "These policies emerge gradually, as the industrial problems become more complex and the political system loses its ability to synthesize a variety of goals and constraints, subjects, and rules of the game" (CER/IRS 1986:141).
4. Institutional weakness and lack of consistency in the interventions.
5. Weak selective capacity of the policies and poor coordination of responsibilities and weak institutionalization of collaboration among different social actors.
6. Little attention to intersectoral policies.
7. Little weight given to demand policies of the state.

8. Substantial weight given to firms with state participation in industrial policy.

From the point of view of forms of regulation, "the 1970s saw a multiplication of centers of triangular consultation over a wide range of issues, but neither systematic concertation of wage policy nor, except in cases of little importance, experiences of industrial bailout where all interested actors made sacrifices developed during these years" (CER/IRS 1986:142). The most important attempt at reform of the institutions of industrial policy was that of Law 675 of 1977. However, the restructuring program tied to this law can be considered a failure. The only thing that remains is an indication of method, "a method of consultation with the social parts which would be wrong to discard rather than correct, given that the process of restructuring will remain important and will require coordination and consensus" (CER/IRS 1986:170). The two principal lines of industrial policy in the 1980s – the recapitalization of the system of industry with state participation and the financing of mobility through the *cassa integrazione* and various forms of early retirement – certainly have not been institutionally innovative with respect to the models of regulation adopted. What remains of the models, at least for the second type of policy, is hardly selective and not very associative-collaborative. If anything, they are "collusive."

Some interesting developments, from an institutional point of view, can be seen at decentralized levels. Various experiments at the regional level have developed from the consultation mechanisms foreseen by the Union-IRI Protocol, from various solutions to the problem of redundancies in industrial restructuring created by the solidarity contracts, and from regional interventions, particularly in the special regions, in the labor market. Nonetheless, these have not altered the overall institutional framework of Italian industrial policy.

In conclusion, compared to the trends in industrial relations, the regulatory criteria of industrial policy manifest a notable homogeneity: there have not been developments toward deregulation (for which firms express only an ideological, and certainly not unified, interest), and political criteria have become more extensive, but show the same limits that operate in the industrial relations system. Missing in industrial policy are the associative criteria that were tried, with limited success, in industrial relations in the early 1980s. The lack of institutionalization of these experiences hindered their transfer to the field of industrial policy and did not favor processes of vertical concertation.

I will not discuss labor market policies, whose relationship to industrial relations is analyzed in sufficient detail in Chapter 5. But even in this area of regulation, the conclusions concerning the operational criteria are similar to those for industrial policy. If one difference is noteworthy, it is the greater diffusion of associative criteria at decentralized levels of the industrial relations system. These are linked not so much to deregulation as to a de-bureaucratization of control of the market.

4. Concluding considerations

The aim of this chapter was to identify the changes in the regulatory criteria of Italian industrial relations over the last decade. As a theoretical point of reference, we embraced roughly the typology of forms and criteria of regulation elaborated recently by Streeck and Schmitter. This typology reflects a tradition of social theory stemming from the work of Karl Polanyi, and foresees communitarian, market, political, and associative forms and criteria. It leaves substantially indeterminate, from a theoretical point of view, the reasons particular issues pass from one form to another. To fill this gap, we proposed the use of "transaction cost" analysis, derived from the historical-economic studies of North. This analysis, while designed for other purposes, has a certain degree of explanatory utility even for industrial relations. The theoretical framework was completed by the introduction of the category of institutionalization, which takes on central importance in understanding the Italian case.

Over the last decade, market criteria, in the narrow sense and especially in the neo-liberal sense of the term, did not significantly spread. Cases of deregulation (for example, in the labor market) were compensated for and the destructuring effects were controlled by a new openness of the unions to negotiate the extension of legislation. However, political and associative criteria became more diffused, even when combined with an insufficient degree of institutionalization of industrial relations at both the horizontal level (in relations between actors) and the vertical level (the internal integration of organized interest groups and their participation in bodies of economic and social policy). This shortcoming continues to make industrial relations unstable and their evolution unpredictable, especially given their exposure to the political system. In order to reduce this exposure and attempt to correct this shortcoming, negotiations among the different leadership groups might be used rather than legislation.

Political criteria are insufficiently selective and unable to order demands hierarchically. It is likely that they are affected by "pluralist stagnation," aggravated by party mediation. Associative criteria have not been consolidated into new institutions, at least at the central levels. However, concertative accords were employed or attempted at these levels in 1983 and 1984, with questionable success from the viewpoint of stable relations between organized groups, but with positive results at least for the control of inflation, which was one of the two principal manifestations of the crisis. The weak institutionalization of associative criteria, however, has hindered their coherent transfer to the fields of industrial and labor market policy. Important indications of change can be seen in particular areas of the system, like the sector of firms with state participation, but it is still too early to evaluate the extent and durability of these changes.

The explanation for these shortcomings can be found in the difficulties associated with the formation of a collaborative coalition between parties and organized interest groups in the Italian political system. Such coalitions could permit a depoliticization of relations internal to, and interventions aimed at, the productive system. But at this point it is difficult to foresee whether or not Italian political parties will deprive themselves of that "resource," which the weak institutional autonomy of industrial relations provides and which they spend in mediations and interventions in civil society.

Notes

1 It is impossible to exchange ill-defined goods and rights on the market.

2 For more on these issues, see Streeck (1986). While not employing transaction cost analysis, the author reaches the same conclusions. Nonetheless, the link between this essay and the typology proposed in an earlier work with Schmitter still needs to be explained. For an analysis of the diffusion of these criteria in collective bargaining, see Negrelli (1985).

3 This refers not to the pure market of individualistic competition, but to the market of organized competition.

4 The success of state intervention can be seen through an international comparison of unemployment rates.

5 For a different interpretation, based on aspects of internal bargaining, see Regini (1985).

6 An example would have been significant changes in the *Statuto dei Lavoratori* (Statute of Workers' Rights) that would have limited workers' bargaining rights. Such changes did occur in Britain in the 1980s.

7 The issue of the decimal points refers to the disagreement that occurred slightly after the 1983 accord on varying the wage indexation system so that wage increases would be inferior to increases in the rate of inflation.

8

The representation of business interests as a mechanism of social regulation

ANTONIO CHIESI AND ALBERTO MARTINELLI

1. The importance of business associations in relation to other regulatory mechanisms

The issue we propose to analyze in this chapter is the role business associations play in processes of social regulation as compared with the role played by other major regulatory mechanisms discussed in the Introduction to this volume.

The competitive system of firms and that of associations of interest representation are forms of social regulation since they possess the power to invest and can guarantee the coordination and control of economic activities. Social regulation cannot, in fact, ignore the efficient governing of the economy, or the need for a certain degree of consensus among economic actors over the rules of the competitive game and a certain degree of coordination between the activities of firms and their socially relevant environment. This environment is composed of the suppliers of factors of production, consumers of the goods and services produced, and the public institutions that direct and control economic life.

In addressing the issue of business associations as institutions of social regulation, we must keep in mind the following:

1. Business associations occupy a non-exclusive role alongside the other, traditionally more efficient, institutional mechanisms (Martinelli et al. 1981b).
2. This role can be more or less central according to the particular national context (Windmuller and Gladstone 1984).
3. The regulatory field concerns both the external environment and the other collective actors with whom firms must establish relations, as well as the internal environment, i.e., the arena of associations in which the system of interest representation plays a role of self-regula-

tion and mediation among the various groups present within the economic leadership class (Schmitter and Streeck 1981).

4. The objects of external regulation are concerned with industrial relations issues, through the representation of firm interests in interaction with union organizations; and political-economic and financial issues, through forms of exchange, concertation, and pressure on political institutions.

5. The ability to efficiently pursue external regulatory goals is based on the internal mediation and unification of business interests (Martinelli et al. 1981a).

Alternative or complementary regulatory mechanisms to associative systems are the market, the state, organizational hierarchies, the community, and clans. This framework is analogous to that discussed by Lange and Regini in the Introduction to this volume. Nevertheless, since our goal is to analyze the mechanisms of social regulation of economic interests, the specificity of this arena requires, in our opinion, a partial reformulation of that typology.

In the specific area of economic behavior, there exists a widespread consensus that the self-regulating market, especially as it is conceived in the model of perfect competition, has gradually lost its central and prevalent function to other mechanisms, in particular the state and organizational hierarchies (Williamson 1975; Chandler 1977). The state replaces the external impersonal mechanism of the invisible hand with conscious regulation by political intervention aimed at stabilizing the economic cycle and limiting the threats against collective consensus that mechanisms of automatic adjustment can produce. Organizational hierarchies internalize the rules of the market within oligopolistic business organizations, thus reducing the degree of uncertainty, increasing the degree of predictability, and, hence, assuring the continuous flow of resources to the firms (thereby reducing their economic costs of adjustment).

We also believe that conflating the state and oligopolistic organizations into one single model of bureaucratic-authoritarian-centralized regulation represents an excessive simplification for our purposes. This is because oligopolistic organizations, as contrasted with the state, can be considered a regulatory mechanism in the hands of business.

Even the concept of community, which refers to traditional social formations (Streeck and Schmitter 1985), could, in our opinion, be revised to highlight the specific mechanisms being described. In this sense Hollingsworth and Lindberg (1985), borrowing from Ouchi's (1977) formulation, substitute the concept of clan for that of community. Clans are informal organizations whose members, belonging to different organizations, develop long-term reciprocal expectations of exchange of economic advantages, power, influence, and prestige. The logic of clans can effectively replace both market and hierarchical regulation. In the first case, they can simplify overly complex market decisions, and in the second case, they can quickly circumvent bureaucratic rigidities by relying on personal trust rather than formal procedures.

In an attempt to specify the reciprocal flow of mechanisms involved in social regulation, we will thus substitute the concept of clan for that of community, and we will seek to identify the arenas in which business associations play a more or less important role in relation to other mechanisms. Keeping in mind the Italian context, we first seek to evaluate which mechanisms operate in the different arenas of economic activity.

Market

Market is a self-regulating mechanism in which the price system provides the necessary information for the efficient distribution of factors of production, goods, and services. It continues to exercise an important role in advanced industrial economies. The ideology of the market is, however, more extensive in the United States than in Europe. In fact, in Italy, until only a few years ago, a counter-ideology prevailed that tended to emphasize the market's destabilizing effects and its excessive social and economic costs as compared with other regulatory mechanisms, above all the state. Moreover, the effects that the market has always produced tended to be undervalued and ignored. In reality, the market has always been much more present than politicians and scholars admitted (Bagnasco 1985). On the other hand, according to Lindberg, in the United States there exists a counter-tendency that undervalues the effects of mechanisms other than the market. In Italy, the low appreciation of market mechanisms is in part due to the relative weakness of the industrial bourgeoisie (Martinelli et al. 1981a), which was unable to diffuse a shared market ideology.[1]

State

The contradictions of the market have created the conditions for a growing, but not linear, intervention by the state in the government of the economy. In Italy, the range of instruments of political intervention in the economy has been quite wide. This has resulted from their traditionally weak efficiency in reaching their declared goals, which has promoted a tendency towards a layering of successive instruments over time, as the efficiency of each was eventually judged to be insufficient (for example, the various instruments for intervention in the South). Italy differs from other European countries in that it constructed both instruments of direct state intervention in the economy and indirect interventions typical of Keynesian policies. The term entrepreneurial state is used to indicate the acquisition of economic command in certain sectors intended to favor development according to criteria of public utility, in the broad sense of the term, or more significantly, with the aim of directing the flow of resources towards a territorial reequilibrium.[2]

The state also intervenes in order to exploit certain sectors as a source of revenue (for example, the petroleum sector) or to promote social stability (controls over commercial licenses and policies, which buffer the effects of competition on marginal producers, hence favoring the traditional middle classes [Pizzorno 1974]).

Hierarchical organizations

As state intervention grew, large managerial enterprises developed, and these tended to internalize the rules of the market, above all in sectors where the market itself expressed oligopolistic tendencies.[3] These enterprises also implemented firm policies aimed at reducing uncertainty with instruments other than simply growth in scale.

Here we are referring to modern transnational enterprises that developed after World War II, first in the United States and later in Western Europe and Japan, as well as to the large managerial enterprises characteristic of England and North America, which constitute their historical antecedent. We are not, however, referring to the cartels and trusts that dominated the economies of continental Europe in the decades preceding and following World War I.

If, in fact, cartels and trusts historically represented a form of regulation of important industrial sectors, which controlled certain tensions and conflicts generated by the "anarchy of free competition," they also generated other more major contradictions. In particular, cartels and trusts showed themselves to be more capable of regulating sectors circumscribed by national economies, thereby exacerbating international conflicts. The close identification between monopoly capital and the state, derived from the political influence of the former in the mechanisms of government, helped to transform economic competition between industrial groups into a political-military conflict between nations. This destroyed the international economic order based on the self-regulating market (Martinelli 1974).

The effects produced by transnational enterprises are quite different. While also a source of inter-oligopolistic tensions and nation-state conflict, they nevertheless play a fundamental role in the regulation of the world economy and thus of particular national and regional economic systems. This permits the more efficient planning of activities on an international scale and an organization of production in different countries through a diversified but coordinated production process (Makler et al. 1982).

Linked to this type of regulation are extra-firm organizational hierarchies that develop with the strategies of decentralization, subcontracting, financial control through holdings, and the diversification of risks by institutional investors – all aimed at creating a developed and coherent system of hierarchically coordinated firms.

Clans

As indicated above, clans are more or less restricted or exclusive groups that play a regulatory role in the economy and that exist where the need for reciprocal trust renders the use of anonymous market mechanisms less efficient and where personalistic elements are the bases for exchange.[4] Weber (1985) has already emphasized the essential role played by groups that base their activity on the reciprocal giving of their word (stockbrokers) precisely in a context dominated by the purest form of the market: the market for stocks. More generally, Stokman, Ziegler, and Scott (1985) sought to demonstrate how the phenomenon of interlocking directorates is not the mere fruit of a stochastic process, nor can it be explained simply through the dynamics of financial control. Rather, it is derived from criteria of coordination of firm activities at the operative and above all financial levels.

Thus, this regulatory model constitutes not so much the survival of communitarian rules within the capitalist system, but rather the proof that universalistic rules of the game are accompanied, in certain areas, by the presence of internal group ethics that are exclusive, particularistic, and in some way solidaristic. Whoever operates in this type of context, among other things, enjoys the net advantage of operating in a universalistic system with the protection and solidarity of a restricted group.[5]

For Italy, more particularly, Chiesi (1982) sought to demonstrate how the structure of the network of people who occupy leadership positions in major corporations is closed, elitist, and quite limited. In this network, phenomena of co-optation prevail and personal acquaintances are essential. An example of the importance of this institutional mechanism is the credit sector, which is characterized by a relative weakening of competitive market rules and by the importance of personal trust in relationships with regulatory and supervisory bodies.

These latter assume particular importance in cases of bailouts. In sum, the regulation of interests through structures of reciprocal trust is more efficient in certain sectors than in others.

Associations

The typology adopted is far from exhaustive. In fact, a fifth mechanism must be examined for the case of the social regulation of economic interests. This mechanism in certain ways can be considered a subspecies of the organizational hierarchies type and, in other ways, can be seen as a fifth, autonomous type.[6] It involves the system of associations of interest representation for both workers and business. In this chapter we will focus our attention on business associations in relation to other forms of social regulation of economic relations.

The role of business associations is more important in Europe, where hierarchical structures of economic interest regulation prevail, than in America (Windmuller and Gladstone 1984). In complex sectors and in highly turbulent external environments, these associations can constitute an instrument better to manage inter- and intra-sectoral problems (centralized industrial relations, lobbying over government economic policy, etc.).

In general, the regulatory instruments of an associative system are more efficient for smaller firms where actors are not tempted by the relative advantages that a large firm might gain through free riding.[7] Moreover, in Italy the political system tends to legitimate the expression of small firm interests (e.g., artisans, cooperatives, and small-scale industry) through a variety of ideological-political associations. We must emphasize, in fact, that the degree of legitimation given to business associations by the political system is similar to that which is given to labor unions.

To evaluate the regulatory efficiency of associations, we must distinguish between industrial relations functions and economic regulation functions, keeping in mind that in other European nations this distinction has a precise correspondence in the structure of the associative system, with its more clearly distinguished employers' and trade associations. Only recently has a tendency towards the separation of these two functions of representation developed in Italy, most notably with attempts to develop trade functions.[8]

There is a consensus that the functions of union representation exercise a notable influence on the system of industrial relations,[9] and thus business associationalism occupies a central place in the regulatory system of the labor market. In the current period, as we will see in the third section of this chapter, the inclination of the General Confederation of Italian Industry (Confindustria) is deregulatory. This is because the associational strategies tend to emphasize the rules of the market as the most important mechanism, similar to a tendency that seemed to be emerging throughout Europe in the mid-1980s (Streeck 1985). This is once again an example of a strategy aimed at modifying the rapport between different regulatory mechanisms.

It is more difficult to evaluate the regulatory impact of the associations, especially of *Confindustria,* on the economy. The analysis must be broken down by single sectors and by individual components of the economic leadership class. We are dealing with detailed but weak regulation, which plays a more or less marginal role relative to the various other regulatory mechanisms operating in the particular sector. This naturally is related to the often mentioned heterogeneity of interests and behaviors of the Italian economic leadership class, a heterogeneity that the system of representation must contend with through specific internal solutions.

2. The "mix" of regulatory mechanisms in the representation of economic interests

The variability of the regulatory mix, the articulation of the system of representation, and the unequal functions of business associations, depending on the economic context, require us to disaggregate our discussion to the sectoral level, even if the research is not systematic and we will cover only certain economic sectors.[10] We hold, in fact, that macro-analysis would not permit us to illustrate important differences. If we keep in mind the analytic distinction between economic functions and industrial relations functions, it appears evident that it is, above all, the former that lead to the variation in regulatory contexts (presented schematically in Table 8.1). As one can see, the five specific mechanisms assume distinctly different degrees of centrality depending on the sector, and they have different weights depending on the combinations. We will now analyze in more detail the typical situation of each sector with reference to recent Italian developments.

Telecommunications

The communications sector is regulated above all by the state and by hierarchical organizations, especially since it is involved with the domestic market and, hence, is not exposed to international competition. The state occupies a monopoly position before a few firms that reach accords among themselves regarding market shares and product standardization (telephones) or even operate as concessionaires (cable management). In this situation, typical of the 1970s and 1980s, the state as regulatory mechanism is, in fact, irreplaceable. The financial

Table 8.1. *The combination of regulative mechanisms in selected Italian economic sectors*

Sector	Market	State	Organizational hierarchy	Clans	Associations
		Prevalent regulative mechanisms			
Telecommunications		+[a]	+		
Petroleum		+			−
Construction	−	+			−
Chemicals	−	+	+		−
Textiles	+	−	+		−
Machine tools	+				−
Agriculture		+			+
Private finance	−		+	+	
Credit		+	+	+	

[a]Symbols: +, primary importance; −, secondary importance.

problems of the public communications sector, beginning in the mid-1970s, were due, in fact, both to the lack of a development plan for the sector and to the political constraints preventing phone rates from covering cost increases due to inflation. Attempts to increase sales through the development of exports, limited to the telephone department, proved to be inadequate and had unequal results for the few firms operant in the sector. Recently, innovation has been relaunched, as a result of the new telecommunications plan that foresees the complete replacement of electro-mechanical technology by electronics. This is once again due to a commitment by the state, which after years of paralysis (Lizzeri and de Brabant 1983) has decided to intervene not only financially but also in the technological choices adopted. In this framework, the absence of a business association in the sector demonstrates that there is no autonomous space for an organization representing business interests.

Petroleum

In the sector of petroleum derivatives, the role of the state is also central, as a result of the regime of administered prices, the high percentage of taxation included in final prices, the regulation of stocks, transportation and security norms, etc. Nonetheless, in contrast to the telecommunications sector, when dealing with an overview of the sector, the role of the dominant association (*Unione Petrolifera*) emerges as important. In fact, even in an oligopolistic situation, the firms find it convenient to delegate the function of bargaining to the sectoral association if negotiations with the state become important in a political context unfavorable to the image of big petroleum multinationals. The recent competition for representation in the sector between the *Unione Petrolifera* and *Federchimica*[11] indicates the important role the associative system can play. Currently, the proposal to move to a regime of free price-setting for gasoline would lead to a shift in regulatory functions from the state to the market. The consequences of such a move would be to rationalize the network of distributors; this would, in turn, create union problems, which would reinforce the role of the associations in the field of industrial relations.

Construction

Even in the construction sector, state intervention is notable (Maraffi 1985) and concerns rent control laws, the regulatory powers of local governments, construction regulations, and above all public spending and construction projects. The market plays an important but not central role (because of localistic fragmentation) to which the associative structure adapts by providing economic and industrial relations assistance to a universe of mostly small firms.

The size of firms and their distribution throughout the national territory influence the structure and efficiency of interest representation. The diffusion of small firms and artisans renders the associative system in certain ways similar to forms of middle-class representation. The major associations in the sector are, thus, divided on political-ideological grounds. To this dimension we must add two other sources of representational fragmentation: firm size, which is legally sanctioned by the distinction between industrial and artisans' firms; and type of property, whether public or private. The capillary diffusion of firms throughout the national territory also makes "province" an important associative criterion. This responds to the localistic logic of both the final and labor markets.

As a result of this notable fragmentation,[12] the management of diversity constitutes a fundamental associative problem (Martinelli et al. 1985), even if associative competition between the systems of representation is reduced by the compartmentalization described above. Because of this structural situation, the regulatory job of the associations in this sector is relatively secondary.

Chemicals

In the chemical industry, the regulatory mechanisms concern principally the state and the organizational hierarchies of the two major oligopolies (ENI and Montedison). In the past, attempts at regulation through the market led to disastrous competitive results.

State intervention occurs both directly, through the system of state participation and ENI, and indirectly, through copious norms and intensive legislation which, although not specifically directed at the sector, have, in fact, been implemented in this sector and not in others. One need only recall the first attempts at economic planning by the Center-Left governments of 1962 and afterwards followed by the policies to promote locational decisions in the South and successively (beginning at the end of the 1970s) by the programs of labor force reduction and mobility required by the productive overcapacity that resulted from earlier policies. The totality of these policies and the consequent economic decisions of private individuals proved unable to promote the attainment of the declared goals and, in fact, have had unforeseen effects.

The oligopolistic characteristic of the market has also provoked commercial wars between different groups, the state-owned group included, with the result of wasting enormous private, but above all public, resources. Given these premises, the most recent restructuring and reconversion initiatives in this sector were based on strategic accords between the two major oligopolies, which include an agreement on the reciprocal spheres of influence of the public and private firms. The accord between ENI and Montedison occurred after the business failures of private groups like SIR-Rumianca and Liquigas, which had quickly grown gigantic through the exploitation of state finances. Another typical characteristic of the oligopolistic structure of the market is, in fact, the progressive concentration of the sector through fusions and acquisitions, which since 1966 involved the major firms, with a good part of final bailout operations falling to ENI.

We will now briefly illustrate the relations between the collective actors we have identified that are of particular relevance for understanding the characteristics and dynamics of the system of interest representation. The model presented reflects above all the structural crisis of the 1970s (Azzolini et al. 1979) and has undergone substantial changes beginning in the 1980s caused by the crisis of the sector, related both to the overcapacity of the chemical industry and to the fiscal crisis of the state (whose investment funds dried up). In turn, the responses to the crisis by the social actors led to changes in the internal alliances of the associative system, culminating in the transformation of the major association, *Aschimici*, into a federation of associations *(Federchimica)*.

We can identify the following collective actors (Chiesi 1985):

1. A limited number of oligopolies in fierce competition. The strategy adopted was that of growth in scale with the aim of promoting

economies of scale and reducing production costs. Growth was often pursued without taking into account the market's absorption capacity. Growth was further pursued through highly capital-intensive investments, thanks to financial benefits that the state provided to firms which invested in the South.

2. The state, which never implemented specific intervention plans in the chemical sector, but which, in fact, intervened with abundant resources since demands from the sector were consistent with the more general policies of industrial development and job creation in the South.

3. Foreign multinational firms, which did not have access to state aid and, thus, implemented a progressive and general strategy of disinvestment in the base sector following the energy crisis, while at the same time increasing their presence in the more profitable secondary chemical sector.

4. Small and medium-sized private firms, which in certain sectors were in potential competition with the foreign multinationals, but which, in fact, possessed fewer research and development resources.

5. The unions, which supported the state's policies of job creation in the South and which successively defended these jobs in plants that proved uncompetitive in the market.

The specific characteristics of the system of economic interest representation and associational strategies thus reflect a context in which the rules of the market are attenuated and limited to certain (but not all) actors, the state plays an essential role, and hierarchies represent the most important regulatory mechanism.

Until 1980 there existed a highly complex organization of interest representation. This complexity was in part counterbalanced by the greater weight exercised by a limited number of predominant associations. The constitution in 1984 of a federation of associations, adhering to the *Confindustria* system, produced a verticalization of the associative structure and, thus, an increased potential capacity to integrate and manage the variety of business interests. Moreover, the federation came to exercise a centripetal force in relation to the autonomous subsectoral associations not belonging to the *Confindustria* system. The immediate consequence was thus the reduction of potential competition between associations present in the same associative arena. Finally, the assumption of the right to represent the economic interests of firms with direct state participation further integrated the representational system. This created conditions within the federation necessary to allow it to undertake the functions of coordination and mediation of relations between private and public chemical sectors, which previously were managed directly by the oligopolies and the Minister of State Participations outside the associational framework.

It is relatively easy to specify the external and internal (i.e., those inherent in the dynamics of the *Confindustria* system) reasons that promoted the transformation of separate interest associations into a federation. First of all, the end of oligopolistic wars and the redefinition of boundaries between the private and public spheres created the external conditions for stability, to which the associative system adapted. The constitution of the federation was also favored by the preexisting internal diversity within *Aschimici,* and by the organizational reform of *Confindustria,* which foresaw the creation of sectoral federations (*Confindustria* 1983). Finally, two aspects of *Aschimici*'s previous policies need to be taken into account: (1) the progressive absorption of minor associations, and (2) the development of relatively conciliatory positions towards the unions. The latter made possible easier coexistence with the concertative policy traditionally pursued by firms in the State Participations arena.

In substance, we can thus conclude that the business associations did play a role in the restructuring of the chemical sector. This role was nonetheless quite limited, since sectoral policies were not developed at association headquarters. Instead, the latter have primarily implementation functions, promoting cooperation among firms and managing relations with the unions. Further, the associational system helps create a favorable external image of the sector's entrepreneurs. This favorable image was used in strategic bargaining, especially with the state, so that sectoral problems were given a high priority and a satisfactory volume of resources was obtained through political exchange.

Textiles

The textile-apparel sector, highly exposed to international competition, experienced a long period of crisis in the 1960s and 1970s, following the redefinition of the chain of the international division of labor with the entrance of newly industrialized countries in successive phases of the production cycle. Afterwards, there was a period of relaunching following a drastic reduction of employment and major technological changes. These have transformed the sector into a highly capital-intensive and innovative industry.

A mix of regulatory mechanisms including the market and hierarchical organizations is present in the sector, where the latter assume the form of vertical integration of firms through a system of suppliers, subcontractors, and general decentralization. Even in the textile sector, therefore, the associations have played a secondary role over the last decade, tied for the most part to the management of industrial relations during the phases of restructuring and the reduction of the labor force, and to the pursuit of "public" economic goals through pressuring public bodies (the state and, at the international level, the European Economic Community), which have influenced the anti-crisis policies and the relaunching of the sector.

While secondary overall, state intervention was critical to the economic support of the sector during the crisis, through indirect instruments like the Textile Law of 1971 and, at the international level, the multifiber agreements of 1977 and 1981. Direct instruments of state intervention occurred through industrial salvage operations and through acquisitions by the state corporations Tescon and Gepi. In the 1970s, these corporations created the largest industrial concentration in the sector under the control of the Ministry of State Participations (*Federtessile* 1981). Moreover, state intervention policies sought to introduce sectoral plans, which provoked the open opposition of industrialists.

As a response to the aggravation of the crisis and the growing presence of the state in the sector, the system of representation of sectoral business interests was restructured in 1975 with the constitution of a federation of sectoral associations (*Federtessile*). Associational activity led to the following goals (Mutti et al. 1986): (1) containment of the state enterprise in the sector; (2) reduction of credit costs; (3) reduction of labor costs through the fiscalization of social security benefits; (4) tax relief; and (5) adoption of protectionist measures against imports from developing nations by the European Economic Community.

Some of these objectives were included in the sectoral legislation mentioned above, and by the end of the 1970s the state abandoned the idea of a sectoral plan because of opposition not only by *Federtessile* but also by the entire *Confindustria* system (the Carli-Savona line, named after the then respective president and general director of *Confindustria*). Notwithstanding these successes, obtained directly through political debate among the political parties, the role of the sectoral associations remains secondary. This is due to the logic of representation. The business associations of the sector suffer from low membership rates. *Federtessile*, in particular, suffers from limited statutory autonomy vis-à-vis its associates and from insufficient economic resources as a result of competition from territorial associations. These associations operate where there are greater concentrations of firms in the sector[13] and where they are able to aggregate a wider range of selective incentives in favor of associates (Mutti et al. 1986). In sum, as in the chemical sector, associative restructuring follows and accompanies economic restructuring, proving that the former depends on, even if it also aids, the latter.

Machine tools

In the machine tools sector there exists a diffusion of small firms, numerous but poorly differentiated producers, a prevalence of competition based on accords among producers, and productive versatility. The final market is also characterized by the existence of several large clients who condition the market. In dealing with this relatively small sector, the government's principal role is in establishing/regulating security norms for the machinery, which are also subject to international regulation. The associative system, however, is especially active and expresses a sharp distinction between sectorally specialized economic functions and industrial relations functions. The latter are left generally to the Federation of Mechanical Industries (*Federmeccanica*), which belongs to the *Confindustria* system.

By rewarding product quality in international competition, the market constitutes the dominant regulatory mechanism. Technological quality can be obtained through the maintenance of quality standards for the product and is recognized by the quality trademark. The associative system of economic interests[14] plays an important role in this context by certifying standards and promoting the product on the market. The two most important associations of the sector confer a trademark on the products of their associates. The trademark guarantees the specialization of the sector, distinguishing it from products produced occasionally by non-specialized forms. The associative trademark also assures that products possess the technical requirements necessary to belong to the associations.

The enjoyment of a selective good so important for the firms obviously implies the erection of an entrance barrier, a mechanism that has evolved over the course of the association's history. In the 1950s, a new member was accepted on the basis of a referendum among associates. Thus, it was a form of pure co-optation, justified by the restricted number of producers who judged the candidate on the basis of reputation and personal acquaintance (Baglioni 1986). This mechanism is interesting since the association began to resemble a clan, as specified in the previous section of this chapter, with formal entrance criteria and reciprocal recognition both inside the association and in the market. In the 1960s, the admissions criteria lost some of their personalistic dimension, and objective technical parameters required of the candidate began to assume importance. A control commission was established to ensure that the characteristics of the associates met the requirements of admission.[15]

Associative resources were also directed towards the production of public goods related to product standardization, technological improvement, and machine safety. Relations with the responsible ministries and with public research centers became particularly important for these activities. More generally, associative activity spawned internal consultant organizations, technical offices, study centers, and above all association-related services which promote the associations' trademark and products at international fairs and trade expositions. In this case, we have an example of very important selective goods that distinguish between associates and other operators.

Agriculture

If we abandon the industrial sector, the lack of research on interest associations prevents us from completing our analysis. Nonetheless, it is possible to advance some further considerations. The agricultural sector, for example, appears to be characterized by a type of regulation that is relatively well integrated between the state and the associations, as a result of the lack of competition and the state's protection of traditional middle classes in the postwar period. Associations are obligatory and highly political. In this sector, therefore, we find a state-association mix typical of Italian cooperatives and artisans in general. Classic studies on organizations like the *Coldiretti* (La Palombara 1964) demonstrated not only the importance of mechanisms of social consensus and political stability, but also the capacity to influence the political sphere through channels of ideological *parentela*.

Artisans

In the artisan sector there are three confederations that are distinguished by ideological orientation and whose relative importance is directly proportional to the weight their related political parties have in national politics. The confederations' lack of sectoral specialization, the importance of territorial representation and organization, the potential competition at the membership level, their birth, and their history all demonstrate that their origin responds to a logic of party penetration of middle-class organizations. Thus, in the area of economic interest representation, these associations appear to operate on the basis not only of the double logic of influence and of membership (Schmitter and Streeck 1981), but also of the logic of party competition (Martinelli et al. 1985).

Finance

Finally, we would like to indicate the regulatory mix present in the field of finance, whose task consists primarily of the allocation and control of capital. In financial activities, which cut across more or less all sectors, and in the allocation of credit, the clan mechanisms assume a primary role, along with the state and organizational hierarchies.

Market mechanisms have, until recently, been relatively secondary because of the oligopolistic nature of the sector, but they are destined to acquire importance with the recent quantitative and qualitative development of the stock exchange. State action is also notable in this arena. One need only think of taxation, which tends, on the one hand, to gather and direct resources through withdrawals and distributions[16] and, on the other hand, to guarantee the rules of the game through state controls and the safeguarding of foreign trade balances.[17]

We believe, however, that limiting ourselves to these regulatory mechanisms is absolutely inadequate since the instruments of capital allocation and control also appear to be governed by the logic of clans. First of all, we would like to clarify that by clan we do not intend some sort of conspiracy in which restricted, hidden groups act against the universalistic logic of the market through insider trading, or against the authorities by planning fraudulent bankruptcies and by illegally transferring funds abroad. While these phenomena have occurred in the more or less recent history of large Italian financial institutions, and while discretion and obscurity are typical clan characteristics, we must analyze much more extensive, constant, and ordinary mechanisms. These tend to stabilize and enhance the flow of the system through personalistic and elitist networks of reciprocal trust, which the sector appears to need in order to obtain the highest degree of overall efficiency. We hold, therefore, that the mobility mechanisms adopted in 1974 within national finance, aimed at Sindona's takeover of Bastogi (a financial holding company), are very important. These mechanisms arose out of an alliance between bodies of state control and trustworthy figures of the establishment. They were capable of mobilizing latent resources in order to exclude "untrustworthy" figures from the centers of economic power, or to reestablish conditions of external trust, as in the case of the salvage of the Banco Ambrosiano, or in the creation of Gemina (a financial corporation composed of an alliance of the largest private groups) in the salvage of Montedison. These mechanisms were developed within the boards of the most important corporations, connected by extensive stock ownership links (Chiesi 1986), through a web of personal ties among the boards, structured in such a way as to permit a relatively large number of people to meet personally and often[18] through corporate pacts based on alliances between settings and individuals which are part of a game of co-optation based on affinities that are difficult to decipher from the outside.

These mechanisms of trust based on the logic of the clan are particularly important when the threat of bankruptcy or of a generalized crisis (for example, a bank failure) generates distrust in the regulatory mechanisms of the market, creating various cycles with perverse effects on the market itself (panic). Aside from acting as a protective net in the case of crisis, the clan is most efficient as a mechanism of crisis management; through trust, it is more capable of managing complex decisions than either the market or the burdensome bureaucracy of hierarchical organizations.

In this sector, therefore, the presence of associations assumes negligible importance, even if they perform linkage and representation functions for the specific interests of the category. (We need only think of the different associations which organize credit agencies.)

3. The role of business associations in the industrial relations system

Having evaluated the various institutional mechanisms of regulation in different sectors and contexts of the Italian economy, we will now focus our attention on a specific area of social relations, industrial relations (IR). This is one of the most important areas for firms, business and union organizations, the state, and, to a lesser extent, clans, even if market regulation plays an especially prevalent role. It is an area of socioeconomic relations in which we can analyze the various mixes of types of regulation, their changes over time, their causes, and their implications for the macro-systemic level. We will examine these problems within the framework of the broader question of the applicability of the neo-corporatist model of concertation in Italy.

We intend to argue three points. First, we hold that even in IR, which is a typical area of regulatory intervention by business associations, these are far from the only mechanisms of regulation. Between the mid-1970s and today, events in Italy have demonstrated that the role of associations and of centralized bargaining was simultaneous with the role of market competition and of hierarchical regulation by the firm, even while posing constraints on the labor market and on the discretion of business in its management.

Second, it appears that in contrast to the unions, business associations tend to consider concertation and tripartite accords "second best" solutions, which the entrepreneurs would happily do without and which they seek, in any case, to restructure as soon as structural or conjunctural conditions are present for the application of a different combination of regulatory mechanisms. Consequently, the openness with which the associations underwrite these neo-corporatist accords is much weaker and more contingent than for the unions.

Finally, it is our opinion that while in Italy the requisites for a systematic application of the neo-corporatist model of IR do not exist, forms of concertation negotiated at the national (central) level among the government, firms, and unions have continued to be pursued and achieved for several years.

If we quickly review the strategies of business associations in the last thirteen years, and of *Confindustria* in particular, we see how different institutional mechanisms were employed simultaneously by firms in a complementary way. We begin with 1973 when Giovanni Agnelli assumed the presidency of *Confindustria* (and Fiat). This can be seen as a turning point. *Confindustria* managed to reverse its trend towards decreasing efficiency in the representation of business interests and to initiate a strategy that initially emphasized containment and later emphasized reduction of union power. First, there was a realistic acceptance of the extant power relations, with the hope that perhaps union power would be reduced by the incipient economic crisis. The strategy adopted was double. On the one hand, the associative system aimed at striking general accords with the unions at the national (central) level in order to reduce levels of conflict. On the other hand, at the level of individual firms and groups of firms, strategies aimed at restructuring, decentralization of production, capital substitution of labor and the reduction of the strongest categories of workers, etc., were implemented. As a result, the structural process of reducing workers' centrality was accelerated.

The first part of the strategy was short-lived and was characterized by the 1975 accord on wage indexation to inflation levels (*punto unico di contingenza*). This accord achieved its goal of reducing labor conflict in a period of wage instability due to high inflation,[19] and can be considered an example of a neo-corporatist accord without the state. This did not represent a conscious choice in favor of a concerted model by *Confindustria*. It was only a second best solution, which, among other things, was in the interest of only one segment of industrial capital, i.e., large firms with strong and militant unions and with the capacity to cover higher labor costs by raising prices, thanks to the oligopolistic structure of the market (i.e., Fiat). The accord cannot be seen as equally advantageous for smaller firms since it introduced wage rigidities.

The second, micro-level strategy involved market and organizational hierarchies as regulatory mechanisms. It began as a response to the conjunctural crisis of 1974 and took on different paces and modes according to the market, sector, and individual firm situations. Private firms were the first to act, while state-owned firms, committed to the concertation model whose principal episode was represented in the EUR line of the late-1970s, delayed adaptation until the early 1980s.

The EUR accord represented an attempt at long-term centralized concertation.[20] It sought to realize a political exchange between wage moderation and extensive reforms (job creation, the development of the South, reform of the health and social security systems, etc.). Since it was a long-term strategy, it involved the political sphere through a new relationship between the governing coalition and the opposition, represented by the governments of national solidarity (the inclusion of the Communist party in the "governmental area" for the first time since the immediate postwar period). Political exchange remained blocked until 1983, however, for various reasons:

1. The unions did not obtain the long-term benefits they desired in exchange for their immediate concessions,[21] above all because the state was not a trustworthy guarantor of the accord, and because the resources available to the collective actors were scarce during the economic crisis (Regini 1985).
2. Power relations within the firm were already shifting against the workers as a result of increased unemployment rates.
3. At the end of the 1970s an increase in interest rates induced firms to become more resistant to union demands, as opposed to the past when permissive monetary policies permitted firms to bargain as a way of reducing labor union conflict.

During this period *Confindustria* appeared to represent, at the level of centralized relations among the confederal leadership and the sectoral associations, a protective umbrella that permitted other slower, but more profound, regulatory mechanisms (the market, organizational hierarchies) to develop. Industrial relations were managed with the aim of reducing conflict and permitting firms to restructure.

The development of the factors that led to the eventual shift in bargaining equilibria in favor of the firms ended in 1979 and coincided with the abandonment of the period of national solidarity. In 1979, in fact, Fiat re-acquired initiative in IR by asking for a special state redundancy fund *(Cassa Integrazione Guadagni Speciale)*. The unions' defeat in the fall 1980 strike at Fiat reflected the changed power relations, while the "march of 40,000" at Fiat (by Fiat workers against union policy in the firm) was an indication of the difficulties the union experiences in representing highly skilled segments of the labor force.

In the 1980s, the associations assume, therefore, a more articulate role, related, among other things, to significant changes in the organizational structure of the *Confindustria* system (*Confindustria* 1983). On the one hand, there is the relaunching of centralized concertation of wage policy, taxation, and social security reforms, but this is accompanied by the simultaneous restructuring of union representation and redefinition of demands reflecting the changed power relations, the industrial restructuring in process, and the political strategies of the governing coalitions led by Republican and Socialist party leaders. Bargaining issues thus concern public goods in which government intervention is essential in legitimating, guaranteeing, mediating, and directing the results of concertative bargaining and policies. On the other hand, the associations play a role at the territorial and sectoral levels in assisting and directing the handling of firm-level industrial relations. Because of the increased complexity of the competitive system, the impact of new technologies on the organization of labor, and firm needs for greater flexibility, collective bargaining becomes increasingly differentiated by sector, geographic area, and type of firm. In other words, the trends present elsewhere in Europe, which Streeck (1986) defines as "an extensive decentralization of the IR system and its integration with the organization of labor and rules of the competitive game," become manifest in Italy as well.

Along with the increase in direct bargaining relations between the firm and individual workers, typical of a resurgence of market rules and the return of hierarchical forms of control, there is, nevertheless, a legitimation of the union as a necessary partner on the part of certain firms. This is illustrated by the 1986 accord at Fiat. This double-tracked strategy, which exists to different degrees in many sectors, is also linked, in a simplified and polarized way, to the internal debate within *Confindustria* between those favoring a concertation line and those advocating increased market regulation (deregulation and delegitimation of the union).

A review of recent events in Italian industrial relations reveals the existence of certain significant obstacles – including, above all, the preference of business associations for a different combination of regulatory modes – to the affirmation of a neo-corporatist system. The neo-corporatist model is based on the combination of two mechanisms of regulation, specifically the policies of interest group associations and state action, not only in the definition of the normative framework for the game among the actors, but also in the determination of the contents of collective bargaining. This requires certain fundamental conditions that have already been outlined extensively in the literature on the topic (Lehmbruch and Schmitter 1982).

These fundamental conditions are only partially present in Italy. Favorable conditions that exist in Italy include: the capacity to aggregate and coordinate interests by both unions and business associations, the legitimation of their actions in the eyes of the state, a high degree of representational centralization, and a tight connection between economics and politics (Regini 1985). However, other essential requirements are missing. For instance, the plurality of interest organizations, composed of union and business associations with different ideological traditions and political alliances, reduces the predictability of the bargaining partners' actions. The government also possesses less authority and capacity to act as guarantor of accords as opposed to occasional mediator. Moreover, Italian unions are less open to collaborative behavior and attitudes, as a result both of their ideological origins and of the division within the Left between government and opposition. Finally, in certain sectors of Italian industry, above all in the areas of small firms with new entrepreneurship, there is a greater trend towards using the processes of industrial restructuring and the problems of the economic conjuncture to weaken unions and decisively alter power relations. This behavior contrasts with the behavior of the business class of North-Central Europe.

This combination of factors results in the more or less limited role for trilaterial political exchange in Italian industrial relations, as contrasted to its dominance in certain recent periods in countries like Austria, Germany, and Sweden. We hold that this subordinate role of trilateral bargaining conforms more to the expectations and interests of the business associations than those of the unions. Political action constitutes, in fact, a second choice for business interests, to be made only when individual action oriented towards the market does not provide sufficient results (Martinelli et al. 1981b). The different structural positions of capital and labor in the productive process promote relevant differences in their strategies. While the former has at its disposal three areas of social regulation for the pursuit of its proper interests (the hierarchical organization of the firm, informal cooperation, and representative associations), labor possesses only this last resource (Offe and Wiesenthal 1980). Moreover, business interests have greater chances of bargaining individually, rather than through associations, with the government by virtue of their power to invest. Finally, business associations have less control than the unions over the behavior and opinions of their membership, and this is a source of instability in political exchange (Mutti 1982).

This helps explain why Italian businesses, with the partial exception of state-owned firms, have assumed a critical attitude towards political exchange and have underwritten tripartite accords only in the presence of substantial partners (i.e., the government). This has occurred in a period of major industrial restructuring and rapid technical-organizational innovation, linked to less sustained growth rates and a decrease in concertation among unions, firms, and the state, even in countries with neo-corporatist experiences.

In the context of the absence of several essential requirements for the neo-corporatist model and of business reluctance towards political exchange, what needs to be explained is not the difficulties experienced over trilateral accords, but the opposite: the persistence of concertation, even if limited, in the regulation of industrial relations, as opposed to countries where the market and state decree are especially dominant (Great Britain and France).

We believe that the principal reasons for this persistence concern the unions and the state of the business associations. Aside from residual ideological resistance, unions have, in fact, manifested a constant tendency towards involving the state in negotiations. This has been the case both in periods of economic growth and/or union power (because the unions want legally to institutionalize current power relations and collective bargaining gains) and in periods of economic recession and/or union weakness (because they seek partially to manage the effects of restructuring and the implications of technical change through an intensification of interaction with local and central government bodies).

The government and the party system, on the other hand, are interested in developing forms of concertation in order to obtain political consensus. The goals of political exchange with the unions have changed. They no longer concern bargaining moderation and political consensus in exchange for social reforms and the development of the welfare state. Rather, they concern an openness to accept certain effects of industrial restructuring and the deregulation of industrial relations in exchange for state interventions protecting employment. Concertation is destined to last, since the unions continue to control ample resources of organized political consensus, notwithstanding their recent problems with representation, and they continue to be privileged interlocutors with parties and the governments. This, more than the government's desire to control labor conflict, which in the present period has substantially declined in all advanced industrial states, seems to be the major reason for the longstanding political influence of the unions and, thus, for the active role the government plays in promoting forms of trilateral concertation.

Some authors have recently denied this continuing union importance in government policies, pointing out that many governments have demonstrated that they can do without the unions in economic and wage decision-making. This is because the unions are less capable of aggregating consensus, crippled as they are by the extensive industrial restructuring, and also because governments seek their own legitimation in different ways than in the past. Governments, in fact, give less importance to social and wage policies that require the previous consensus of the unions, preferring monetary and industrial policies and forms of consensus that are directed toward social groups different from those traditionally represented by the unions, or at individual citizens who do not require the mediation of mass organizations (Crouch 1981a; Carrieri and Donolo 1983).

These analyses are more appropriate to the North American and English contexts than to Western Europe. Executive autonomy from union action is exaggerated, and it applies less to Italy than elsewhere. We believe, in fact, that the unions' capacity to organize consensus remains the most important reason for the government's preoccupation with favoring forms of bargaining and concertation at the national (central) level, even inducing business, the reluctant partner, to participate in these accords in return for financial and tax benefits.

This is not, however, the only reason for the continuation of concertation at the national level, even in the presence of a relative decline in the importance of industrial relations at the firm, geographical area, and productive levels. There are at least four other causes:

1. Representational organizations, on both sides, tend to gain more legitimation from the state, and thus to obtain benefits from the third actor when they accept concertation at the national level.
2. The negotiation of public goods and the obtainment of state indemnities in exchange for accords can occur only at the center.
3. Certain sectors, like the chemical industry, are in fact attracted by the model of industrial relations elaborated in the arena of state-owned enterprise and thus practice moderate and concertative strategies.
4. The logics of organizational persistence within the respective representative systems fosters bargaining moderation by *Confindustria*, in the present period of balance of power in favor of firms, in a way similar to that practiced by the unions between 1977 and 1979.

Confindustria, moreover, has clearly followed the industrial relations policies of the largest private oligopolistic group (Fiat), of multiplying the settings and occasions of meetings with the unions without, however, any concrete negotiation results. It also decided to abandon the 1975 accord on wage indexation, copying at the confederal level Fiat's strategy at the firm level.

Finally, *Confindustria* has opted for bargained moderation in a period of favorable power relations, but it has demanded and obtained substantial benefits from the government in exchange for its willingness to support the tripartite accord of January 1983 and to give its assent to the decree law of February 1984.

4. Conclusions

In the preceding pages we have sought to analyze the specific role played by the associations of economic interest groups in a reality in which highly variable regulatory mixes prevail. These mixes depend both on the specific context in which they operate, as described in section 2 of this chapter, and on the phases of the economic cycle, as we illustrated in section 3 of this chapter. The regulatory efficiency of the associative systems is thus unequal. First of all, in distinguishing between economic and industrial relations functions, it appears that the role of defending economic interests is central in certain sectors, but not in others. In periods of sectoral crisis, state intervention, elicited by the need to restructure, can induce business, as the textile and chemical sectors demonstrate, to develop forms of collective representation capable of counterbalancing state action and lobbying in a socially accepted and efficient way. We are dealing with the efficiency of large numbers in a context of parliamentary democracy, for which it is more legitimate to take into account the representative interests of many actors, rather than of the individual, no matter how big.

In other sectors, however, the associations play a very different role. This is both because the associations acquire certain typical traits of a clan (e.g., co-optation, entrance barriers, reciprocal knowledge of members, and external recognition through trademarks), as in the machine tool sector, and because situations resembling the neo-corporative model can be identified at the sectoral level, as in the case of artisans' firms or where middle-class forms of representation prevail. Here, however, we also find interparty competition, which, for other reasons, takes us away from this model. In other fields, different regulatory mechanisms prevail, as is the case with the clans in the fields of finance and credit. Here, the associations play only a marginal role.

While the logic of bilateral concertation appears to prevail in the field of economic interests, in the sphere of industrial relations there is a greater trend towards trilateral concertation. This trend is conceived, however, only as the second best solution to other, more automatic regulatory features traditionally preferred by business. The hypothesis sustained in section 3 of this chapter concerns precisely the contingent and provisional character of business' disposition to sustain neo-corporatist accords at the center, waiting since the late 1970s for conditions to mature so that the competitive rules of the market can be relaunched at the firm level.

These considerations can, among other things, better clarify the relationship between regulation and control. It is obvious that the regulatory mechanisms of control are not neutral, *super partes*, and that there exists a problem of their control by interested organizations or particular institutions. In this light, it appears useful to analyze what degree of control business exercises over different regulatory mechanisms. Business associations are as such instruments of control over the external environment for business, but they also belong to the more ample regulatory system based on bargaining relations with other associations and on political exchange with the state.

Every actor has an interest in developing the regulatory mechanism most convenient to that actor, that is, a situation of structural advantage in which the actor can use the increased *atout* that the mechanism itself offers. Business generally prefers market regulation. This occurs more easily in the transaction of goods and service since each operator reacts according to an individual logic of maximization of its comparative advantage. When action is geared to the acquisition of factors of production (above all labor), business, in fact, finds itself operating in a context where politics, collective action, and organized interests prevail (Martinelli et al. 1981b). But even in this case political action constitutes a second choice. Business adopts this only when individual market-oriented action does not provide sufficient results, generally because of state intervention in the economy. Thus, even if they possess strong interest associations, business interests prefer to use them to modify the regulatory mix to favor the role of market rules, or of organizational hierarchies, or of clans.

One last aspect that merits further discussion, especially in light of related recent research, concerns the functions of internal regulation played by business associations vis-à-vis their associates. In confirmation of the hypothesis advanced by Offe and Wiesenthal (1980), business associations appear to exercise less control over the attitudes and behavior of their membership than do unions. Nonetheless, the structural characteristics of the different associative systems are capable of modifying in part these general rules, introducing more or less efficient mechanisms of control.

The most important characteristic of the associative structures of Italian business may be summarized as follows: (1) the importance, in terms of resources and membership, of territorial-based interest organizations; (2) the separation of interest representation between public and private firms, as a consequence of state interference in the associative system; (3) less functional differentiation between representation of economic interests and industrial relations concerns; and (4) less vertical integration of the associative system as an indication of the difficulties in unifying the interests of the various components of the economic leadership class.

Elsewhere we have discussed the internal organizational variables, and the factors inherent in the history and the structure of the Italian political system that produced them. Here we want to emphasize that these distinctive features of the associative system have contributed to the underdevelopment of neo-corporatist features in Italy, while not impeding forms of trilateral concertation.

Notes

1 One need only think of the strong historical impact the planning ideologies of the Left and the solidarism of catholicism had in Italy.

2 One need only remember the policies promoting localization, investment, and employment in the South.

3 The instruments adopted are those typical of organizational development, like divisionalization, incorporation, fusions, and joint ventures.

4 Think of the role of the Chinese overseas business communities or of mafia-like forms of economic organization, which constitute a sort of degeneration or extreme of this type.

5 Mutti (1986) recently described the weak formalization of the concept of trust. In this context, among the various definitions, we use the term trust as the expectation of cooperative behavior, within the theory of social exchange. It is important to note how trust becomes "an important savings factor in transaction costs in that it reduces the need for information, for control and for supervision" (Mutti 1986:8). In this sense trust is part of an alternative regulatory mechanism.

6 Even Streeck and Schmitter (1985) are uncertain whether or not to consider this a fourth type distinct from the other three of their typology.

7 The behavior of members of business associations appears, at first, counterintuitive to Olson's (1965) logic. An empirical analysis of certain associations (Chiesi 1985) shows how often large firms take initiatives that usurp the official functions of the collective organization of the sector. This behavior is obvious in the pursuit of individual advantages, more easily obtainable by large firms that can present themselves with authority before the unions and that possess sufficient economies of scale to support a lobbying structure or an autonomous technical-political apparatus during bargaining rounds. Smaller firms instead must lean on the associations for such services, which are provided as selective incentives.

Different is the discussion of public goods, for example, collective contracts. Here, according to Olson's well-known rule, in a context with many actors, smaller actors can obtain a relative advantage in reaching agreements outside of or even against the platform of the association (see, for example, the 1983 contract renewal in the textile sector [Guidotti 1986]), while larger actors, because of their greater political visibility, are constrained to follow in a more orthodox way the line of the association. On the other hand, the large actor is better able to influence the positions of the association. In sum, the logic of collective action of business interests appears more influenced by firm size than by the number of actors. This is especially true in the Italian case, which is characterized by the classic dualism between large and small firms, often reflected inside the associations.

8 See, for example, the Giustino Reform, which ran into difficulties because of the opposition of the territorial interest associations, traditionally preponderant in Italy.

9 As opposed to the economic functions that are less visible and difficult to evaluate, notwithstanding recent research on the subject. See Martinelli et al. (1985) and Mutti et al. (1986).

10 This discussion draws on an international research project directed by P. Schmitter and W. Streeck on the organization of business interests in several advanced industrial nations. The Italian part of this research, conducted by M. Baglioni, A. M. Chiesi, and M. Maraffi and coordinated by A. Martinelli, was funded by ASAP of Rome and the Ministry of Public Education (40 percent funding).

11 The 1984 constitution of *Federchimica* has given origin to an association of producers of petroleum derivatives, in potential competition with the *Unione Petrolifera*. The constitution of the association affiliated with *Federchimica* caused the passage of members from one organization to the other and the later mediation by *Confindustria*, which sanctioned a de facto specialization of the two associations: *Unione Petrolifera* is more oriented towards representing foreign multinationals, *Federchimica* closer to national producers (Chiesi 1985).

12 The associative universe is composed of nine associations, some of which have ample internal specialization (Maraffi 1985).

13 The textile-apparel sector is distinguished, in fact, by the highly localistic and homogeneous (mono-product) character of its industrial poles. In these areas the territorial associations serve a function of providing services for the firms.

14 The two associations present in the sector are UCIMU, which organizes producers of machine tools, and ACIMALL, which organizes wood-working firms (Baglioni 1986).

15 For more on the role of these committees, see Baglioni (1986:69).

16 In the credit sector, the state directly controls the majority of banks.

17 While others emphasize the heterogeneity of the state actor vis-à-vis the central bank (see Epstein and Schor in this volume [Chapter 7] and Addis [1987]), for simplicity in this chapter the various bodies of state regulation have been collapsed together.

18 For more on this see Chiesi (1982) and Stockman et al. (1985).

19 It is not important for our purposes to analyze the perverse effects this mechanism of undifferentiated indexation later brought about.

20 EUR is an area of Rome where the accord was reached.

21 Think of the deluding results of Law 675 of 1977.

Part IV

The welfare state

9

Public and private in the Italian welfare system

MASSIMO PACI

1. The continental European model of the welfare state

Only recently has the welfare policy of the Italian state become an object of study for sociologists and political scientists in Italy. In fact, for a long time this task was left to students of labor law and social insurance, who developed an interesting body of information, but who stuck to an analysis of the evolution of positive rights (law).

Thus, reflection upon the welfare state as an instrument of social and political regulation has – in Italy – just barely begun. It is also true, however, that this work has already passed that preliminary phase in which (as is usually the case when a new field of study develops) there is an enormous indebtedness to foreign literature, in terms of both models and research hypotheses. On the basis of studies and empirical research conducted in recent years, an analysis of the institutional characteristics of the Italian welfare state has begun, allowing us to describe with reasonable approximation the "historic form" of the latter and to place it within the typological framework offered by the comparative literature. In particular, a consensus emerges concerning the definition of the public system of welfare in Italy as a clientalistic variant of the "particularistic-meritocratic" model of the welfare state characteristic of continental European nations.[1]

The "particularistic-meritocratic" model is characterized on the institutional level by the fact that benefits are conferred primarily on the basis of the occupational status of the beneficiary. The distributive principles that inspire it are sectoral solidarity and a correspondence between care offered and work performed (or contributions paid). Thus, this model contrasts with the "universalistic-egalitarian" model (prevalent in the Northern European nations) in which benefits are distributed with respect to need, according to principles of equality and solidarity among all citizens. (Other differences regard systems of financing and distribution of services. In the "particularistic" model, financing is primarily contributive and services are constituted in large part by monetary transfers, while the "universalistic" model is financed though the generosity of the Treasury and the provision of services is clearly of greater importance.)[2]

In the scientific and academic debate, numerous factors have emerged enabling us to explain the different routes taken by the European nations. Many such factors date from the crucial period of the formation and consolidation of modern nation-states and from the era when the Industrial Revolution and the market began to threaten traditional society and its institutions of social insurance. Of particular importance in discussing the problem at hand, i.e., of the relationships between diverse systems of social regulation, are those analyses that have drawn attention to the persistence (in continental European countries in which the "particularistic" model of the welfare state became predominant) of traditional institutions, such as professional corporations or the Church, which have entered into a complementary relationship with new public forms of social security, while retaining ample space for autonomous control (Rimlinger 1971, 1982; Heidenheimer 1981; Marshall 1965).

Thus, it is easy to understand the reasons behind the low degree of state intervention and central control in the assistance sector in France during the last century as compared to England during the same period. Nineteenth-century French society displayed greater solidity and "togetherness" of community and family ties and lesser secularization, in part as consequences of a less tumultuous and altogether less prolonged exposure to the Industrial Revolution and the market. Analogously, in Germany, public intervention in the social security sector, while having great impact upon day-to-day reality, could remain, as compared to what happened in England, largely hidden, since it was mediated by strong traditional "intermediary" institutions (Heidenheimer 1981). In particular, while the traditional institutions of control over the market and labor (the guilds and corporations) could evolve in the Germany of Bismarck to the point of assuming a "semi-public" status in the administration of national security programs, nothing of the sort occurred in England. There the "friendly societies" transformed themselves rapidly into strictly associative organisms that lost any real regulative or administrative power at the time of the institution of national security programs (Paci 1982b).

The advent of the "particularistic-meritocratic" model of the welfare state in Germany, as elsewhere in continental Europe, thus occurs subsequent to, and in combination with, the role played by "intermediate" solidarities – confessionally or professionally based – and their interpenetration with forms of public regulation. As a result, a complex of institutional bodies develops that is fragmented, heterogeneous, decentralized, and characterized by administrative and financial autonomy, and in which sectoral organizations are recognized to have regulative authority over their own members. Thus, one witnesses the institution of "semi-public" entities and systems and the growth of a bureaucracy, traditionally prepared and efficient, that is distinct from that of the central apparatus of the State.

These historic characteristics of the welfare state in continental Europe must be taken into account in order to understand why, notwithstanding the "particularism" of its institutional structure, it remains inspired by criteria of impartiality and meritocracy in the distribution of social benefits. Indeed, it has been observed that "the continental type [of welfare state] . . . selects and fragments the concerns of the citizens based on their occupational status, and yet it tends nonetheless to distribute its own services following standard and unequivocal criteria, with impartial procedures which are very difficult to manipulate" (Ferrera 1984:272).

The public allocation of the resources of social security, in other words, is differentiated from the existing social and occupational inequalities, but it is not therefore less "certain" or "objective." The "particularism" of welfare institutions does not automatically involve the existence of discretionary power by the central administration, nor the dependence of beneficiaries on the favors of the political class. The existence of strong sectoral representation, with financial and administrative autonomy and with regulatory powers, reduces the risk of "slippage" from the "particularistic-meritocratic" type of welfare, to the "assistential-clientalistic" type, which instead characterizes the Italian situation.

2. The specifics of the Italian case

In order fully to understand the specifics of the Italian welfare system, one must go back to the roots of social legislation in Italy, to the crucial phase of its formation and the beginnings of the process of modernization, during which the principal characteristics of the social intervention of the state emerged. As I have shown elsewhere, all the premises existed for the evolution of the Italian system of public social insurance to forms similar to those followed by other European nations.[3] Traditional institutions, particularly those of religious origin, were strong in the assistance sector. The development of the Workers' Mutual Aid Societies (*Società operaie di mutuo soccorso*) from the remaining traces of the professional guilds (*corporazioni di mestiere*) was also extremely promising. This situation evolved only formally in the direction of the "particularistic-meritocratic" model of the welfare state typical of continental European nations. From this model, the Italian welfare state adopted only the features of institutional fragmentation and heterogeneity, not the relative financial and administrative autonomy – within the public regulative context – of the organizational entities that emerged from civil society. From this point of view, the Italian case presents itself clearly as one of "party government" (see Chapter 1) or, better yet, of an early hegemony of the political class over every instance of potential self-government in civil society. As I have already noted,

the "particularistic-clientalistic" expansion of social intervention by the state in our nation [Italy] has resulted in the exhaustion of local level initiative which was extensive throughout society, thus increasing demand for services from the public administration. This is part of a more general phenomenon of scarce autonomy of civil society from the state in our country, which has been described as "clientalistic dependence" and whose traits were evident since the first post-unitarian decades (Paci 1984, with relevant bibliography).

In this light, what happened to the *Opere Pie* and the Workers' Mutual Aid Societies, while in many ways quite different, appears emblematic. In both cases, state intervention was intended to direct these societal initiatives at assistance into legal channels and an administrative system highly susceptible to wide-ranging political controls (Paci 1984, with relevant bibliography).

With these premises, one can understand why, when the principles of obligatory insurance were spreading in Italy and the rest of Europe, the type of institutional solution that was chosen was the model of mutual funds which, behind the form of autonomous control, favored a substantial control (politico-clientalistic more than administrative) on the part of central authorities. The *Cassa Nazionale di Previdenza* for aged and infirm workers, approved in 1898, was characterized by its status as a state institution of popular insurance and by a formally autonomous board whose members, however, were (as it was said then) "morally dependent upon the government" (Merli 1972:349).

This basic character of social policy under the Italian state was congenial to the "transformism" of the historic Left that brought it into being. It would remain unaltered during the course of successive administrations. The acceleration in social legislation under Giolitti must clearly be seen as an attempt to politically integrate the working class of the North, thereby facilitating a definitive takeoff of national industry (Ascoli 1984:26). Analogously,

the impulse given by Fascism to the Mutual Funds, together with the dissolution of the Workers' Mutual Assistance Societies and the creation of the Enti

Nazionali Autarchici di Assistenza e Previdenza are signs of a similar strategy of political and social control. The State now restores relationships of politico-clientalistic connivance . . . between middle-level professionals, public bureaucrats and the party of the regime (Paci 1984:315).

From this point of view, Fascism favored the open display of the process, already under way, of confounding aims and functions of private insurance and social intervention by the State and cleared the way for the "upcoming total enmeshing of the national welfare apparatus in the logic of the developing system of parties and lobbies: this extreme politicization of the critical nodes of the welfare system came to represent from then on a stable 'difference' of the Italian case from the other western nations" (Ascoli 1984:29).

On the whole, one could say that the welfare system of the Italian Republic as inherited from Fascism was already clearly characterized by two general principles that we may respectively call "corporative-guarantistic" and "clientalistic-assistential." The former expressed itself in the primacy of professional solidarities based on private insurance, which, once inserted into the public code (specifically the Fascist corporative one), assumed "guarantistical" institutional characteristics. The latter manifested itself primarily in assistential programs left to the political and administrative discretion of the public authorities, thus leading to the clientalistic dependence of the beneficiaries. As I have observed elsewhere,

these two logics are not, in themselves, contradictory. Instead, they have the same common tendencies toward expansion of the public role, through the creation of regimes, bodies, and institutions aimed at satisfying jointly the sectoral needs of groups and categories, and the interest of the political class in maintaining stable consensus, leaving intact, in the meantime, the structure of inequalities inherited from the market (Paci 1985:153).

The evolution of Italy's public welfare system since World War II did not substantially alter this state of affairs. Favored also by the relative disinterest of the workers' movement in insurance legislation (which was not considered by them to be connected to the problem of unemployment), the centrist postwar governments were quick to thwart any attempt at reform in this arena, notwithstanding the innovative, if formal principles expressed in the Constitution (Paci 1985). Thus, we can describe the postwar development of the welfare system as an incremental process through which the petitions advanced by the most diverse of groups have obtained institutional recognition with the creation of diversified public or "para-public" entities and regimes. In this way, an expansion in the public sector, through the incorporation of "private blocks," occurred. In the last forty years, attempts to introduce changes inspired by principles of equality into the Italian system of social welfare institutions have been extremely rare. Mandatory schooling, "social bracket" pensions, the national health service, etc., were all attempts that were subsequently contradicted in their implementation and management (Ascoli 1984).

These are some of the historic and institutional characteristics of the Italian welfare state. As has been said before, what sets Italy apart from other European nations is not so much the "particularism" of programs and their management (even though, at the level of values, a greater dose of "universalism" in Italian social policies would certainly be preferable). Rather, it is the extensive clientalistic character that the provision of services has taken on, in both its "corporate" and its "assistance" components. As Ferrera (1984:271–2) concludes: "In no other context (even in those characterized by high institutional fragmentation between schemes and programs) can such a particularistic variety of distribution and benefits be seen. . . . The party-clientalistic manipulation of insurance services is a phenomenon virtually unique to our nation."

3. The regulative area left to the private sector

The study of social policies that has developed in Italy in recent years has clarified, therefore, some of the basic modalities of the welfare state in Italy. Still, this has remained primarily within the boundaries of the public regulation of welfare. The scientific debate has assumed public regulation to be the problem (most likely pushed in this direction by the urgency and political weight of the problem of public spending).

This has led to an underappreciation of the role and importance of certain areas of the private regulation of welfare in Italy, which appear to lack any coordination with the forms of public regulation. In truth, the idea that in Italy today there exists a cumbersome and all pervading welfare state that has disproportionately compressed private initiative and the market does not correspond with reality. If it is the case that with the passage of time an overextended public insurance system and certain major social services (especially in the areas of health and education) have been instituted, it is also true that important gaps in the Italian system of social protection exist. In the housing and assistance sectors, for example, Italy lags far behind other European nations. In particular, there exists a vast private area that has been resistant to any intervention of social policy.

I am referring essentially to three areas: tax evasion or elusiveness, the underground economy and "black" (undeclared) labor (moonlighting), and private and family assistance. Italy has lacked not only a comprehensive reform of these three areas, as well as many others, but also simple intervention to order and rationalize them. Instead, there has been a chaotic flow of legislation that has embodied substantial inequalities and, above all, left enormous loopholes that have proved impervious to any state intervention to a degree unknown in any other major western countries.

I will not now discuss the institutional characteristics of the Italian tax system, which also are emblematic of the space left to the "private." I would like, however, to recall certain figures, in order to give some sense of the enormous dimensions of tax evasion. A conservative estimate would put the sum at around 50 billion lire annually, that is to say, about one-half the national budget deficit. The newspapers have unrealistic statistics on the declarations of IRPEF (Personal Income Tax) and the IVA (Value Added Tax) for a series of sectors, among which professionals and shopkeepers figure prominently. The same could be said of IRPEG (Corporate Income Tax): 50 percent of the S.p.A. (corporations) and S.r.l. (limited companies) and entities subject to the IRPEG declare a loss or near-loss and thus do not pay taxes. That loss, in addition, can be subtracted from taxable income the following year. The result of this massive form of evasion is that 60 to 70 percent of the State's tax income comes from wage labor (Tremonti and Vitaletti 1986).

Another area worthy of discussion is the jungle of tax deductions. The greater part of these are to the advantage of the middle and upper brackets as well as businesses and firms. It is well known that businesses, especially investment firms, have many ways of avoiding taxation. But consider as well the various allowable deductions that may be taken off taxable income: passive interest of money loans on mortgages, premiums on life insurance, taxes for higher education, and specialized medical visits in Italy and abroad. Certainly, the middle and lower income brackets are not the most likely to benefit from such tax breaks.[4]

More generally, the space left to the "private" in Italy is manifested in scarce or nonexistent laws concerning inheritances, capital gains, reinvested profits, bonds and financial rents, and stock market earnings.[5]

Another vast area of private autonomy, also arising from omissions and loopholes in public regulation, is that of "black labor" *(lavoro nero)* and the hidden economy, about which entire volumes have already been written. ISTAT (the Central Statistics Bureau) has estimated the underground economy in Italy at about 15 percent of the gross national product. As a matter of fact, the figure is probably greater and shows no sign of decreasing. We are witnessing a boom in small-scale business and self-employment (in particular in the service sector), which are a fertile ground for the continued growth of the hidden economy. A recent survey by *Confcommercio* (Confederation of Commercial Businesses) of so-called "clandestine" businesses estimates an equivalent of 45 billion lire in turnover from clandestine commercial firms. There are millions of individuals involved in some sort of moonlighting. Some recent studies on the subject, for example, demonstrate that this varies between 10 and 15 percent of the workforce in different sectors and areas of Italy (Gallino 1985). From this perspective, it might be said that there is ample room in Italy for "*ante-litteram* deregulation" of the labor market.

Naturally, moonlighting means "hidden tax revenue." This is a considerable sum, although not as high as that previously mentioned for tax evasion. I will mention only one survey conducted by the National Institute for Social Security (INPS) showing that 40 percent of the businesses surveyed had irregularities in their (benefit) contribution payments (45 percent of these had completely abused the law) (*Previdenza Sociale*, Official Journal of the INPS, 1982:511–15).

A third area in which the state has done little is that of assistance. This has constituted a traditional "sanctuary of the private sector" left to the family and religious and charitable institutions (David 1984, 1985). The Italian state has clearly opted for a policy of assistential transfers to families, rather than a policy of social services distributed throughout the country. To be sure, during the course of the 1970s, following strong social mobilization (in which women were leading players), this situation was partially modified as a result of the initiatives taken by the local authorities in different parts of the country. But the demand for social services (day care, consultation, visiting services for the elderly, etc.) has not been satisfied. Even where a network of basic services has been set up, they continue to be questioned. The general reform in this sector, as promised by Law 616 of 1977, was never implemented. The transferral of IPAB (*Instituti di Pubblica Assistenza e Beneficienza*) to the regions was prevented by the Supreme Court (*Corte Costituzionale*).

The health reform has remained a dead issue, especially with respect to the integration of social and health areas. Indeed, the Local Health Boards (*Unità Sanitarie Locali*) have not been allowed to finance assistance other than hospitalization through the National Health fund. The situation, moreover, is bound to get worse given the enactment of recent budget laws that cut the budgets of local governments. Therefore, in Italy the family remains to a great extent the institution upon which assistance depends.

On the whole, all the phenomena just mentioned are deeply inter-twined, and the discussion of any one of them would inevitably lead to the discussion of others such as family, off-the-books labor, hidden economy, fiscal evasion, etc. These make up a sort of "firm foundation" upon which the private sector may build, which state regulation cannot or will not penetrate. Such a "foundation" has grown in recent years into a sort of specific culture, to which we might apply a phrase coined by Banfield (1958) many years ago with reference only to the South: "amoral familism." In effect, a most "particular" culture that legiti-mizes the pursuit of family interests to the point of illegality has spread throughout a rather broad social stratum in Italy.

4. Dualism in the Italian welfare system

The presence of a public sector left entirely to private regulation along-side a formal public welfare sector underscores the "dualistic" charac-ter of the entire Italian system. This conclusion can be reached through an analysis of labor and social security policies (Paci 1982a; Regalia 1984) as well as from an analysis of fiscal and contributions patterns (Pedone 1979; Ferrera 1984).

If we look, for example, at the development of social security policies (in particular, those regarding pensions) or even at the labor policies of the 1950s and 1960s, traits of a dualistic system clearly emerge. "Guar-antistic" regimes were, in fact, introduced for the protection of specific categories of workers (with strong built-in corporate inequalities), while a large part of the active population was either deprived of pro-tection or left with partial or insufficient protection. The result is a sys-tem in which the principal differences exist between the public sector and large private businesses, on the one side, and small businesses and the self-employed on the other. These are further subdivided along gender and generational differences, and between "strong" and "weak" suppliers of labor. In substance, public regulation mainly offers privileged protection to those interests represented by strong organi-zations or directly by the state.

The conceptual duality "excluded/guaranteed," which developed in relation to the evolution of such welfare policies and of the job market, does not fully take into account the institutional characteristics assumed by the Italian welfare state. Parallel to the "guarantistic-cor-porative" tendency of state intervention, in fact, several counterten-dencies have developed over this same period. In fiscal policy, for example, notwithstanding the official attempt to introduce more pro-gressive forms of taxation, public and private employees continue to bear growing tax burdens, while the small businesses of the underground economy, together with a wide stratum of self-employed work-ers and professionals, continue to enjoy generous degrees of fiscal "freedom." In this regard, it should be remembered that the financing of many Italian welfare programs through the National Health System (SSN) is of a contributive and not fiscal nature and bears down with great force on these productive sectors of the population and in partic-ular on wage laborers.[6] In addition, numerous transfers of a substan-tially assistential nature, often masquerading as a pseudo-agrarian (Becchi Collidà 1978; Boccella 1982) or insurance policy (Paci 1987), were made in the 1950s and 1960s to those same subjects who already benefited from the fiscal policies just described.

That this policy of "assistential" transfers is a strategic choice becomes clear in several ways. Indeed, this has represented an alter-native to the provision of public social services offered to all citizens. It has signified an option in favor of the family and the "private," with particular reference to the self-employed. In the second place, it has favored the expansion of micro-businesses and the "underground" economy, which rely on a strong family, and has provided incentives for non-institutionalized forms of labor and the related phenomenon of evasion of taxes and social security contributions. Finally, this has brought about a substantial redistribution of income from the area of institutionalized wage laborers to that of the self-employed and the non-institutionalized. The "assistential" transfers in question, in fact, have been financed to a great extent by contributive means, that is, through the tax contributions paid to INPS by the productive, above-ground categories (wage laborers and businesses).[7]

Thus, the conceptual dichotomy "guaranteed vs. excluded" must be integrated with that of "contributor vs. evaders-assisted." If the 1950s and 1960s, together with the transition to a fully industrial society, have brought with them the emergence of a "guaranteed" social area, notwithstanding the strong "corporative" inequalities within it, then the 1970s and 1980s have demonstrated ever more clearly the exis-tence of "the other side of the coin." On one hand, in fact, the greatest burden for the financing of the welfare budget rests on the "guaran-teed-corporative" area. On the other hand, the area of those excluded from guarantees appears to be an extremely dynamic one, at the center of which are social groups and categories that grow by taking advan-tage of tax evasion and assistential transfers (if not actually through activities connected, directly or indirectly, with organized crime).

The crisis in the "guaranteed-corporative" area, the direct object of public welfare regulation, has emerged by means of processes of ero-sion and "back-sliding," under the weight of the underground econ-omy and those "evasion-assisted" categories. In particular, the onus of fiscal and contributive pressures on dependent employees and businesses has progressively promoted tendencies to try to "escape" to the area of private regulation. This is how we are to understand the phenomena, ever more evident in the 1970s, of subcontracting from the large firms to micro-firms, of the growing supply of non-institutional "moonlighting" by public and private employees, and of the search for tax loopholes on the part of businesses, often in silent agreement with the labor unions (Regonini 1984).

In sum, if the analysis just presented corresponds to reality, we can say that to understand the specific "historic form" of the Italian welfare state it is not enough to outline the characteristics of the "particularistic-clientalistic" system. It is also important to know that along with the "guarantistic-corporative" component, which is the most direct expression of public intervention and on which most studies of this problem have until now focused, there exists a "privatistic-assistential" area – which can only be expected to assume a growing role – characterized by the absence of direct state intervention or by an indirect intervention intended to maintain the conditions for private regulation in this field.

5. From complementarity to crisis in the relationship between public and private

In spite of its dualistic nature, the system just described more or less functioned for many years. Apart from the social crisis in the years following 1968 and the "battle for reforms" that characterized it, Italian society does not seem to have felt the need for more unified and rational public intervention in the welfare field. Until the beginning of the 1980s, the two "spirits" of our welfare system, the "guarantistic-corporative" and the "private-assistential," were able to coexist without contradiction.

At the micro-social level, families found the existence of such a dualistic welfare system convenient. In time, a sort of "division of labor" developed between public and private in this area, and found acceptance among families (as long as certain basic conditions remained unchanged). True, the state did not offer extended and efficient social services to families, but this in a certain sense was "reciprocated" by the job possibilities offered to the head of the family through the clientalistic route within the "guaranteed-corporative" area. It is true that schools and hospitals do not function well, but it is also true that these institutions provide "secure" salaries to employed personnel, without examining the finer points of their professional competence. Analogously, it is true that welfare services offered by the state are inadequate, but it is also true that the state looks the other way regarding tax evasion, illegal construction practices, and off-the-books labor.

At the sociocultural level, the existence of a regulative double-standard – in which the state, with its institutional network of occupational and insurance guarantees, is juxtaposed against the world of the hidden economy, of fiscal evasion, and of private assistance – was not seen as a contradiction by the generations of the 1960s and 1970s. The "culture of the workplace" that dominated the world of institutional labor was impregnated by "particularistic" or "corporative" values, which were, in turn, congruent with the privatistic and familiaristic orientations prevalent in the world of the underground economy, assistential subsidies, and fiscal evasion. From this point of view, a welfare state worthy of its name (as a cultural achievement more than as an institutional program) has never existed in Italy. The "culture of welfare citizenship," with its values of equality and solidarity among all its citizens, is still an experience to be achieved.

This dualistic system of welfare and the complementarity between public and private have grown from certain basic conditions that today are fading. The policy of assistential transfers, for example, was a real alternative to the public provision of social services only in the presence of the traditional family, with its network of parental assistance, its division of roles by gender, the "service labor" of women, and, often, its agricultural subsistence base. Only in these conditions (insofar as they were a useful complement to the resource of social protection already provided by the family) could the monetary transfers of the state play a role. The same might be said for the opportunities of black/undeclared labor.

A second fundamental condition that sustained the financial features of the system until the 1970s was the expansion of institutionalized wage labor, upon which, as has been said, the burden of the fiscal and contributive payments to the state weighed the heaviest. Only the growth of wage labor in industry and the public sector allowed such a system of social benefits to go on for so long, on the basis of this partial and discriminatory mode of financing.

The third basic condition has been the possibility of obscuring the extent and selective nature of fiscal contributive payments. Recourse to the wage laborers' Pension Fund (*Fondo Pensioni Lavoratori Dipendenti*) of the INPS (National Institute for Social Security), for example, to finance all sorts of assistential programs has never occurred in a way that was clearly perceptible to those directly concerned (Trentin 1986). Besides, in order to compensate for tax evasion and the subsequent difficulty in financing social services, the state has increasingly sought refuge in borrowing. Therefore, the scarce visibility of financing through hidden and increasing debt has constituted an increasingly important factor in the maintenance of the system (Ferrera 1984:248).

These "prerequisites" of this "Italian-style" welfare state are, however, fading today. The family is, indeed, undergoing radical cultural and demographic changes. The women's movement is certainly not spent, even if it is no longer the source of the kinds of visible results of the successful mass movement of the 1960s and 1970s (equal pay, new family rights, divorce, abortion, etc.). It remains one of the great cultural revolutions of our time, whose traces are clear today in the behavior of contemporary women. Recent surveys (including the official findings by the *Istituto Centrale della Statistica*) show a rapid spread in the 1980s of a more modern family model, characterized by the loss of the "extended family," falling birthrates, the concentration of births in a narrower maternal age bracket, and, above all, a much larger and steadier supply of female labor than before, in spite of a competitive and difficult job market and the high rates of female unemployment. Under these new conditions, it is obvious that the policy of monetary transfers to families (as supported by forms of private assistance) is no longer valid and that what is needed is a policy of available and efficient welfare services across the nation, which the Italian state has neither wanted nor known how to offer.

Moreover, the second basic condition upon which the national insurance-assistance apparatus is built is less common today: the occupational base (fiscal and contributory) of employed labor is, in fact, progressively and sharply diminishing. On one hand, unemployment has grown dramatically, and now seems to have stabilized at two-digit levels. On the other hand, the prospects of autonomous labor and small businesses (the micro-businesses) continue to grow. Today, more than 30 percent of the Italian population active in the labor market consists of autonomous labor and their assistants. (This percentage does not include off-the-books labor and the micro-businesses of the underground economy, which are always in significant expansion.) It is true that this corresponds to a related structural process involving the so-called information and electronic technological revolution and the advent of micro-organizational structures in services and new independent professions. The fact remains that while the number of citizens destined to avail themselves of social services is rising, the number of those who finance it – should the existing mechanisms of fiscal and contributive funding remain what they are – is diminishing.

The relative decline of the fiscal and contributive base of employed labor is occurring, in other words, while public expenditure is growing steeply. (This appears, in substance, in the form of ever-growing interest paid on the state's debt.) This has brought to light, at the level of public opinion, a "perverse" circuit of financing (INPS payments and public borrowing) that had remained largely hidden until a few years ago. INPS (which bore a particularly heavy part of the burden of the costs of this "assistential" policy) is experiencing very serious budgetary problems. The question of the relationship between insurance in the narrow sense and "assistential" transfers from the INPS budget has thus become an important political issue of which Parliament and the mass media have become well aware.

Also, the integration of the system at the micro-social level is decreasing. The "silent agreement," which existed between "guaranteed" and "evaders" and which affected many Italian families, is in crisis. What is now emerging is an awareness on the part of certain social categories (wage laborers, in particular) that they contributed for years to the fiscal and insurance well-being of the other brackets (those of the self-employed and independent professionals). The unwillingness of these latter groups to "continue to play the game," expressed through their refusal or resistance to cooperate in explicit forms of fiscal and insurance solidarity (such as financing reforms) requested by the government, also illustrates the erosion of this micro-social logic.[8]

Symptomatic of this situation is the unitary document approved by the three metalworkers' unions in the autumn of 1986. In reference to the law on the national budget, the unions sought (among other essential requests of the moment)

... Definite measures of fiscal reform aimed at establishing conditions of equity by increasing the contributions of totally or partially exempt incomes; concrete reductions in the totality of fiscal and contributive deductions from salaries on which the burden has unfairly fallen in the past; reduction in the "per time" costs for medical analyses, especially for those with low incomes; implementation of an equitable reform of the pension system, after years of delay, which have made the situation in the insurance sector unbearable (META 1986:24).

Surely, it seems that the balance between the two different components of the welfare system has been upset: the relationships between "guaranteed" labor and underground economy, between "corporative" insurance and fiscal evasion, between contributive and assistential systems are no longer complementary but instead in contradiction. The critical threshold in the relationship between private and public regulation beyond which elements of inequality and social tension become predominant has probably been surpassed. It is for these reasons that Italian governments today find themselves faced with difficult choices that imply comprehensive rationalization and reform within the entire sector.

6. The current direction of welfare policy

The current "neo-liberalist" orientation in social welfare reform promoted by the parties of the government over the last two or three years, especially through the budget laws, needs to be evaluated on the basis of the problems and contradictions described above.[9] This orientation has had its most explicit formulation in the so-called "Goria draft," a text with which the then Minister of the Treasury (and, subsequently, Prime Minister) intended to outline the general principles of the 1986 Budget. This text (partially reproduced, afterwards, in the document prepared by the Minister of the Treasury for the 1987–1989 budget planning process) presented an image of a major compression of the private sector by the Italian welfare state and affirmed that

... social protection should be concentrated in an effective way upon those who truly have need for it and not over such a vast range as to render the entire system extremely costly and the protection of the individual irrelevant; ... the funding for many public services for individual needs should be reduced and the same services be paid for in proportion to their cost in such a way as to measure their efficiency, even by the consumer (Minister of the Treasury 1986:55).

In effect, the measures adopted by the 1986 Budget Law tried (even with many contradictions) to apply such a line. The first part of budget maneuvering was aimed at compressing the demand for public services by means of an increase in their cost to the user. On one hand, scholastic taxes and the tariffs on centrally offered public services (such as transportation and the postal and telephone systems) were raised, which, in turn, forced many local services to do the same because of the reduction of state allocations to them. Nor should it be forgotten, in this context, that a new "tax on services" was introduced on the community level in 1987. On the other hand, the exemptions on health-care vouchers were reduced, with drastic outcomes for a great number of the aged and infirm. (Only after an actual threat of a general strike by the unions was a partial retraction enacted.)

A second part of this "neo-liberal" maneuver in social welfare policy consisted of the creation of space for the expansion of the private sector of services and insurance. For example, the "tax on health," introduced by the Budget Law of 1986, instituted the principle of "regressive contributions" so that the people with the most wealth would have an incentive to pay for their own private health plans. Such a principle has significantly shaped the pension reform plan presented by the government (a correction of the plan developed by the special committee created by Parliament). This project proposes to progressively "freeze" the ceilings on pensions and to introduce a "contributive ceiling" in order to create wide margins for the expansion of private integrative insurance, which would also be favored by the sensible removal of the cost of insurance premiums from taxable income.

A third aspect of the modification of welfare policy, guided by recent financial laws, introduces selective measures of social services, contingent upon a monitoring of the beneficiary's income. The document presented by the Ministry of the Treasury aimed at modifying the 1987–1989 budget states: "of great importance in this discourse is certainly the moment of the selection of who is to benefit . . . as far as conditions of need are concerned" (Minister of the Treasury 1986:81).

The government has already introduced a series of measures aimed at subordinating the provision of welfare services to a monitoring of the beneficiary's income. This was the case for social pensions and, more recently, for family support checks and invalid pensions. Now this strategy – defined by "social brackets" – is to be used as a general directive, in such a way as to include, according to this document, health services and old age pensions.[10]

More generally, the government appears unable (above all because of internal divisions) to implement any real measure of rationalization or reform in the fiscal or contributive sector: recent efforts aimed at self-employed incomes and investment earning have been partial or ineffective. Furthermore, with respect to employment, there is an absence of an economic policy capable of appreciably bolstering dependent employment (aside from the general indications contained in the "Ten Year Plan" presented by the Minister of Labor in 1985). Instead, a policy has been proposed that favors – as an ideological premise more than an economic one – the micro-entrepreneurship (individual or associated) of youths looking for work. Thus, the absence of a fiscal reform policy aimed at reducing evasion, combined with the tendency towards labor policies that provide incentives for forms of micro-enterprises and self-employment that largely evade the monitoring of earnings, certainly does not seem consistent with the need to increase the fiscal "take" of the state.

In summing up, we find ourselves facing a twofold strategy. On the one hand, it affirms, if not increases, the situation of fiscal and contributive latitude of the middle and upper brackets by steering their incomes toward the private sector of services and insurance (a reasonable objective when tariffs of public services are increased without providing better services). On the other hand, there is a tendency to create a social fracture between the greater part of dependent workers, who principally bear the largest fiscal and contributive burden, and the relatively limited stratum of the needy and assisted, who today benefit from the free distribution of social services that were previously offered to all citizens.

In reality, the government has not developed a set of social policy principles as such; what emerges under the encouragement of the Minister of the Treasury is an "accountant's" line, exclusively inspired by the need to cut public spending in the larger context of the heavy national budget deficit. This basic design has forced an acceptance of a "neo-liberal" philosophy of welfare politics, in tune with certain trends observed in other nations. Thus, in the years 1982–6, a series of measures were undertaken to reduce the scope of public regulation of welfare and to enlarge (as has already been seen) that of private regulation. We can, therefore, speak, on the whole, of "slippage" in the Italian welfare system towards a "residual" model of the social state.[11]

Yet, it will be difficult to succeed in resolving the actual problems with such a strategy since it, in fact, seems more likely to aggravate than reduce the antinomies and contradictions that afflict the Italian welfare system. Certainly, the revamping of forms of private assistance, together with the maintenance of current fiscal and contributive "sanctuaries," will allow those in the middle and upper income brackets to reinforce, to their own advantage, the already conspicuous margins of private regulative autonomy. This will not occur, however, for the middle and lower strata, and especially for the mass of dependent workers. The fiscal and contributive pressures that weigh on them will remain more or less unchanged.[12] Furthermore, these brackets will find available fewer of a series of supports and free welfare services, which from now on will be reserved only for the "needy." Nor will they have access to the costlier private substitutes offered by the market. And this will occur while certain types of family structures and local communities, which previously provided "internal economies" of social protection, are in dissolution and thus will prove less supportive.

What is emerging appears to be an operation of drastic redistribution of income and of "life chances" to the detriment of the middle and lower classes of our society. This could set off, even in Italy, the phenomenon of welfare backlash where the guilty finger is pointed not so much at the state and its social policies as at the stratum of the "needy," towards which the public "assistential" transfers are more visibly directed.

Notes

1 As is known, we owe the definition of the "particularistic-meritocratic" model of the welfare state, as well as the other models to be cited later, to Richard Titmuss. In such a model, "the welfare institutions play an important role as a complement to the market economy and social needs are satisfied according to merit, work performed and productivity" (Titmuss 1974:18–19).

Various authors have contributed to the definition of the Italian welfare state as a "clientalistic" variant of the "particularistic model": Esping-Andersen (1982a), Paci 1982a, 1984), Ascoli (1984), and Ferrera (1984).

The reference to such models of welfare states is made with the understanding that they are preliminary conceptual constructs, with a limited heuristic capacity. Besides, it is true that in the last twenty years there has been a process of progressive convergence among European social welfare states that has reduced the "salience" of the models developed by Titmuss (Flora and Heidenheimer 1981).

2 The model of the "universalistic" welfare state, or even that of the "institutional-redistributive," according to Titmuss, "sees welfare as a prioritized institution integrated into society, aimed at providing universalistic services outside of the market, in conformity with the principle of pure need" (Titmuss 1974:19).

3 For a deeper understanding, refer to the paragraph "The historic roots of the Italian welfare system" (Paci 1984:315–16).

4 The integrative pension insurance seems destined to become a part of this jungle of fiscal facilitations, as the projects under discussion in Parliament would make use of a generous defiscalization.

5 In this situation, the provision made regarding the BOT (treasury bills) coupons appear to be a drop in the ocean, and will not modify the weakened situation of public regulation in this sector of fiscal policy.

6 The relationship between contributions and taxes in financing the welfare state is a good indicator of the relationships between the historically existent classes in a given country. As Philip Abrams has written with reference to England: "They are the relationships of power that explain why, in the end, we have found ourselves with a system of social security based upon fixed contribution and not a direct taxation proportional to income, or rather, with a system that imposes a comparatively greater rate on categories of lower income" (Abrams 1983:34). In this regard, it is interesing to compare Italy with England: the two countries have roughly the same percentage of total revenue of the state on the gross national product (45.5 percent for Italy, 44.9 percent for England), but welfare contributions amount, again as a percentage of GNP, to 8.2 percent in England and 16.2 percent in Italy (Visco 1986:105). The considerations of Abrams, therefore, are somewhat valid for Italy too.

7 We refer here, above all, to "one-way solidarity" (Regonini 1984:96) between the preventional management of dependent workers and those of farmers, artisans, and shopkeepers.

8 Think of the opposition stimulated by the provisions aimed at increasing the fiscal and contributive pressure on the self-employed and free-lance workers for the rechanneling of their preventional management into the general regime.

9 On this point I refer to some of my recent writings: Paci 1986a, 1986b, 1986c).

10 Among the "perverse effects" of the system of "social brackets" is that of providing an ulterior incentive for the already strong tendency of certain groups to underdeclare income: in fact, one may add to the fiscal advantages of this practice that of better access to social services (Paci 1986b).

11 According to Titmuss, the model of the "residual" welfare state is ". . . based on the premise that the private market and the family are two 'natural' or 'socially given' channels through which the individual normally satisfies his needs and that, only when these two fail, public institutions must intervene, but only temporarily" (Titmuss 1974:18).

12 It should be noted that the recent measures against fiscal drag undertaken to ease their situation actually leave the structural inequalities of the welfare system intact.

10

Public intervention and health policy: an analysis of tendencies in progress

ELENA GRANAGLIA

At the end of 1978, when most OECD (Organization for Economic Cooperation and Development) nations had already begun openly denouncing the dilemmas facing the welfare state, the Italian Parliament initiated one of the most radical possible measures within the framework of traditional social reform. Apparently in tune with the "universalistic" model of Titmuss (1974), Parliament passed Law 833 creating a National Health System (SSN for *Sistema Sanitaria Nazionale*) that sought to guarantee equality to all citizens with regard to health needs.

As stated in Article 1 of the law, "the SSN comprises the complex of functions, structures, services, and activities for the promotion, maintenance, and recovery of physical and mental health for the entire population without distinction of individual or social conditions and according to norms that assure the equality of citizens in terms of service."

The event might seem somewhat peculiar given the attacks on egalitarianism simultaneously occurring in other nations. Yet, it is not the authoritative enactment of strong social rights that is astonishing, but instead the total faith placed by Law 833 in the public system.

A new awareness of the limits of state intervention was developing in other nations. At the same time, in Italy, planning-programming and operational responsibilities were respectively delegated to Parliament, Regional Councils, Communities, and Local Health Districts (USL for *Unità Sanitaria Locali*) supported by politically appointed Administrative Committees. Meanwhile, hospitals, clinics, and all remaining publicly run diagnostic and treatment centers became technical branches of the USL. Doctors were removed from the more administrative aspects of health care. In other words, the entire health-care service became the responsibility of the political-administrative apparatus.

In 1986, after seven years, the SSN, with funds of over 40,000 billion

235

lire, remains the framework for the distribution of health service. Hence, one might well ask whether Italy represents a case of the crisis of the welfare state or an isolated bulwark of dedication to the public good in an international context where the state seems increasingly to limit its duties to the provision of minimal security. This is the central question that I seek to address in the following pages.[1]

1. Boundaries between "public" and "private" in the health sector from the origins of the SSN to the present

In contradiction to what is often thought, any implementation process can significantly alter the legislative measures undertaken by decision-making bodies. This can occur in several ways: through operational decisions that are insufficient to carry out the legislative norms or even contrary to them, through administrative delays, or even through mere apathy and indifference in the performance of prescribed duties.

Thus, in order to answer the question posed above, one must take a closer look at the actual or presumed interventions of health-care policies in Italy, from the beginning of the SSN to today. The aim is to verify whether or not such measures have altered the boundaries between public and private assistance.

Synthetically, implementation of the post-reform health care system can be divided into three stages. The first introduced forms of private sharing of health expenses, thanks largely to the establishment of the fee system. The second attempted to contain budget expenses. The third, of most recent origin, sought to improve the actual management of organizational-operational procedures.

The fee system (Tickets) first appeared with the enactment of Law 833. On this first occasion, a contribution for all citizens was set at 1,000 lire per prescription, except for those medicines exempt by law. Social pension holders, however, paid only a refundable deduction of 10,000 lire. In 1981, the fees were increased to a maximum of 3,000 lire per prescription. Moreover, the exemption from payment was extended to all citizens with a yearly net income of less than 4 million lire, or of 6 million lire in the case of retired or dependent workers. In the case of family units, an exemption of 500,000 lire could be added per dependent individual. The disabled were likewise granted an exemption. In 1982, charges for fees covering instrumental and laboratory tests were set at 15 percent of cost, but they could not exceed 15,000 lire per medical visit and 40,000 lire for the sum total of the treatment. Included with all this were the same exemptions as those for medication.

In 1983, the entire system was restructured to guarantee free distribution of a determined group of medicines, in order better to take into account various health risks. For a second group of medicines, composed essentially of antibiotics, payment was fixed at 1,000 lire per prescription. For a third group, there was a fixed contribution of 1,000 lire per prescription as well as 15 percent of the fee. This system was adopted in order to avoid crossover transfers of differently valued fees. Similarly, the maximum possible charge was increased to 20,000 lire per visit for diagnostic services and 50,000 lire per treatment.

The exemption was likewise increased for those with an income of up to 4.5 million lire. The following year, retired and dependent employees were exempted from all charges if they had an income of less than 9 million lire. Also, the group of prescriptions exempted from charges was enlarged. In 1985, fee charges rose to 1,300 lire per prescription. With the budget law of 1986, there was yet another increase for both medications and diagnostic services, to 2,000 lire per prescription and to 20 percent of the cost of the treatment. For diagnostic services, the maximum was raised to 30,000 lire per visit and 60,000 lire per treatment. The exemption based on health needs did not change, while those relative to income were modified. In fact, exemptions were allowed only to nuclear families with an income of up to 5 million lire, or up to 19 million lire for families with more than seven members.[2] For those over sixty years of age, such limits were increased by 20 percent. Besides this, fees were also applied to specialized services.

The declared objective of these measures was to save the National Health Fund (FSN for *Fondo Sanitario Nazionale*) about 2,500 billion lire, that is, about 15 percent of the total estimated budget. Yet, in order to achieve such savings, it would seem necessary to combat the high levels of evasion of fees and of health-care overconsumption. Let us examine, for instance, the case of medications. A 1985 study (Ministry of Health 1985) shows that in the regions of Veneto, Emilia, and Marche, there were, respectively, 4.5, 3, and 6 times as many families benefiting from exemption of fees as were entitled. As for overconsumption, the same report shows that, for example, in Bolzano, citizens exempt from fees represented roughly 3 percent of the total population but consumed at least 23 percent of total prescriptions in the area. In Calabria, those exempt were about 19 percent of the total population and actually consumed 60.4 percent of the total prescriptions. As a result, in 1984, the distribution of pharmaceutical fees represented less than 1 percent of the FSN, against a pharmaceutical expenditure of 13 to 14 percent of the FSN. In such a situation, it is obvious that the restrictive budget-oriented norms do not have a serious prospect for success.

Political measures controlling financial interventions of the post-reform period can be summarized briefly. On the one hand, there was an attempt to contain expenditures by limiting appropriations for the

FSN, hoping in this way to provide incentives for more prudent financial behavior. In reality, setting excessively low limits has had the opposite effect, i.e., that of inducing carefree spending habits, given the confidence of local administrators that hoped-for revisions in the budget would resolve the problem of possible deficits. This has consistently occurred.[3] On the other hand, a series of eligibility controls was imposed on the USL (France 1985). For instance, the institution of the *Collegio dei Revisori di Conti*, an accounting review board, was made part of the USL. Similarly, a sanitary and financial regional inspection service was constituted, and regions were granted deputy authority over USL units with budget deficits. Regions, moreover, have to pay penalties when USL units under their control do not present quarterly reports on time. Other measures taken included the institution of regional control committees and the attribution to the region of responsibility for maintaining a balanced budget, even if this meant imposing local taxes. This last norm, however, was later judged unconstitutional. As a result of such measures, the USL today is formally under eleven different controls. Nevertheless, there continue to be high degrees of inefficiency in the entire system.

The tax burden has also been continually increasing, especially for self-employed workers. In fact, the fixed tax for artisans and shopkeepers rose from 100,000 lire to about 300,000 lire between 1980 and 1984, and the variable tax from 1.5 percent to 4 percent of taxable income. Similarly, for professionals, the increases were from 125,000 lire to 300,000 lire and from 2 percent to 4 percent of taxable income. The ceilings for taxable incomes have since been abolished.

Since 1986, according to the budget laws, artisans and shopkeepers must pay 7.5 percent of their taxable income to the SSN through the IRPEF (Personal Income Tax). A maximum of 40 million lire may be raised in this way. Also towards this end, income from land rights, holdings, and capital gains was added to the 4 million lire ceiling and taxed accordingly. On income rates between 40 million lire and 100 million lire, a 4 percent flat tax must be paid.

Such measures were also applied to retired dependent workers, although pre-taxed income and pension income were exempted. In other words, dependent workers with an income of up to 40 million lire are subject to a 10.95 percent tax rate, of which 9.6 percent is paid by the employer (5.6 percent effectively, thanks to the fiscalization of social benefits) and 1.35 percent is charged directly to the employee. Of the 4 percent tax on incomes between 40 million lire and 100 million lire, dependent workers pay 0.2 percent, while the rest is paid by the employer. Altogether, all workers share a considerable part of the burden.

As far as structural measures are concerned, after a five-year delay, Law 595, enacted in 1985, finally defined the general orientation and binding norms of the National Health Plan *(Piano Sanitario Nazionale)* and provided for a law concerning long-term financing. Thus, in the future, the SSN would not continue to be governed with the short-sighted perspective of annual budget laws, as had been the case up to then. In the meantime, the very structure of the USL was also reexamined, the goal being to overcome the widespread sense that it had become bureaucratic and clientalistic. The result was the reduction of administrative committees and the dissolution of the assemblies. The role of the political bodies, however, remained central. Moreover, the first steps were taken towards the creation of a Health Information System *(Sistema Informativo Sanitario)* and towards the pursuit of a territorial realignment based on demographics, as opposed to the historically based allocation of resources. A new policy for controlling pharmaceutical and diagnostic prescriptions was also initiated.

Thus, a Committee of Regional Professionals was established to oversee the prescription practices of doctors and the automatic distribution of medical prescriptions. Not all of these measures have necessarily improved the system; indeed, some of them have definitely proved insufficient, as, for example, the reform, or more appropriately the mini-reform, of the USL, which still awaits a more comprehensive restructuring aimed at bolstering technical competence.

Additional reforms have been executed only formally. For instance, the professional committees have been set up, but they have yet to begin to operate effectively. Others still have to be drafted, as is the case, for example, with the National Health Plan, which is still being discussed. Finally, there are many other fundamental issues yet to be resolved, such as control in a non-hierarchical system, the allocation of responsibility from the center to the periphery, and even the preparation of a suitable information system. It is easy to understand the negative consequences of these failings in terms of low efficiency, effectiveness, and equity relative to the expenditure of the current system.[4] Notwithstanding their inadequacies, these measures have, however, reinforced the role of the SSN.

At the same time, there seems to be an increasing demand for services in the private sector. For example, according to a recent survey by the National Council on Economy and Labor (CNEL 1982), between 1979 and 1982, the private health sector grew by 34 percent, which represents 1.1 percent of the Italian gross national product (GNP). According to the survey, 52.6 percent of those interviewed in the sample maintained that after the reform there was an increase in the use of private services, while only 26.6 and 10.2 percent, respectively, thought that demand for private assistance had remained stable or had diminished. These findings are particularly interesting given that the sample consisted of labor union members, who are traditionally more sympathetic towards public services than the general population. Similarly, a survey conducted in 1984[5] indicates that in the period 1981–4 about 30 percent of all citizens changed their behavior by seeking some sort of private service for general and specialized medical visits. Although private health insurance continues to have a small impact in terms of percentage, it appears to be registering a strong rate of increase. Between 1983 and 1985, for instance, the rate was 27 percent.

In sum, there seems to be little evidence of significant alterations in the boundaries between public and private sectors. On the contrary, the SSN remains the center of distribution of health services. The growing use of the private sector, far from representing a coherent process of integration between private and public health care, seems to constitute a perverse, but limited, consequence of the declining confidence in the SSN itself. This hypothesis seems to be confirmed by a recent ISTAT (Central Statistics Bureau) survey which indicates that as far as specialized medicine is concerned, of all the citizens who sought services, 25 percent sought them in the private sector and only 8 percent turned to both private and public services. As for diagnostic services, 6 percent used exclusively private services while 10 percent looked to both private and public providers.

2. The "private" sector within the SSN

Until now, the term "public" has been used explicitly as the opposite of private. This definition is faulty since major parts of the different forms of regulation are characterized by the existence of both public and private features (see the Introduction to this volume). From this point of view, an examination of the boundaries between the public and the private within the SSN reveals a substantially greater rate of growth of the "private" in recent years.

Let us consider first of all the importance of private health care operating within the National Health System. About 100,000 doctors are part of the SSN, including general practitioners, pediatricians, and specialists. Moreover, a notable portion of part-time hospital doctors, 40 to 50 percent of the total, also provide services in private clinics operating within the SSN. Ninety percent of private health clinics work within the SSN (on a subcontracting basis), composing about 15 percent of the total number of hospital beds in Italy. This translates into a burden for the FSN of about 1,800 billion lire compared to the 1,600 billion lire burden for hospital assistance (university clinics, research institutions, etc.) and the 10,000 billion lire cost for public hospitalization (1984 data). Indeed, such a burden continues to grow, notwithstanding the Minister of Health's exhortation to use public facilities.

As far as the day clinics are concerned, two-thirds of the total operate within the SSN, generating a cost of about 1,200 billion lire compared to an expenditure of about 400 billion lire for public specialized medicine. These 1984 data are particularly interesting given that in 1983 a system of joint-sharing had been introduced in order to reduce the use of private specialists. The result seems to have fallen far short of expectations.

By itself, such data should not be disconcerting to those who view public and private as a continuum. Indeed, the private sector could have a positive effect on the SSN by filling holes in the latter's services or by providing the same services at lower costs. In the case of Italy, however, the private sector fulfills neither of these functions. Rather, it seems to be regulated in a manner entirely inconsistent with the collective objectives of the SSN.

Let us take the case of private health clinics integrated in the SSN. Data for 1981[6] and other disaggregated regional studies and information from other sources seem to confirm that the old problems persist. First of all, it is wrong to affirm that publicly subsidized private hospitalization costs less than public hospitalization, even though it is true that the average daily cost of hospitalization in the subsidized private sector is one-half that in the public sector. In fact, such costs are not comparable because of the profound differences that exist in the "case-mix" product. To be more specific, even though the private sector is progressively improving itself by offering Emergency Room services and equipping itself with CAT scanners, which are very costly, it remains true that the private sector is specialized in providing relatively low-cost in-patient services for neuropathology, gynecology, and surgery, which are not capital intensive. Therefore, without more comparable data, it is not fair to state that private care costs less than public care.

Second, the lower number of hospital personnel per bed found in the private sector does not in itself imply more efficiency since much depends on the composition of the personnel itself. For instance, it is just as possible that the lower number of auxiliary staff indicates a scarcity of nurses. This fact, as is well known, represents a negative phenomenon for service productivity.

Third, within these private clinics there are great differences in terms of costs relative to certain efficiency indicators, such as the average length of hospital stay and rate of occupancy. For example, for general medicine the average expense per case varied in 1981 from over 2 million lire in Tuscany to less than 800,000 lire in Molise; for surgery, from over 1 million lire in Piedmont and Lombardy to 420,000 lire in Umbria. Similarly, in general care units, hospitalization varied from 12 days in Puglia to 23.7 days in Tuscany; for long-term treatment units from 26 days in Piedmont to 113 days in Tuscany. On average, private institutions taken as a whole have statistically shown longer hospital stays than public sector hospitals. For example, the hospital stay for general care in the public sector was 13 days, compared to 19 days in the subsidized private sector. This fact, independent of its specific causes, constitutes another sign of the inefficiency of subsidized practices.

Fourth, the data at hand indicate a greater demand for private sector services in places where both public and private services are most inefficient (as measured by considering together the average length of stay, usage rate, and turnover rate). A 1984 study of the Lazio Region, (Regione Lazio 1984) adds very useful information in this regard. Once again, the costs of subsidizing private institutions are most alarming, especially given that such institutions are located in areas in which the presence of public hospitals is greater, thus going against any logic of equitable territorial dispersion. The average length of hospital stay in private institutions is significantly greater than that registered in public hospitals. The occupancy rate is almost always very high. But, instead of indicating high productivity, these facts seem to indicate – according to surveys conducted by the Regional Overseeing Service (SIR) – a "forced" occupation of the beds, with the recovery of long-term patients taking place in facilities intended for intensive care, and an excess of occupied beds relative to those authorized or subsidized.

There is also much room for improvement of services in the subsidized sector. For the most part, the medical personnel are employed on a free-lance basis, which in itself may indicate a greater availability of doctors from the public sector. Data concerning their on-duty schedules is virtually nonexistent. Moreover, the parameters included in the subsidy agreements for paramedical personnel are seldom respected.

But this is not all. Another type of "private" seems to be invading the SSN. It consists of a certain type of behavior aimed at satisfying private ends and interests rather than collective goals. One might claim that this is obvious and that no one should be so naive as to think that the "public" effectively pursues collective goals. On the contrary, are we not all now convinced of the applicability of market standards, collective choices, and the attribution of individual utility functions to bureaucrats?

Such an objection would seem disputable, however. On the one hand, the privatization of the public, even if it is a well-known phenomenon, has yet to be fully understood. On the other hand, such privatization, besides bearing considerable responsibility for the faults enumerated in the introductory section of this chapter and for those of the subsidization policies, seems to take on peculiar characteristics in Italy's SSN. This privatization is due not so much to disobeying the law – sometimes for private gain, sometimes not – as to the presence of laws so inefficient that they encourage self-interested behavior instead of collective goals.

Let us take the case of USL administrators. Even at the highest levels they are underpaid. They are placed under eleven different supervisory controls and are obliged to work in a context that is complicated, intricate, and characterized by constraints and rigid rules regulating the use of resources. Even worse, when these administrators take initiatives to implement some improvement in the allocation of resources, they receive no financial bonus or raise, since pay increases are a function of a predetermined salary scale. The USL also does not benefit from savings, since in the present system, not only must savings be handed over to the FSN, but less spending one year often means less funding the following year. In such a context, the primary incentive is to reduce one's efforts to a minimum, and to create one's own comfortable niche and status by establishing clientalistic relationships and unloading one's responsibilities onto the next person.

Similar arguments pertain to dependent medical personnel. Doctors must often work in malfunctioning hospitals and are stripped of their role in the administration of health care. Moreover, they are essentially paid wages that are completely independent of the effectiveness of the services provided and hence offer little incentive to contain costs. In this last respect, not even the integration of bonuses with wages seems structured so as to achieve expected results. Much the same is the case for members of the Administrative Committee and all other personnel.[7]

Leaving the specifics aside, considerations similar to those concerning the subsidized private sector apply. Here, too, one cannot simply object to the pursuit of personal ends per se since this seems inevitable. On the contrary, the SSN manifests an institutionally sanctioned and systematic gap between self-interest and collective ideals. In other industrialized nations, the trend appears to be the opposite, and the two tendencies are reconciled through an appropriate system of incentives and disincentives, of individual and public goals.[8]

The private sector was understood in this section as both the subsidized private sector and the pursuit of private ends and interests by different actors within the SSN. It has been shown to be much more widespread than an analysis based solely on an examination of the formal financing, administrative structure, and regulatory guidelines would suggest.[9]

3. "Public" and "private" in health care: a glance at the future

The discussion of the preceding section should have satisfactorily responded to the central question posed in the introductory section. In the post-reform period, save for a notable increase in the private contribution to the FSN financing and a considerable but still limited dependence upon the private sector, the SSN remains as it was in 1979, when it was founded. It is, above all, a service that is three-fourths financed by compulsory, risk-free contributions and that offers no choice in terms of health plan. For the remaining one-fourth, the SSN is financed through the national budget, except for the fiscalization of social security payments, which make up a fourth of the obligatory contributions.

The SSN is also a service governed by public bodies, that is, by Parliament, the Ministry of Health, the Regions, local governments, and the USL. It is, finally, a general and homogeneous service, offered to all citizens on the basis of need, at least in principle.

However, today, as in 1979, it is also a service whose existence is a source of revenue for a large number of subsidized (subcontracted) personnel, for the greater part of all private laboratories, and for the overwhelming majority of private care centers. Within the service, the rules of the game and remunerative practices continue to promote the pursuit of self-interest instead of the collective goals of the Service itself. However, we should not consider our simple retrospective analysis sufficient. It would, in fact, seem more useful to conclude by sketching some possible evolutionary tendencies for the SSN.

Signals coming from the health sector are not reassuring. The present state of the SSN and the difficulty in initiating any serious process of actual reform would seem to a large extent related to the balance of forces at play. Despite the fact that doctors are legitimately claiming a greater role in the administration of medicine, they continue to appear primarily interested in defending their contractual position and status. The subsidized sector has everything to gain from an inefficient and uncontrollable public sector. While the administrative bureaucracy and the dependent personnel demand increased responsibility and autonomy, they remain attached to all the security and "rents," attached to the very same positions that would need to be abolished in any process intended to increase responsibility based on the provision of incentives and disincentives. In the meantime, citizens, who are always dissatisfied with the SSN, rather than protest, tend to privatize their collective problems, seeking favoritism in the public sector or "exiting" to the private. At the same time, reformist interests, while they exist, do not succeed in organizing themselves.[10]

The most likely outcome in such a situation would seem to be either the triumph of the needs of the strongest groups, such as the doctors, over severe control policies, or a decision-making stalemate, as in the redistribution of powers between the center and the periphery. There could also be, for example, a non-decision regarding the modernization of the public administration.

Such a conclusion should not surprise anyone. On the one hand, the health-care universe is populated by a plurality of actors, motivated, at least in part, by conflictual interests that would involve either diffuse costs and concentrated benefits, or concentrated costs and benefits. As is well known, such conditions tend to favor respectively the triumph of solutions favoring the strongest or a decision-making stalemate. On the other hand, reformist goals to rationalize services represent not only a collective good – a characteristic that in itself discourages collective action – but a collective good whose realization appears highly costly.[11] For example, consider the importance of the relevant costs for (1) the negotiations that would have to take place among the supporters of reform interests; (2) the organization of the opposition that would have to be mounted against those on whom the burden of such rationalization measures would fall; and (3) the realization of those changes necessary to tearing down all the juridical, institutional, and cultural barriers that today prevent the modernization of the public administration. Clearly, the costs would be extremely high.

If the pluralistic alternative has been barred, so too have the neo-corporatist and policy community strategies (see the Introduction to this volume). For such strategies, even those who could promote such innovative projects are missing. For example, the National Health Council, which could have constituted a truly appropriate policy community, is instead primarily a body for voicing regional interests. The only route left seems to be the political one, but certain fundamental obstacles exist even for this strategy.

First, in the public arena, inflated as it is today by social demands, political intervention tends to react against external stimuli rather than acting as an autonomous promotor of change. In national health care, the existent pluralist balance does not appear likely to stimulate much change. In fact, the only plausible improvements would seem to be those that favor the interests of those with the greatest power.

Second, the political parties are directly involved in the financing of health services by means of the levies imposed by the Administration

Committees. Since any policy of rationalization would result in a reduction in the power of such committees,[12] it seems somewhat improbable that those who would be hurt most by such measures would support them.

Third, and partially independent of issues of power, the political milieu seems erroneously influenced by a growing faith in the self-regulating capacity of the market. Two proposals submitted by former Ministers Degan and Goria, both members of the Christian Democratic party, provide proof of this trend.

Briefly, according to Degan's proposal, the contributions of dependent workers would be fixed at 12 percent of gross salary (of which 10.75 percent would be charged to the employer and the rest to the employee) while self-employed workers would be charged 9 percent of their declared earnings. The contributive responsibility of the employers would remain invariant. Workers, whether dependent or not, having paid a solidarity contribution of 50 percent of the charged rate, would pay the remaining half only in case they decide to avail themselves of all the services of the SSN. If one should instead opt for private assistance, one would pay 25 percent less if one renounced public hospital services, 15 percent less in the case of general assistance, and 10 percent less in the case of specialized services.

The Goria proposal was even more drastic. It would limit public responsibility to supplying hospital services. The only exception would be for those citizens who fall below a certain income level, for whom the full range of services would be covered by the state budget. Healthcare contributions, on the other hand, would be reduced to about one-third with an advantage for the employer as well.

The fundamental issue with these and other proposals that confine the public role to the safeguarding of basic needs is that they do not take into account that what is important in health care is not *ex ante* choice between the state and the market or even the simplistic reduction of the public role in favor of private responsibility. Rather, what is important is to identify those special mixes of public and private instruments that seem best suited satisfactorily to implement the objectives of efficiency, effectiveness, and equity, since neither the state nor the market, understood as ideal types, represents an optimal solution.[13]

The market, for example, might prove very inefficient as a result of the presence of externalities, economies of scale, limits of insurance mechanisms, and, above all, a significant asymmetry in the ownership of information. Such factors, instead of favoring the development of a truly competitive free-market system, tend to promote those pseudo-competitive aspects dominated by health-care producers to the detriment of the consumer, with negative effects as well in terms of effectiveness.

Moreover, the interaction between public and private would seem often to generate perverse effects rather than productive cooperation. In this regard, certain limits could arise due to: (1) excess capacity; (2) overproduction and overconsumption of medical services, which seem particularly alarming because of both low effectiveness and the danger of extended medicalization of health needs; (3) fragmentation of supply; (4) pressures on the growth of public expenditures since competition in health care is based not so much on price as on quality, and since the health-care sector is one in which technological developments, far from diminishing costs, tend to significantly raise them; and (5) loss of the best personnel to the private sector. Together, these present a very serious risk when recourse to the private sector is understood, as is generally the case, as a means of unloading responsibilities of the public sector, which nonetheless remains unchanged because it cannot be easily rationalized.[14]

Finally, even if this is an obvious consideration, the hypotheses of privatization and of new combinations of private and public would bring about sharp increases in costs – monetary and otherwise – paid especially by the poorest and most infirm.

To avoid such consequences, further public regulations would seem inevitable.[15] But hardly a trace of such regulations appears in the proposals cited above. This absence is predictable, given the previously described structure of costs and benefits related to any policy of rationalization.

The problem is very serious because no political actor seems to be able to develop appropriate alternatives, not even among the parties of the Left. These, on the one hand, seem to be attracted by the idea of the market for reasons of efficiency and, in this way, underestimate the risks of creating pseudo-markets. On the other hand, for reasons of equity, they persist in opposing the private sector, thus ignoring all opportunities that are related, in a world of scarce resources and unlimited desires, to the development of distributional rules aimed at an equitable functioning of the market itself.

In sum, the picture of the interests and forces at play does not suggest any significant changes in the near future. In the not-so-immediate future, however, one could imagine the implementation of pseudo-competitive proposals such as those mentioned above. The new pro-market trend, the growing interest of consumers to avail themselves of the private sector, and the active support of the doctors and private clinics that would benefit the most from privatization could contribute to their success. If this were to happen, the outcome would be troublesome. Little would be accomplished by the introduction of poorly regulated markets alongside a public sector that, albeit reduced, would continue to manifest the same shortcomings as today.

Notes

1 In this sense, this chapter does not occupy itself with an examination of the socio-political factors that led up to the launching of the reform in 1978. For that, the reader is referred to Piperno (1984).

2 Such modifications with respect to income, aside from the scantiness of the stable social brackets, brought with them, when compared to preceding dispositions, certain positive effects. On one side, discrimination based on earnings was abolished. On another, they take into account better the case of family dependents by considering differentiated increases based on the number of family members.

3 In 1983, for example, the difference between projected and actual costs was about 4,000 billion lire.

4 Among other things, the various reports of the Ministry of Health – Central Service for Welfare Programming (Servizio Centrale della Programmazione Sanitaria) – and Censis elaborated in different years the relations of the Corte deo Conti (1983–1984: the UIL report on Health, Rome, 1985).

5 See Piperno (1986). Similar tendencies are also recorded by Censis (1986).

6 For a more detailed exposition, refer to an analysis by Granaglia (1985).

7 Refer to a study by Granaglia (1986) and to ISIS (various issues).

8 Regarding attempts to congruently harmonize private and collective ends, see Enthoven (1980, 1986), Greenberg (1978), Havighurst (1982), and Olson (1981).

9 A third recognized role of the private sector could refer itself to the voluntary sector. Regarding this, although comprehensive and detailed data are lacking, available information would seem to indicate an increase of volunteer workers, especially in hospitals. One reason might lie in the dequalification of hospital service staff that took place following the subordination of the hospitals themselves to the USL.

10 See the bibliographical indications of notes 5 and 9.

11 Concerning this, see Olson (1965), Wilson (1980), and Lindbeck (1985); as far as the health-care sector is concerned, see Alford (1976), Feingold (1980), Klein (1984), and Hyatt (1975).

12 This fact, given the nature of collective choice in allocative and distributive decisions that take place in the health-care sector, does not necessarily signify a total transferral of directive responsibilities to so-called technicians. It simply means a diminishment of political party leanings in the SSN and a corresponding evaluation of the technical role from within an equal division of capabilities. See Williams (1985).

13 See, among others, the classical analyses of Arrow (1963), Culyer and Cooper (1973), Cullis and West (1979), and Van Der Gaag and Perlman (1981).

14 See Granaglia (1987) and bibliography therein cited.

15 Concerning the same need for regulation in both public and private sectors, see Maynard and McLachlan (1982).

Conclusions: the Italian case between continuity and change

PETER LANGE AND MARINO REGINI

The essays in this volume examine the role of different mechanisms and institutions in regulating the production and distribution of economic resources in Italy and show how these have changed over the last decade. They provide, therefore, a systematic overview of changing modes of regulation in a single national case. In this concluding chapter we want: (1) to draw some descriptive generalizations about the Italian case; (2) to make some causal inferences about the nature and sources of the overall pattern of change and stability; and (3) to explore the issue of the extent to which and how our findings regarding Italy might be generalized to the other advanced industrial democracies.

1. Overview of the Italian case

Several descriptive generalizations can be drawn from the preceding chapters in this volume. These concern how the regulation of activities and relationships among actors in the economic sphere occurs in Italy and what have been recent trends in regulative patterns. Let us look briefly at each of these in turn.

Regulatory mixes

There has been a tendency in recent years to discuss regulation of the economy in the advanced industrial democracies in terms of the contraposition between state and market: where one rises, the other declines. By implication, these are the only two regulative modes worthy of attention in the economic sphere, and, more polemically, where the state "interferes," economic inefficiency is the primary result. If state and market were actors rather than institutions, one would say their relationship has been characterized as a zero-sum game, with a preference for more market and less state.

Much of what appears on the preceding pages, however, suggests that the contraposition between state and market is a false dichotomy that distorts more than it reveals about how regulation occurs. In one area after another, we have found mixes of regulatory modes and institutions. As we noted in our Introduction to the volume, these mixes include solidarity – not just authority and exchange – modes of regulation and social – not just market and state – institutions. Perhaps most important, the mixes are often intricate and symbiotic, reflecting interdependency and mutual reinforcement, rather than debilitating "invasions" of competencies.

The mixes of institutions and modes are apparent in the policy areas covered in all the chapters. Nowhere have we seen either unfettered regulation through the market or by the state. Even in a policy arena such as macro-economic management by the Bank of Italy, where market forces might be expected to be predominant and where there certainly have been significant trends in this direction (see below), state authority continues to play a role. Here, however, the popular dichotomy might be said largely to apply.

Not so in other arenas. The chapters on health, the labor market, social policy, industrial relations, the management of social movement and industrial conflict, and even industrial policy show a mix of mechanisms which defies simple characterization. In each of these cases, state, market, and social institutions – and, more generally, the principles of authority, exchange, and solidarity – are bound by complex relationships in which the functioning of one is at least partially and often positively dependent on the existence of the other. Thus, for instance, the recently growing role of market considerations in the hiring of labor cannot be understood without a recognition of the role played by the Italian state in regulating the labor market and in providing social benefits.

The complex and at least partially symbiotic relationships are not confined to market-state relations, however. In one case after another, it is clear that other modes and institutions of regulation also play a prominent role. Solidarity, particularly through family, kinship, and other interpersonal ties, is widespread. Reyneri (Chapter 5) shows clearly that this applies not just in southern Italy, where stereotypes and the character of local economic structures might have led us to expect it, but in parts of northern mass production industry as well. Furthermore, the role of family and other solidarity networks is not just the residual product of sociocultural resistance to the "cold but efficient" logic of the market. Quite the contrary. Often it is only through these institutions that markets can operate (Bagnasco 1985). Analogous forms of symbiosis can be found in other cases. Once we set aside simplistic and unrealistic models of an entirely atomized market society, mixes of regulatory modes and institutions become not just the rule but often a necessary component of efficient and effective production and distribution of economic resources and the management of potential or manifest conflicts.[1]

Of course, the extant mixes that have been identified are not always economically functional and should not be rationalized as such. Several of the chapters show how the particular mix of modes and institutions of regulation, while perhaps tempering potential conflicts, produces highly inefficient outcomes that often are unsatisfactory to most of the participants or make impossible the achievement of both their individual goals and identifiable collective ones. Ferrera (Chapter 4), to cite one example, shows how the role assumed by the Italian state in industrial policy, when combined with the institutionalized rules of decision-making within the Italian state, has frustrated the goals of that policy by sharply limiting the (appropriate) role that might be played by "technical/substantive" criteria in industrial policy decisions. Here certainly the regulative mix is inefficient and the state role is a primary source of such inefficiency, and this without even satisfying other public goals that might provide alternative rationales for the outcome.

The case described by Ferrera highlights the potentially perverse role of the state in regulation of economic activities. But it highlights as well the fact that a great deal depends on the specific nature of role that the state is playing in regulation. In fact, the preceding chapters show not just that intricate mixes of regulative modes and institutions are generally present but also that the state itself can play different roles, and that it is extremely important to identify what *kind* of role the state is playing if one wishes to understand the regulatory mix and how and with what consequences it operates.

State regulation in the form of direct authoritative control through binding and universalistic rules is the historically most common Italian mode (Cassese 1987). It is also the style of state regulation most often criticized in the anti-statist literature in recent years. There is little in the preceding chapters which would suggest that, *in the Italian case*, such criticisms are misplaced. In most cases, we have seen that such regulation by the Italian state tends to produce inefficient outcomes and perverse effects in terms of designated goals of policy. Yet, we would emphasize that several chapters (those by Ferrera, Paci, and Granaglia, for example) suggest that these results are at least in good part the product of the particular character of the Italian state and how it functions (see below). It is quite possible – certainly this is an implication to be drawn from Paci's discussion and studies of public policy in other advanced industrial democracies (Korpi 1983; Hibbs 1978) –

that direct state regulation in the social policy and other areas can be decidedly effective both in terms of the egalitarian provision of services and the efficient functioning of the labor market and the economy more generally.

Furthermore, as we suggested in the Introduction and the subsequent chapters made clear, the state can play other roles that can make a positive contribution to regulation by complementing and/or reinforcing other modes and institutions. Cella's discussion of the attempts at concertation and the allocation of state resources to facilitate oligopolistic bargaining among associations (Chapter 7) highlights such a state role, as do a number of the other essays. What must be stressed is that while these state roles are often unintended, they can also be – and often are – intended ways of making regulation more effective and efficient through the market and norms of solidarity.

To conclude, what the essays in this volume suggest is that one must expect mixes of regulatory modes in most arenas of policy and that the efficiency/inefficiency of such mixes is not something that can be known a priori. Simplistic criticisms of the state as a source of regulation are misplaced both historically and in evaluating regulation of the production and distribution of economic resources in contemporary society. *And this is so even in the case of Italy and the Italian state.* Instead, it is clear that a good understanding of how and with what effects regulation occurs must be the product of careful investigation based on expectations that "mixed" modes of regulation are the norm and that the state's role can be of different degrees and types.

Trends

There is no question that ideological trends in the 1980s have been toward a reduced role for the state in the regulation of economic and social activities. While most apparent in the United States and Great Britain, similar tendencies have appeared as well in continental Europe. Changes in actual policy may not have been as dramatic, but here too there is considerable evidence of a decline in the state's use of its authority to direct and control social processes. There seems, in other words, to have been a trend toward a narrowing boundary of the political in the advanced industrial democracies (Maier 1987).

The findings for the Italian case presented in this volume are only partially supportive of this image. The patterns, rather than being uniform, vary both across policy areas and over time. They show some cases of an increased state role in regulation, of shifts in the type of state regulation, and also of decline in the state role.

In a number of areas – health, industrial policy, industrial relations – the late 1970s were marked by legislation increasing the interventionism of the state. In health, for instance, there was a dramatic shift in the mix of modes of regulation with the creation of a national health-care delivery system. Similarly, the industrial policy law centralized an already large state role in industrial development and further expanded the instruments for such intervention. In industrial relations, the state assumed a higher profile in the efforts to establish concertative agree-ments between capital and labor. Here, however, its role was less to use its authority to establish specific outcomes than to use its financial and other resources to facilitate agreements between the industrial and union confederations. Thus, even where we have evidence of an increased state role, it is important to remember that the type of state regulation varied and that it generally was comingled with other reg-ulative modes and institutions.

We also have at least one example from other policy areas of a long-term trend toward a declining role of state regulation. In the case of the Bank of Italy, the "divorce" of 1981 culminated a longer trend (Addis 1987) of incremental policy changes that gave, and were intended to give, a much greater scope to market forces in the determination of interest rates, the growth of the money supply, and Bank policy more generally. This case emerges as a particularly interesting one, precisely because the change in the role of state intervention was both explicit and intended. We will return to it below.

As the attentive reader will have observed, however, trends toward a shifting and/or declining role for the state and an increase in the role played by market forces in the regulatory mixes was not confined to the banking area, and only sometimes was the result of explicit policy initiatives. In the health-care system, for instance, the nationalization of health care was soon accompanied by the introduction and spread of fees for various kinds of services, a trend that has continued. In addi-tion, the new rules created opportunities for providers to expand their private activities at the expense of the national system, thereby increas-ing the role of market factors and non-state institutions in the overall health delivery system. In social services, more generally, Paci (Chap-ter 9) shows that the already large role assumed by non-state modes and especially solidarity norms and the family has tended to grow. In the labor market, recent years have been marked by a growing aware-ness, and most recently, the actual introduction of greater flexibility and responsiveness to market forces has occurred. As Reyneri (Chapter 5) points out, however, regulation through the market has continued to be tempered by the role played by kinship and other solidarity link-ages, at least in some areas. In industrial relations too, the mid-1980s were marked by a growing role for market factors in the determination of wages and working conditions, but here this resulted less from explicit policy initiatives – much less concerted action – and more from the impact of changing demands of international competition and the effects of labor market conditions on the bargaining power of labor and capital.

By the time the essays in this volume were written, therefore, the swing toward a growing role for state regulation – including regulation through authoritative control – that was evident at the end of the last decade had been reversed. While regulation in all policy areas continued to be characterized by complex mixes of modes and institutions, the relative role played by the market and by norms of solidarity was clearly on the rise. In only a few areas, however, did this appear the result of explicit policy initiatives on the part of the state, a pattern seemingly more characteristic of the Anglo-American democracies as well as some other continental European systems. What this observation prompts, therefore, is a shift in our analysis at this point from a description of outcomes to a discussion of processes and causes.

2. Patterns and processes of change

How does change in the mixes of modes and institutions of regulation occur in Italy? What are the principal patterns? What appear to be the major processes? What can be identified as the major sources of change and stability? These questions are addressed in the pages that follow.

Patterns of change

Even a cursory examination of the preceding chapters in this volume reveals a contradictory but quite understandable pattern of change in regulatory mixes across the policy areas examined. On the one hand, there have been numerous efforts at large-scale change through state action. The late 1970s, in fact, were marked by major legislative efforts at systematic reform intended to alter the mix of regulatory modes and institutions and thereby increase economic efficiency and/or social equity. The reforms of the health-care system and of industrial policy are only the clearest examples.

On the other hand, with the notable exceptions of the reform of the system for the making of monetary policy (see below) and, earlier, the reform of workers' rights in the workplace (see Stefanizzi and Tarrow, Chapter 3), the outcomes of these reform efforts were much less extensive than expected and much less effective than intended. Consistent with the prevailing stereotypes, the formal *dirigisme* of these state-sponsored reforms was belied in practice. One is impressed, instead, with the capacity of the individuals and groups whose interests seem threatened to resist changes through evasions or to get subsequent changes in policy or its implementation that frustrate the global intentions of the reforms.

Yet, beneath the surface of the relative failure of major state efforts at sweeping reform, there is a reality of constant change in how affairs are regulated. These changes are sometimes through state action, sometimes in response to it and sometimes in spite of it. The Italian system stifles intentional state-directed systematic change but permits the vitalism of society to be transformed into relatively constant incremental changes in regulatory modes and the regulatory roles of different institutions.

There seems little reason to provide extensive examples from the individual chapters to support this characterization. Almost every one provides evidence both of the frustration of major regulatory innovations and of the constant flow of changes in how specific problems are regulated. What seems more useful is to explore the processes that seem to lie behind this pattern. In doing so, three questions seem most pertinent. Why is change generally incremental, either in initial intent or subsequent implementation or both? Why, occasionally, are more sweeping efforts at change undertaken? And how do the relations between groups in society get translated into the mix of regulatory modes and institutions that govern their relations?

Processes and causes – the Italian system of policy-making

We argued in our Introduction that two salient dimensions for understanding the policy process and the factors affecting it are the extent of isolation of the decision-making institution(s) from external pressures and the comprehensiveness (indicated by the degree of aggregation of inputs and interdependence of outputs) of the decisional process. The scheme seeks to capture the character of institutions for decision-making, social interests, and their interaction. It also leads us to predict that, to the extent that policy is the outcome of either pluralistic pressure or policy networks, change is likely to be incremental and often internally contradictory.

General institutional structures. Much of the pattern of frustration of major regulatory innovation seems well explained by this framework. The Italian system is overwhelmingly characterized by decision-making institutions that are highly permeable and/or decision processes in which inputs are highly disaggregated and outputs fragmented and relatively isolated from one another. The result is policies likely to change only in incremental fashion and in response to marginal shifts in the political resources and influence of countervailing social forces. In one policy area after another – health, social policy, industrial policy, labor market policy – we have seen fragmented interests exercising their will either through state action or through evasions that are not impeded by, and are subsequently sometimes incorporated into, state policy. Aggregation of inputs and linkage of outputs are the exception. The extent of policy-making autonomy is in dispute (see Chapters 1 and 2) but may make little difference from the standpoint of the incrementalism and incoherence of policy outcomes. The combination of aggregation, linkage, and sufficient autonomy to produce and implement major changes in regulatory mixes is likely to be rare indeed.

How is this pattern to be reconciled with the common characterization of Italy's policy process as one dominated by mass parties, relatively centralized interest organizations, themselves linked to the parties, and a centralized Napoleonic state? Attentive studies of *il caso italiano* have already recast this traditional image (LaPalombara 1987). And the preceding chapters provide additional support for the development of a revised perspective. First, the parties – with the possible exception of the Italian Communist party[2] – act at least as much as agents for fragmented social interests as aggregators of those interests. While best exemplified by the factional structure of the Christian Democratic party, other examples are easily found. Second, even if some large interest organizations have been able at times to undertake coordinated action, their degree of effective centralized control appears, upon close examination, rather low.[3] So too, therefore is their capacity over the longer run to aggregate the more particularized interests they represent (see Chiesi and Martinelli [Chapter 8] in this regard). The party linkages of many of these interest groups certainly cannot be taken to mean that they constrain their demands to conform to a larger party strategy. Capture from below seems a better metaphor than control and sometimes even constraint from above.

Third, an already historically fragmented interest structure has tended to be further fragmented by state policies undertaken in the postwar period and especially after the major expansion of state intervention from the 1960s onwards. These policies, reflecting the already existing structure of interests and their interaction with policy-making institutions, have tended to be particularistic and/or clientelistic rather than universalistic (Paci, Chapter 9), thereby creating new fragmented constituencies seeking support and protection from the state.

Finally, Italy's multi-party system as a whole has tended further to fragment the inputs to policy-making. Interests that, in two-party systems, *might* be squeezed by an aggregative process induced by party competition have often been able to find effective representation directly through small parties or indirectly through their blackmail potential in the context of diffuse interparty competition within governing coalitions. The implications of this pattern are clear. There is little, either in the social structure of interests or the organizations through which this structure becomes translated into political pressure, to encourage aggregation of inputs or interdependence of outputs.

As our approach stresses, however, it is not just the fragmentation of interests but also the structure of the state decision-making institutions to which they have access that is important. Here again, we know that the permeability and willingness to service particularistic interests of these institutions are relatively great.

For reasons that will not be reviewed at length in this context, postwar Italian republican institutions were designed to assure that there would be few if any opportunities for the centralization of political power. The status of the Prime Minister relative to the cabinet, of the Parliament to the executive, of the *Camera* to the *Senato*, the existence of judicial review, and numerous other examples that might be given suggest the diffusion of power in the system. Furthermore, the internal rules of the Parliament itself tend further to encourage diffusion and to provide opportunities for fragmented interests and for the opposition to exercise their influence (Cazzola 1972; DiPalma 1977). Finally, one should not overlook the "culture" of the political elite, which seems to favor distributively based consensus over majoritarian decision and behind the scenes compromise over confrontation, the latter most often serving essentially symbolic functions.

This diffusion of power, as well as the culture of compromise that it tends to foster, has several important implications. It is important for our purposes for two reasons. First, one of its consequences is the existence of innumerable points of access for interests to the formulation of policy. Losing in one arena, they can seek redress in another. Second, even where policy is made through relatively less permeable policy networks, the fragmentation promotes relatively narrow specializations – especially within the public bureaucracy – and obscures public responsibility for decisions, even as it discourages linkage between policy decisions. No surprise then that systematic policy innovation, much less implementation, is rare.

But even when major reforms are formulated and implemented, there are many opportunities for those interests who consider themselves the losers in such a process to gain redress. Not only can they return to Parliament to seek protective "corrections"; they can also operate directly on a bureaucracy that, beneath a veil of centralization and rigid universalistic rule-making, is available to penetration and ready, therefore, to interpret the law in a way that allows exceptional treatment or to delay its implementation. Scarcity of time or the limited resources of personnel and skills are often used to justify this behavior. Thus, even when – as is shown in a number of chapters – major reform of regulatory modes is undertaken, there are numerous opportunities for damaged interests to deflect its intended consequences.

Of course, the combination of structures and institutions just outlined would have less marked consequences for the issues we are examining were there effective mechanisms in the system that constrained legislators, governments, and bureaucrats to restrain the inherent tendencies of the system toward fragmented policy. There are, however, few such mechanisms. The dynamics of the postwar party system have encouraged a great deal of symbolic partisan political conflict based on broad appeals to principle. But they have also produced relatively weak electoral accountability, with the parties in governing coalitions facing few threats of displacement due to voter disaffection. The social embeddedness of party electorates has fostered a combination of rhetorical mobilization based on principle and a more hidden politics of exchange (Barnes 1977; Tarrow 1977b; Mannheimer and Sani 1987). Furthermore, the complexity of government decision-making and the opaqueness of bureaucratic processes and outputs have provided few opportunities for success for political appeals to universalistic policy values. Thus both the visible and "invisible" politics (Sartori 1976) of the system has been permissive of the kinds of policy process and outputs to be expected in a political structure characterized by highly fragmented interests with easy and multiple access to a decision process that little encourages policy linkage and interdependence.

Images of policy-making. How does the argument just outlined reflect on the discussions by Pasquino (Chapter 1) and by Dente and Regonini (Chapter 2) of how policy-making actually takes place in the Italian system? After all, at first blush, they would appear to offer sharply contrasting views. As we suggested in the Introduction, however, this need not be the case.

Two points should be emphasized in this regard. First, much of Pasquino's argument relates to *who* decides and what their primary points of reference are in determining the positions to take on particular policy issues. There is little reason to believe that he is wrong when he argues that the political parties have been and remain pervasive in both these respects. "Party men" are everywhere throughout the policy process, and even when they are not, those responsible for making policy decisions may well find it in their interests to identify where different parties stand on the issues under consideration and how they can be satisfied.

But the implications of this for policy outputs depend critically on both the "logic" of interparty politics and the nature of the parties' control over those making policy decisions. With respect to the first, there is ample evidence that while the "visible" side of Italian party relationships has been dominated by partisan conflict, "invisible" politics has much more often been marked by reciprocity and, at times, even cooperation (Cazzola 1972; DiPalma 1977; Tarrow 1977a, 1977b). Even Sartori (1976), who has most often stressed the polarization of the Italian political system, has noted the potential importance of far more cooperative behavior behind the scenes. Furthermore, his own analysis of the dynamics of a "polarized pluralist" system makes clear that within the set of parties who govern, the system encourages clientalism and the satisfaction of factional interests. Sartori's model tends to pay less attention than does ours to the permeability of the partisan system to social interests, which are themselves fragmented, and to the policy process more generally, but in either case, the *outcomes* of the policy process would under many circumstances look similar to what we expect in a model of "pluralistic pressure." This would especially be the case if, as so much of the Italian party literature stresses, the parties themselves often act more to *articulate* social interests within the policy process than to *aggregate* those interests into a coherent program or set of programs based on ideological principle turned to purposes of partisan conflict.

Such a pattern of policy outputs would be all the more likely in those policy-making processes dominated by what Dente and Regonini describe as policy networks or communities. Here, as we have argued in our Introduction and as they elaborate both empirically and theoretically, the policy-makers may be relatively insulated and their competencies relatively specialized and segmented. The logic of their ongoing relationships with one another dominates any priority they might assign to partisan concerns or party dicta *even when they are party men*.

Of course, in some cases the insulation of decision-making arenas is not complete and the participants in such policy communities do look elsewhere to determine the goals they want to pursue through the policy process. But, to the extent that they look to parties where they have themselves become the "experts" on the policy issues and the primary persons linking social interests represented by the party to the office in the party structure responsible for policy on those issues, the outcomes would seem likely to differ little from a process in which the policy community was wholly isolated. Thus, whatever the extent to which one believes that one or the other of these "models" of the policy process applies to the areas of state regulation covered in this volume, the outcomes would generally be likely to resemble the fragmented, incrementalist, and internally contradictory pattern described in the preceding chapters.

Exceptions to the rule. As has already been mentioned, the chapters in this volume highlight what at first sight appear as four "exceptions" in the last decade to the general pattern of Italian policy performance we have described: the health reform of 1978 (Granaglia, Chapter 10); the industrial policy reform of 1977 (Ferrera, Chapter 4); the "triangular" concerted agreements between *Confindustria*, the three major labor confederations,[4] and the government in 1983 and 1984 (Cella, Chapter 7, and Chiesi and Martinelli, Chapter 8); and the reform of central banking policy culminating in the "divorce" of the Banca d'Italia from the Treasury Ministry of 1981 (Epstein and Schor, Chapter 6). The questions that naturally arise are what is the relationship of these "exceptions" to our previous argument and, more generally, what can they tell us about the conditions under which significant innovations in regulatory mechanisms are to be expected? Our discussion will necessarily be synthetic. It is intended to be suggestive rather than exhaustive.

In what sense were these four cases similar? All represented major efforts to make relatively coherent changes in the mix of modes and institutions regulating important areas of policy, and all were ostensibly motivated by broad-gauge public purposes. In all four cases, furthermore, some formal successes were achieved: laws were passed; regulations were altered; accords were reached.

Here, however, the similarities end. Two differences are centrally important to our concerns here. First, only the bank reform can be considered a "success" in the sense that the principles embodied in the reforms were attained once the new regulatory system was put in place. The chapters on the other three make eminently clear the deviations from original principles that took place and/or the breakdown of the regulatory mechanisms put in place. Second, while in three cases reform was initiated through a single major policy initiative, in the banking case it resulted from a series of incremental changes spanning a number of years but all based on an underlying set of principles about the appropriate mix of state authority and market criteria.[5] This suggests that the banking case should be treated separately from the other three, and this is what we do in the discussion that follows.

In looking at the three cases, one characteristic stands out above all others: decision-making was taken out of the hands of diffused policy-making centers and either centralized in the hands of party leaderships or made the object of political exchange between the government and

Conclusions

261
a few encompassing interest organizations. The houses of Parliament and their committees, on the one hand, and bureaucratic officials, on the other, appear to have played relatively minor roles in the formulation of policy. In these cases, in other words, concertation and party dominance, the latter understood as the making of decisions based on partisan goals and interparty maneuver at the highest levels, were imposed on what is otherwise a fragmented and diffused policy-making process.

Of course, the circumstances of the three cases were somewhat different. For the health and industrial policy reforms, the party leaderships took control as a result of the partisan dynamics that accompanied the inclusion of the Italian Communist party (PCI) in the "governmental area" following the major PCI electoral gains of 1975 and 1976 (Lange and Tarrow 1980; Hellman 1978). The programmatic demands of the Communists – which were a condition of their participation in the arrangement – had to be mediated among the government coalition parties. Furthermore, the relationship of cooperation/conflict between the coalition partners – especially the Christian Democratic party and Prime Minister Giulio Andreotti – and the PCI was *publicly* played out on policy grounds. Both the Communists and the coalition partners felt they had to show that they were dealing with the national crisis which had been used to legitimate the peculiar coalition, and both wanted to appear as the primary source of the "extraordinary" policy measures intended to deal with that crisis. At the same time, the then very powerful trade unions showed their changed attitude toward both the new coalition and the need for economic crisis management by reaching agreements with the government (on the industrial policy reform, on youth unemployment measures, etc.), later to be transformed into laws.

This was not "politics as usual." It was, instead, the politics of highly *visible* and *symbolic* partisan competition/cooperation. Under these conditions, the party leaderships seized the initiative, superseding the normal channels of fractionated policy-making within the parties and formal legislative institutions and bargained between themselves the terms of policy agreements. The reforms reflected carefully drawn compromises within the parties of government and the PCI, with an additional important role played by the unions, whose opposition might have proved fatal to the reform efforts. There was, thus, little scope for changes through parliamentary action, all the more so because the parties were engaged in public "credit-taking" for the decisiveness of the reform and the capacity for effective response to crisis that it displayed.

From the standpoint of our earlier discussion, what is important to note about this process is that it tended sharply to increase the insulation from fragmented pressures and, especially, the comprehensiveness of the decision-making process. On the one hand, the institutional settings most susceptible to fragmented pressures were cut out of the formulation of policy. Of course, the parties are themselves quite permeable, but both the centralization of decision-making into the hands of the political leaderships and the highly public and symbolic cooperation/competition among the parties reduced the possibilities for influence by party factions, internal policy networks, or privileged external interests. Certainly the latter were consulted, but these were primarily the major encompassing functional interests, themselves represented by relatively centralized organizational leaderships (e.g., *Confindustria*, and especially the three union confederations, at that time operating in relative unison). On the other hand, the party leaderships, precisely because of their authority within their parties and the strategic logic of the interparty bargaining, were able and willing under these conditions to pursue a more comprehensive approach to reform, with significant linkage between policy issues that might, under other conditions, be treated separately.

The specific situation and dynamics of the efforts to reach concerted agreements in 1983 and 1984 were different from, but analytically bear considerable resemblances to, those just discussed. First, decision-making again was centralized in the hands of a relatively few officials, *acting outside of the parliamentary and bureaucratic arenas.*[6] The roles played by specific actors were different. The party leaderships were less important, specific government ministers more so; the parties took a lesser role,[7] the leaderships of the unions and of *Confindustria* a larger one. Yet, the effect was similar: decision-making was centralized. Second, the processes and decisions were highly public and visible, and the stakes of the decisions were understood by the decision-makers and public as being as much symbolic – involving reciprocal legitimation – as substantive. Third, the bargaining agents (the government ministers taking the most active roles, and the leaderships of the union and *Confindustria*) were, under these conditions, able to incorporate a large number of often separated issues into a single policy package, trading off concessions in one area for advantages in another. These were, in other words, "package deals," which meant that they were both more comprehensive than normal and less susceptible to parliamentary or bureaucratic tinkering.[8] In sum, like the reform legislation of the late 1970s, the two efforts at concertation of the early 1980s appeared to have at least partially "succeeded" because they were able to increase both the relative insulation and especially the comprehensiveness of the decision-making processes through the concentration of power to make decisions in the hands of relatively few decision makers whose strategic goals were partisan, symbolic, and comprehensive and whose actions and decisions were highly public.

The natural question that arises at this point is what were the broader political and other conditions that facilitated this kind of decision-making, overriding the normal institutional constraints. No simple answer can be given. Two conditions should, however, be mentioned. First, in all cases, at least one, and generally more, of the actors saw advantages and succeeded in portraying the situation as a "crisis" or an "emergency" that required extraordinary action. In the late 1970s, the sense of crisis was pervasive, but it was the Communists who drew the greatest advantage from such a characterization. In the mid-1980s, it was the leaderships of the two governments and *Confindustria* who portrayed a sense of crisis.[9] The role of the crisis atmosphere was sharply to constrain the demands of the contending parties and to justify and legitimate the use of extraordinary processes to reach decisions.

Second, in both periods, the atmosphere of crisis promoted a highly visible politics of partisan competition/cooperation in which winning or losing became less dependent on substantive than symbolic policy outputs and less linked to the satisfaction of narrowly articulated interests than to seeming to serve the "public" interest.[10] In combination, these two factors appear to have been critical preconditions to the kinds of decision process we have described, which led to the attempt to implement major revisions in the mixes of modes and institutions used to regulate policy areas.

It remains to be explained, however, why there was an almost unanimous agreement in these years on the need for "centralized management" of the crisis by means of a combination of state regulation and concerted agreement leading to a series of comprehensive reforms. This strategy was not confined to Italy in the late 1970s. It was also pursued in other European countries such as Britain under the "social contract." There appear to be two reasons for this seeming convergence. The first is linked to the political and cultural prevalence of a strategy with the following components: incomes policy, and therefore moderation on the part of the social partners, in exchange for state intervention aimed at expanding or rationalizing welfare provisions with an inevitable increase in the public role in the regulation of important aspects of economic activity. The contrasting strategy, aimed at deregulation, larger scope for the market, and a partial dismantling of the welfare state, had not yet achieved cultural legitimation or political hegemony.[11] The second reason (which may be causally prior to the first) is that trends – so evident in the 1980s – toward labor market segmentation, the search by capitalists for flexibility in the workplace, and social differentiation had not yet become fully evident (Berger and Piore 1980; Piore and Sabel 1984; Accornero 1984; Regini 1988; Carrieri and Donolo 1983). These social and economic changes created major problems for encompassing organizations in aggregating the demands of their constituents and for defining, much less winning support for, programs of "general" reform. Or it may be that while the manifestations of these trends had already begun to appear, the "culture of crisis" of the late 1970s postponed their organizational and strategic effects. In any case, solutions built on centralized and relatively consensual management of the crisis still seemed relatively "obvious" and "necessary" at that time; and they led to the search for basic innovations in the prevalent modes of regulation.

The case of the Bank of Italy reform was markedly different, but it again shows the importance of the variables of insulation and comprehensiveness. As described by Epstein and Schor (Chapter 6; see also Addis 1987), the reform of Bank policy resulted from a series of incremental reforms made over a lengthy period of time. The incrementalism of these reforms does not, however, appear to have been the product of countervailing external pressures on the Bank's policy process. Rather, it resulted from a gradual evolution of policy strategy among the Bank's leadership in response to a changing economic environment. The grounds for this change seem to have been "technical" in the sense that they were driven by the particular ideology – based on economic theory – of officials within the Bank itself.[12]

What is striking in the accounts, in fact, is the high degree of insulation – in part due to ignorance and in part to deference – among those outside the Bank whom one might have expected to be most concerned about the increasing role of the market and declining role of state control and "public" goals in Bank policies. The absence of any real concern by the Communist party – a traditional supporter of the Bank's staff, which it has viewed as an island of autonomy in a sea of highly partisan and inimical institutions and pressures, including those from government – or the trade unions meant that the Bank was able to pursue its change in regulatory strategy largely immune from political or interest pressures from the Left. To the extent that the changes being undertaken were consonant with the economic interests and ideology of elements of the business community, there was no need for them to seek to exercise pressure.

Thus again in the Bank case, insulation appears to be important in explaining the emergence of a sharply reformed mode of regulating (in this case monetary) policy. The problems of fragmentation were overcome by the fact that the Bank leadership – both technical and political

– was largely in control of all the instruments necessary to accomplish their policy goals. Under these conditions, policy intention could be translated into policy implementation. The "technical" character of the policy area – and, more importantly, the tendency of the political parties and interest groups to treat it as such and to accord the Bank a good degree of policy autonomy – allowed a significant reform to take place without the kinds of special conditions we have seen are necessary in more permeable and politicized policy areas.

In concluding this discussion of exceptional cases of major innovations in regulatory approach, it is worthwhile remembering their fate: in all but one (the Bank "divorce"), the ambitions were frustrated, the innovations undermined, the initial goals of the reform largely defeated. The formulation of policy and the passage of legislation or achievement of formal agreement among contending parties proved easier than the sustained implementation of new policy procedures involving marked departures in the mix of regulatory mechanisms and institutions. In thinking about why this was so, we observe once again the pervasive impact of the highly permeable and fragmented character of Italian policy-making institutions.

In the chapters by both Granaglia and Ferrera, it is clear that the reforms broke down because the "extraordinary" conditions that permitted the insulation and comprehensiveness of the process leading to the reforms were not and, we would argue, could not be sustained once the implementation process began. The reasons for this are threefold. First, precisely the symbolic, centralized, and highly partisan character of reform efforts engineered by the top party leaderships meant that once the political returns of appearing decisive in the face of crisis had been realized, attention was likely to shift elsewhere, with implementation passing into other hands proceeding in "normal" ways. Such normalization, however, could be expected to have precisely the consequences outlined by our authors. Preexisting policy networks and/ or highly permeable decision-making structures reasserted themselves, opening the way for the influence of fragmented interests seeking to change the general direction or divert specific impacts of the reforms. Furthermore, even to the extent that parties continued to exert their influence, in the "invisibility" of normal politics it would be in the parties' interests to satisfy specific, negatively affected constituencies, the returns of symbolic politics having already been gained. They could, so to speak, have their cake and eat it too. This was all the more the case with the breakdown of the national solidarity governments, Communist electoral losses, and more general political defeat after 1979, which altered the terms of political competition, putting it on a more normal footing. Finally, as both authors indicate, the reforms themselves were flawed by a lack of effective linkage between principles and institutional structure. These weaknesses only amplified the opportunities for fragmented interests to reassert their influence.

The sources of the breakdown in the concertation agreements are more complex, but nonetheless show the importance of institutional structures in explaining the pattern of policy outcomes. On the one hand, it is not at all clear to what extent the unions and especially *Confindustria* were really committed to implementation of the agreements. In 1983, signs of decay of the agreements undertaken appeared almost immediately. In 1984, the CGIL (Confederazione Generale Italiana del Lavoro) did not agree to sign and the PCI mounted an immediate, and highly public and symbolic, opposition (Regini 1987a; Lange 1986). The agreements had some short-term effects on wage and employment practices, but failed completely as efforts to reorganize the modes and institutions for the regulation of industrial relations.

Cella (Chapter 7) suggests that this outcome was the result of the low degree of "institutionalization" of Italian industrial relations and the related politicization of this policy arena. Such an explanation already points to the lack of insulation. Yet we would mention in addition the ways that the more general fragmentation and lack of insulation of the Italian policy process contributed to the failure to implement structural changes. For concertation to work and become the established way of reaching major industrial relations decisions, the government must be able to offer *reliable* tradeoffs and/or guarantees in a variety of policy arenas. Yet, under normal conditions we have seen that it cannot make such commitments with sufficient credibility to reduce the risks faced by the actors. Furthermore, the actors themselves can expect to be able to gain direct access to policy-making procedures on issues most important to them. Thus, the fragmentation and permeability of the policy process feed back negatively on the possibility of reaching and stably implementing agreements that require reliable inter-policy area commitments.

The Bank case is again different. Here insulation created the possibility of significant change and also appears to have allowed effective implementation over time. The "technical legitimacy" of the Bank and the insulation of the policy processes and criteria established by the "divorce" have protected the reform from the decay of original intentions we have seen in other areas. It is also possible, but this is no more than a speculation, that the predictability associated with post-reform Bank policy is preferred, even when the outcomes are undesirable from the standpoint of actors' short-term interests, to the uncertainties – both about who might predominate and how stable policy would be – that would result from more politicized and/or permeable central bank policy-making procedures.

To conclude, the four "exceptions" to the normal process of policy-making in Italy reinforce our understanding of the conditions under which major changes in modes and institutions of regulation are likely in Italy. Moreover, it is clear that even when major reforms can be undertaken, their implementation remains problematic. The lack of insulation of the policy-making arenas, the high fragmentation of the interests that make inputs to the policy process, and the lack of linkages between the different arenas result in policy change that is more a reflection of changes in the political resources of the actors seeking to influence the policy process than of concerted efforts to make major changes. The mixes of regulatory modes and institutions will be likely to change, but only in incremental, marginal fashion.

3. Closing observations

"Unintended" is perhaps the word that best characterizes the patterns of regulation we have observed in Italy. By this we do not mean that the actors involved in policy-making do not have goals, but that the outcomes do not reflect the intentions of any single actor or coalition. When we look at the regulatory mix in a particular policy area, much less at the mixes across policy areas, we find few signs of design, governing vision, ideology, or even predominant cultural patterning. Instead, there is a crazy quilt of sometimes contradictory, sometimes complementary modes and institutions for regulating the production and allocation of resources and the conflicts among interested parties.

In the most immediate sense, we have seen that this can be explained as the outcome of the push and tug of relatively fragmented social and political actors pressing their interests. Operating in an institutional environment that offers them ample access to multiple decision points or encapsulates them in relatively stable policy networks, they can defend their particularistic interests but find few chances to impose broader regulatory ideologies.

From a longer perspective, these institutions can themselves be explained as outcomes of the postwar political and economic development of Italy and the Italian party system. Constitutional and other compromises reached among the predominant postwar "social-political blocs" created an institutional framework that reflects the postwar balance of power among them. Unwilling or unable to impose a unique structure of social and political order, the two blocs, led respectively by the Christian Democrats and the Communists, settled on institutional compromises that might not allow them wholly to predominate but that would certainly enable them to extract desired resources from the polity and above all to survive.[13] When combined with the historical tendency toward a pervasive but only partially effective *etatisme* (Cassese 1987; Paci, Chapter 9), the result has been a decidedly complex set of regulatory mixes reflecting social and political pressures, symbiotic and evasive reactions to state intervention, and a highly incrementalist process of policy influence.

In concluding our discussion, however, we need to touch briefly on two questions. The first concerns whether and how systematic change occurs in such a system; the second, what our findings from Italy can and cannot tell us about regulatory processes in other advanced industrial democracies.

It might appear that stalemate is the rule in policy and regulatory mixes in Italy. Yet the essays in this volume suggest that this is far from being the case. Certainly, if the standard is the grand designs for reform that occasionally appear for different policy issues, stasis is the predominant image. Even when – as we have seen – extraordinary conditions permit efforts at major reform, they appear, with very few exceptions, rapidly to run afoul of the underlying social, political, and institutional structure. But when we look with a finer lens and set aside grand reformist ambitions, we find that there is considerable change and that, occasionally, it even appears to have a consistency of direction. Examples of the former appear throughout this volume. One cannot, in fact, but be impressed by the dynamism and resourcefulness of Italian social and economic actors who seem able to develop often highly innovative and effective policy responses to emergent problems and opportunities. These responses often occur outside of, in spite of, or in negative reaction to actions undertaken by the state. But they are also often aided, sometimes intentionally, more frequently unintentionally, by state policies. The mixes we observe generally reflect these processes of interaction between society and state.

We see as well instances of incremental but consistent changes in the character of regulation. The studies on the labor market, for instance, note a growth in the role of market mechanisms for the regulation of entry and exit, wages, and employment conditions in the mid-1980s and speculate on the possible continuation of such trends. If one employs a solely institutionalist explanation of policy outcomes, such trends seem inexplicable. The permeability and lack of comprehensiveness in the policy process should enable those whose interests are damaged by such trends to defend themselves through countervailing action in one or another institutional setting.

What this fails to recognize, however, is that even in the fragmented policy framework we have identified, external, sometimes structural, changes in the distribution of power resources can have profound and consistent effects on how regulation takes place. Just as in the first half of the 1970s the effects of the immense increase of the mobilizational and political capacities of the labor movement were translated into a set of changes across policy areas (see Stefanizzi and Tarrow, Chapter 3), so too in the mid-1980s a shift in power resources toward capital and toward a policy agenda dominated by questions of economic competitiveness rather than distribution has been reflected in numerous policy and regulatory changes. Grand designs for innovation generally fail, but change is a constant, and consistent change can emerge as a reflection of broad-scale shifts in social and political power and their translation into incremental policy initiatives. Indeed, the less public and explicit the rationales behind such changes, the more likely that they will not run aground of countervailing pressures.[14]

Precisely this kind of discussion, however, tends to suggest that there is something "unique" about the Italian case we have presented. What then are the possible generalizations that might be drawn to other countries? We would suggest three primary ones. The first concerns our finding that regulation in Italy occurs through a highly complex mix of modes and institutions. There is little reason to believe that this would not also be the case in other countries. These mixes appear to reflect the complexity and multiplicity of interests that are commingled in any policy area, and there is no reason to think such underlying realities will not also be present elsewhere. Two qualifications should, however, be entered. To the extent that power relations among critical social actors have been consistently to the advantage of one or another or some coalition of them, and to the extent that these actors have operated with a consistent regulatory ideology, mixes might be more coherent and uniform in different policy areas. One might think here, for example, of regulation of labor relations as well as a set of economic and social policies in the American South. Furthermore, we would stress that it will be difficult to understand the mix of regulatory modes and institutions without paying close attention to the institutional structures through which state policy with respect to regulation is established. It is, in fact, the interplay between the structuring of social relations of power and institutional structures that appears to determine the character of regulation and how it is likely to change over time.

Second, it seems clear that the Italian political system is particularly likely – one could even say appropriately designed – to produce the kinds of regulatory outcomes we have illustrated. Both the political and institutional structure of the country make complex regulatory mixes reflecting a multiplicity of fragmented interests probable and major reforms unlikely. We have seen that, under special conditions, the latter are possible, but even when undertaken, they may not be implemented over time. If we look across the advanced industrial democracies, the Italian system seems peculiarly without the kinds of institutions that are able to impose relatively consistent policy directions. The absence of either a potentially strong presidential office that can, under certain conditions, claim a mandate and operate on it (as in the United States) or of strong, disciplined, and relatively predominant parliamentary parties linked to the political executive (as has been the case in Britain and Germany, for instance) make the imposition of coherent policy initiatives unlikely. Where these latter institutional conditions are present, even a highly fragmented interest structure and/or highly permeable legislative and bureaucratic institutions may be turned to major innovations in regulation or overridden.

Third and last, we return to the broad historical question that initially provoked us to undertake the project which led to this volume: is there any general trend away from the state and toward the market, away from authority and toward exchange, in the advanced industrial democracies? Our study of the Italian case would urge caution in pressing such a thesis, in two respects. On the one hand, the contraposition of state and market seems misplaced both because the two often have highly symbiotic relationships (which extend well beyond the traditional state economic functions of guaranteeing property rights, defending national capital on the world market, and providing infrastructural support) and because we have consistently found the presence of other – than authority and exchange, and state and market – modes and institutions of regulation. Simplistic formulations of how regulation does, and even more *ought to*, take place seem belied by the Italian case. The terms of the contemporary political debate seem likely to be out of touch with the reality which they are thought to capture and for which they prescribe. Second, to the extent that there have been shifts, within these complex mixes, towards a greater role for the market and exchange relationships in the last decade, there seems little reason to believe they will necessarily endure. Because, we would argue, they are primarily the reflection of particular constellations of power during the current decade and not of long-term structural or even secular transformations, trends may change. What needs to be done, therefore, is not so much to describe current trends but to try to understand their underlying structure and causes. We need to compare how shared issues and similar shifts in power resources have been translated into changes in regulatory mixes across the advanced industrial democracies. And we need to examine how patterns of outcomes have differed across policy areas within countries and across them and what role institutional and political structures play in explaining these different outcomes. We need, in other words, to move from polemic and prescription to analysis and explanation. In that task this volume is a first, tentative step.

Notes

1 One can undoubtedly develop theoretical arguments for why this is the case. One promising direction in which to look for such theoretical insights is the work of Williamson (1975) on transaction cost analysis in micro-economics and the research and further theoretical elaborations that it has spawned.

2 Even for the PCI, there has been considerable evidence that the party has in the last fifteen years become less able to impose a highly aggregative strategy on the multiple interests that it incorporates and represents.

3 Stefanizzi and Tarrow (Chapter 3) show that this was even the case for the Communist party and the members and mass organizations whose behavior it could putatively control.

4 In 1983, all three major labor confederations joined in the final accord. In 1984, the Communist-led CGIL, the largest of the confederations, refused to enter into an accord, setting off a protracted struggle within the union movement and the political system more generally (Regini 1987a; Lange 1986).

5 Another set of differences concerns the goals of the reforms. In two cases (health and industrial policy) the effort was to centralize and expand regulation by state authority. In a third, the effort was to use the state's authority and its financial resources to promote concerted agreements (oligopolistic bargaining) among the principal industrial relations actors. In the fourth case, the changes were designed to reduce markedly the role of the state relative to the market. As will be clear, however, these differences seem relatively unimportant in explaining why reform occurred and why it succeeded or failed.

6 In both years, the respective Ministers of Labor, strongly backed by the authority (and at points intervention) of the respective Prime Ministers, took the lead in hammering out the agreements. For the necessary technical support and negotiation of detailed portions of the bargains, they sought outside advice and/or the help of ad hoc internal committees made up of those whose advice they respected *and* trusted and/or who would be useful in legitimating the agreements to the other interested parties and the public. "Normal" channels were circumvented, and final bargaining was carried on almost exclusively between the Labor and Prime Ministers acting for the government and their own party (in 1983 both were from the Christian Democrats; in 1984, from the Socialists), the leadership of the PCI, and the leaderships of the unions and *Confindustria* (Lange 1986).

7 Exceptions in this regard are the parties of the Prime Minister and Labor Minister in each year, which had a major stake in a successful outcome, and the PCI, whose interests were heavily bound up both with what role it was allowed to play in the bargaining and with the substantive outcomes. The Communists were regularly consulted in both years. In 1984, however, they chose to oppose the agreement (Lange 1986).

8 A number of the aspects of the agreements of both 1983 and 1984 eventually required parliamentary approval, but Parliament's role was largely reduced to a formal one. In interviews conducted by one of the authors in 1986, Communist party officials complained of this, particularly with respect to the 1984 agreement, which they opposed.

9 We do not here wish to enter into arguments about whether or not a "crisis" was present. Rather, what is important is that some of the key actors gained advantage from communicating a sense of crisis for the nation and getting the public to accept it.

10 Again, our point here is not whether such a public interest existed or was served but that it was perceived to and became a critical standard by which the parties in conflict could measure their gains or losses.

11 In Italy this did not even occur in 1983–1984 when concertation was still being pursued there while other countries were changing to policies more in accord with the second strategy.

12 What we are suggesting here is that policy change was not the product of direct interest pressures. This does not, of course, mean that the policy did not serve a particular constellation of interests and damage others, but only that these were effects, but probably not causes, of the changes. To the extent that they played a role in causing the evolution of Bank policy, the mechanisms were highly mediated.

13 In the case of the Christian Democrats even more than for the Communists, it is also clear that the internal social coalition that the party represented could not be represented by a single predominating and coherent pattern of regulatory modes and institutions (see, for instance, Paci's discussion of social welfare [Chapter 9] and Chiesi and Martinelli's of industrial interests [Chapter 8]). It might, more boldly, be argued that any dominant social and political bloc in the advanced industrial democracies is certain to have internal contradictions with respect to the "appropriate" way to regulate social affairs that are likely to be reproduced in policy outcomes combining different mixes of regulatory mechanisms across policy areas.

14 This may seem to contradict our analysis of the four "exceptions." It does not, however, for two reasons. On the one hand, we are discussing here not discrete efforts at major reform but incremental changes driven by a shifting balance of power resources which, when looked at over time, result in major changes in how particular policy areas are regulated. On the other hand, as we saw in those cases, major highly public and symbolic initiatives can rapidly run afoul of countervailing fragmented pressures once out of the glare of public scrutiny.

Bibliography

Abbate, M., Lo Moro, V., and Marconi, P. 1985. *I finanziamenti pubblici all'industria.* Rome: FOR.

Aburrà, L. 1984. "Liberalizzazione senza riforma, lavoro senza formazione (i contratti di formazione-lavoro e la Legge no. 79 in Piemonte)." *Quaderni di rassegna sindacale,* No. 106.

Aberbach, J. D., Putnam, R. D., and Rockman, B. A. 1981. *Bureaucrats and Politicians in Western Democracies.* Cambridge, Mass.: Harvard University Press.

Abrams, P. 1983. *Sociologia storica.* Bologna: Il Mulino.

Accornero, A. 1967. [Published anonymously] *I comunisti in fabbrica: Documenti delle lotte operaie,* No. 1. Florence: Centro G. Francovish.

1984. "Fra stabilita e flessibilita: sindacato e modelli di tutela." *Quaderni di rassegna sindacale,* No. 108-109.

Addis, E. 1987. "Banca d'Italia e politica monetaria: la riallocazione del potere fra Stato, mercato e banca centrale." *Stato e Mercato,* No. 19 (April).

Alford, R. 1976. *Health Care Politics.* Chicago: University of Chicago Press.

Allum, P. A. 1973. *Italy: Republic Without Government?* New York: Norton.

Amato, G. (ed.). 1971. *Il governo dell'industria in Italia.* Bologna: Il Mulino.

1976. *Economia, politica ed istituzioni.* Bologna: Il Mulino.

Amendola, A., and Jossa, B. 1981. "Italian Economic Development: Comment on an Interpretation." *Review of Economic Conditions in Italy,* No. 3, pp. 481-512.

Arrigo, G. 1983. "Occupazione giovanile: dai progetti di riforma alle riforme senza progetto." *Contrattazione,* No. 3.

Arrow, K. 1963. "Uncertainty and the Economics of Medical Care." *American Economic Review,* 53.

1974. *The Limits of Organization.* New York: Norton.

Ascoli, U. (ed.). 1984. *Welfare State all'italiana.* Bari: Laterza.

Astrologo, D., and Ricolfi, L. 1981. "Governare il mercato del lavoro," in S. Scamuzzi (ed.), *Riforma del collocamento e mercato del lavoro.* Milan: F. Angeli.

Azzolini, R., Di Malta, R., and Pastore, R. 1979. *L'industria chimica tra crisi e programmazione.* Rome: Editori Riuniti.

Bachrach and Baratz. 1963. "Decisions and non-decisions: an analytical framework." *American Political Science Review* 57:632-42.

Bade, R., and Parkin, M. 1980. "Central Bank Laws and Monetary Policy." University of Western Ontario. Mimeo.

273

Baglioni, Guido. 1976. "Il cammino e le difficolta dell'unita sindacale," pp. 873–90 in Accornero, A. (ed.), *Problemi del movimento sindacale in Italia. 1943–1973.* Milan: Feltrinelli.

Baglioni, M. 1986. *L'azione collettiva.* Milan: Giuffre.

Bagnasco, A. 1985. "La costruzione sociale del mercato: strategie di impresa ed esperimenti di scala in Italia." *Stato e Mercato,* No. 13 (April).

Balbo, L. 1986. "Falsa tematizzazione: il PCI e la vita quotidiana," pp. 3–14 in L. Balbo and V. Foa (eds.), *Lettere da vicino.* Torino: Einaudi.

Bananian, K., Laney, L., and Willett, T. 1983. "Central Bank Independence: An International Comparison." *Federal Reserve Bank of Dallas Economic Reviews,* March, pp. 1–13.

1987. "Making the Fed More Politically Responsible Isn't Likely to Reduce Inflation: A Comparative Study of Central Banking Arrangements and Inflation in Industrial Countries," in T. Willett (ed.), *Political Business Cycles: The Economics and Politics of Stagflation.* San Francisco: Pacific Institute.

Banfield, E. 1958. *The Moral Basis of a Backward Society.* Glencoe: The Free Press.

Bank of Italy. Various years. *Annual Report,* abridged version.

Barbagli, Marzio, and Corbetta, Piergiorgio. 1978. "Partito e movimento: Aspetti del rinnovamento del PCI." *Inchiesta* 8:3–46.

Barberis, C. 1973. *Sindaci, assessori e consiglieri nei municipi d'Italia.* Rome: Cinque Lune.

Barnes, S. 1977. *Representation in Italy.* Chicago: University of Chicago Press.

Becchi Collidà A. (ed.). 1978. *Lavoro, sussidi, Mezzogiorno.* Milan: F. Angeli.

Benedizione, N. 1984. "Il ruolo del Presidente del Consiglio nel rapporto governo-parti sociali." *Annali della Fondazione G. Pastore,* XI (Milan: F. Angeli).

Benoit, A. 1984. *La politique de l'emploi. Organisation et moyens.* Paris: La Documentation Francaise.

Berger, S. 1979. "Politics and Antipolitics in Western Europe in the Seventies. *Daedalus,* Winter, pp. 27–50.

Berger, S., and Piore, M. T. 1980. *Dualism and Discontinuity in Industrial Societies.* Cambridge: Cambridge University Press.

Blau, P. M. 1964. *Exchange and Power in Social Life.* New York: J. Wiley.

Bobbio, Luigi. 1979. *Lotta Continua: Storia di una organizzazione rivoluzionaria.* Milan: Savelli.

Boccella, N. 1982. *Il Mezzogiorno sussidiato: reddito prodotto e trasferimenti alle famiglie nei comuni meridionali.* Milan: F. Angeli.

Bolasco, S., Cerase, F. P., Mignella Calvosa, F., and Rella, P. 1983. *Istituzioni, giovani e lavoro.* Milan: F. Angeli.

Boltho, A. (ed.). 1982. *The European Economy: Growth and Crisis.* Oxford: Oxford University Press.

Bordogna, L. 1985. "Tendenze neo-corporatiste e trasformazioni del conflitto industriale," in G. P. Cella and M. Regini (eds.), *Il conflitto industriale in Italia.* Bologna: Il Mulino.

Bordogna, L., and Provasi, G. 1979. "Il movimento degli scioperi in Italia, 1881–1987," pp. 169–304 in G. P. Cella (ed.), *Il movimento degli scioperi nel XX secolo.* Bologna: Il Mulino.

1984. *Politica, economia e rappresentanza degli interessi.* Bologna: Il Mulino.

Boyer, R. 1979. "La crise actuelle," Critiques de l'économie politique, Nos. 7–8.

Boyer, R., and Mistral, J. 1978. *Accumulation, Inflation, Crises.* Paris.

Brinton, Milward, H. 1980. "Policy Entrepreneurship and Bureaucratic Demand Creation," pp. 255–77 in H. M. Ingram and D. E. Mann (eds.), *Why Policies Succeed or Fail.* Beverly Hills: Sage.

Bruno, Michael, and Sachs, Jeffrey. 1985. *Economics of Worldwide Stagflation.* Cambridge: Harvard University Press.

Button, James W. 1978. *Black Violence: Political Impact of the 1960s Riots.* Princeton: Princeton University Press.

Caranza, C., and Fazio, A. 1983. "Methods of Monetary Control in Italy," in D. Hodgam (ed.), *The Political Economy of Monetary Policy: National and International Aspects,* Conference Series 26. Boston: Federal Reserve Bank of Boston.

Carinci, F. 1985. "Il protocollo IRI nella dinamica delle relazioni industriali," in CESOS (ed.), *Le relazioni sindacali in Italia. Rapporto 1984/85.* Rome: Edizioni Lavoro.

Carrieri, M., and Donolo, C. 1983. "Oltre l'orizzonte neo-corporatista." *Stato e Mercato,* No. 9 (December).

1986. *Il mestiere politico del sindacato.* Rome: Editori Riuniti.

Cassese, S. 1980. *Esiste un governo in Italia?* Rome: Officina Edizioni.

1983a. *Il sistema amministrativo italiano.* Bologna: Il Mulino.

1983b. "Espansione e controllo della spesa pubblica," in *Il Mulino,* No. 3.

1984. "Le due realta della politica industriale italiana." *Mondo Economico,* 22 March.

1987. "Stato ed economia: il problema storico," pp. 45–53 in P. Lange and M. Regini (eds.), *Stato e regolazione sociale: Nuove prospettive sul caso italiano.* Bologna: Il Mulino.

Castles, F. G. (ed.). 1982. *The Impact of Parties, Politics and Policies in Democratic Capitalist States.* Beverly Hills: Sage.

Cazzola, F. 1972. "Consenso e opposizione nel Parlamento italiano. Il ruolo del PCI dalla I alla IV legislatura." *Rivista Italiana di Scienza Politica,* 2.

(ed.). 1979. *Anatomia del potere DC.* Bari: De Donato.

1982. "La solidarieta nazionale dalla parte del Parlamento." *Laboratorio politico,* No. 2–3.

CEEP. 1984. *Dibattito sulla politica industriale.* Rome.

Cella, G. P. 1981. "Tra interesse e solidarieta: L'azione sindacale nella crisi del pluralismo." *Stato e Mercato,* No. 2 (August).

1985. "Tipologia e determinanti della conflittualita," in G. P. Cella and M. Regini (eds.), *Il conflitto industriale in Italia.* Bologna: Il Mulino.

Censis. 1986. "Relazione sulla situazione sociale del paese." *Quindicinale di Note e Commenti,* No. 2–3.

Centre de Recherche Travail et Société. 1983. *Evaluation des politiques de l'emploi en Europe.* Paris: Université Paris IX-Dauphine.

CER-IRS. 1986. *Quale strategia per l'industria?* Bologna: Il Mulino.

Chandler, A. D. 1977. *The Visible Hand.* Cambridge, Mass.: Harvard University Press.

Chiesi, A. M. 1982. "L'elite finanziaria italiana." *Rassegna italiana di sociologia,* No. 4.

1985. "L'organizzazione degli interessi imprenditoriali in un caso di ristrutturazione settoriale." *Studi Organizzativi.* No. 3–4.

1986. *La classe dirigente economica milanese.* Mimeo. Milan: Istituto Superiore di Sociologia.

CNEL. 1982. *Osservazioni e proposte sullo stato di attuazione della riforma sanitaria.* Rome.

Compagna-Marchini, L. 1981. *Nel labirinto della politica industriale.* Bologna: Il Mulino.

CONFINDUSTRIA. 1983. "Commissione per la formulazione della proposta di riassetto per la determinazione degli strumenti giuridici ed organizzativi di attuazione." Rome, October. Mimeo.

Cortese, A. *Il mercato del lavoro fra economia e società.* Milan, F. Angeli.

Cotula, F. 1984. "Financial Innovation and Monetary Control in Italy." *Banca Nazionale del Lavoro Quarterly Review* 37:219–56.

Crouch, C. 1978. "Inflation and the Political Organization of Economic Interests," pp.

217–39 in F. Hirsch and J. Goldthorpe (eds.), *The Political Economy of Inflation*. Cambridge: Harvard University Press.

1981a. "Dal compromesso di classe alla radicalizzazione dei rapporti sociali," in G. Baglioni and E. Santi (eds.), *L'Europa sindacale agli inizi degli anni '80*. Bologna: Il Mulino.

1981b. "Stato, mercato e organizzazione: la teoria neocorporativa." *Stato e Mercato*, No. 2 (August).

Crouch, C., and Pizzorno, A. (eds.) 1978. *The Resurgence of Class Conflict in Western Europe Since 1968*, 2 volumes. London: Macmillan.

Cullis, J., and West, P. 1979. *The Economics of Health*. Oxford: Robertson.

Culyer, A., and Cooper, M. (eds.). 1973. *Health Economics*. Harmondsworth: Penguin Books.

David, P. 1984. "Il sistema assistenziale in Italia," in U. Ascoli (ed.), *Welfare State all'italiana*. Bari: Laterza.

1985. "La politica dell'assistenza tra riformismo e tradizione." *Stato e Mercato*, No. 14 (August).

De Vivo, G., and Pivetti, M. 1981. "International Integration and the Balance of Payments Constraint: The Case of Italy." *Cambridge Journal of Economics*, No. 4, pp. 1–22.

Dell'Aringa, C. 1983. "Ristrutturazione industriale e mercato del lavoro." *Prospettiva sindacale*, No. 49.

Della Porta, D. 1987. "Organizazzioni politiche clandestine: Il terrorismo di sinistra in Italia durante gli anni settanta." Ph.D. thesis, European University Institute.

Della Porta, D., and Tarrow, S. 1987. "Unwanted Children: Political Violence and the Cycle of Protest in Italy, 1966–1973." *European Journal of Political Research* 14:607–32.

Dente, B. 1985. *Governare la frammentazione. Stato, Regioni ed Enti Locali in Italia*. Bologna: Il Mulino.

Diebold, W. 1980. *Industrial Policy as an International Issue*. New York: McGraw-Hill.

Di Gaspare, G. 1981. *Organi, procedimenti decisionali e strumenti di agevolazione finanziaria all'industria agli inizi degli anni '80*. Rome.

DiPalma, G. 1977. *Surviving Without Governing. Italian Parties in Parliament*. Berkeley: University of California Press.

Dryzek, J. S. 1983. "Don't Toss Coins in Garbage Cans: A Prologue to Policy Design." *Journal of Public Policy*, No. 3, pp. 345–68.

Dubois, P. 1978. "New Forms of Industrial Conflict," pp. 1–34 in C. Crouch and A. Pizzorno (eds.), *The Resurgence of Class Conflict in Western Europe Since 1968*, vol. 2. London: Macmillan.

Dyson, K. 1983. "The Cultural, Ideological and Structural Context," pp. 26–66 in K. Dyson and S. Wilks (eds.), *Industrial Crisis*. London: Basil Blackwell.

Dyson, K., and Wilks, S. (eds.). 1983. *Industrial Crisis*. London: Basil Blackwell.

Easton, D. 1965. *A Systems Analysis of Political Life*. New York: Wiley.

Eisinger, P. 1973. "The Conditions of Protest Behavior in American Cities." *American Political Science Review* 67:11–28.

Enthoven, A. 1980. *Health Care Plans*. Reading: Addison Wesley.

1986. *Reflections on Improving Efficiency in the NHS*. London: Nuffield Occasional Paper.

Epstein, G. 1981. "Domestic Stagflation and Monetary Policy: The Federal Reserve and the Hidden Election," in T. Ferguson and J. Rogers (eds.), *The Hidden Election*. New York: Pantheon.

1982. "Federal Reserve Politics and Monetary Instability," in Stone and Harpham (eds.), *The Political Economy of Public Policy*. Beverly Hills: Sage.

1985. "The Triple Debt Crisis." *World Policy Journal* 2(No. 3):625–57.

Epstein, G., and Ferguson, T. 1984. "Monetary Policy, Loan Liquidation and Industrial Conflict: The Federal Reserve and the Open Market Operations of 1932." *Journal of Economic History*, 64(No. 4):957–83.

Epstein, G., and Schor, J. B. 1985. "The Determinants of Central Bank Policies in Open Economies: An Analytic Framework." Paper presented at Conference on the Political Economy of Central Banking, University of Naples.

1986. "The Political Economy of Central Banking." Paper presented at Conference on Global Macroeconomic Policies, World Institute for Development Research, Helsinki.

Ergas, Y. 1985. "Allargamento della cittadinanza e governo del conflitto," pp. 232–65 in G. Pasquino (ed.), *Il sistema politico italiano*. Bari: Laterza.

Esping-Andersen, G. 1982. "The Welfare State as a System of Stratification." Paper given at Conference on Society and the Political Economy of the Welfare State, Aarhus, Denmark, April.

Estrin, S., and Holmes, P. 1983. "French Planning and Industrial Policy." *Journal of Public Policy* 3(No. 1):131–48.

Evans, P., Rueschemeyer, D., and Skocpol, T. (eds.). 1985. *Bringing the State Back In.* Cambridge: Cambridge University Press.

Fazio, A. 1979. "Monetary Policy in Italy." *Kredit und Kapital*, No. 3, pp. 145–80.

Fazio, A., and Lo Faso, S. 1980. "The Control of Credit and Financial Intermediation in Italy." *Review of Economic Conditions in Italy*, No. 3, pp. 459–974.

FEDERTESSILE. 1981. *Il settore tessile e abbigliamento in Italia*. Milan: F. Angeli.

Feingold, E. 1980. "Who Controls the Medical Care System?" *Annals of the Academy of Political Science*, Washington.

Ferrera, M. 1984. *Il welfare state in Italia*. Bologna: Il Mulino.

Fiorina, M. P., and Noll, R. G. 1979. "Majority Rule Models and Legislative Elections." *The Journal of Politics*, pp. 1081–1101.

Flanagan, R. J., Soskice, D., and Ulman, L. 1983. *Unionism, Economic Stabilization and Incomes Policies: European Experience*. Washington: The Brookings Institution.

Flora, P., and Heidenheimer, A. J. (eds.). 1981. *The Development of Welfare States in Europe and America*. New Brunswick, N.J.: Transaction Books.

Fox, A., and Flanders, A. 1969. "The Reform of Collective Bargaining, From Donovan to Durkheim." *British Journal of Industrial Relations* 7(No. 2):151–80.

France, G. 1985. "Controlli esterni sull'utilizzo delle risorse da parte delle USL." Mimeo.

Franzosi, R. 1980. "Strikes in Italy: An Exploratory Data Analysis." *Rivista di politica economica, selected papers*, No. 14.

1987. "The Press as a Source of Socio-historical data: Issues in the Methodology of Data Collection from Newspapers." *Historical Methods* 20:5–16.

1988. *Strikes in Italy in the Postwar Period*. Madison: University of Wisconsin Press.

Galante, W., and Bogetti, M. 1982. "Ricerca sul collocamento di Torino:chiamate numeriche." *Osservatorio sul mercato del lavoro e sulle professioni*, No. 2.

Gallino, L. (ed.). 1985. *Il lavoro e il suo doppio*. Bologna: Il Mulino.

Gallo, R. (ed.). 1983. *Attivita concernente il governo dell'industria*. Rome: Istituto Poligrafico dello Stato.

Gambale, S. 1979. "The Crisis in Public Finance in Italy." *Banca Nazionale del Lavoro Quarterly Review* 32(No. 128):73–90.

Gamson, W. 1975. *The Strategy of Protest*. Homewood, Ill.: Dorsey.

1989. "Political Discourse and Collective Action" [in press], in B. Klandermans, H. Kriesi, and S. Tarrow (eds.), *From Structure to Action: Studying Movement Participation across Cultures*. Greenwich, Conn.: JAI.

Garonna, P. 1986. "Youth Unemployment, Labour Market Deregulation and Union Strategies in Italy." *British Journal of Industrial Relations*, 23, No. 1.

Giavazzi, F. 1984. "A Note on the Italian Public Debt." *Banca Nazionale del Lavoro Quarterly Review* 37(No. 128):151–8.

Girotti, F., et al. 1983. *Rapporto sui consiglieri comunali in Piemonte*. Milan: F. Angeli.

Giugni, G. 1976. "Critica e rovesciamento dell'assetto contrattuale," pp. 779–808 in A. Accornero (ed.), *Problemi del movimento sindacale in Italia. 1943–1973*. Milan: Feltrinelli.

1985. "Concertazione sociale e sistema politico in Italia." *Giornale di diritto del lavoro e di relazioni industriali*, VII, No. 25.

Gobbo, F. 1984. "Comportamento delle imprese e politica industriale," in CESOS (ed.), *Le relazioni sindacali in Italia. Rapporto 1982–83*. Rome: Edizioni Lavoro.

Gobbo, F., and Prodi, R. 1982. "La politica industriale italiana." *Note economiche*, No. 5–6, pp. 199–212.

Golden, M. 1988. *Labor Divided: Incomes Policies, Trade Unions and the Italian Communist Party*. Ithaca, N.Y.: Cornell University Press.

Goldthorpe, J. H. 1978. "The Current Inflation: Towards a Sociological Account," in F. Hirsch and J. Goldthorpe (eds.), *The Political Economy of Inflation*. Cambridge: Harvard University Press.

1983. "I problemi dell'economia politica alla fine del periodo post-bellico." *Stato e Mercato*, No. 7.

(ed.). 1984. *Order and Conflict in Contemporary Capitalism. Studies in the Political Economy of Western European Nations*. Oxford: Oxford University Press.

Granaglia, E. 1985. In E. Granaglia et al., *Quale sanita pubblica*. Rome: Salemi.

1986. "Come spendere meglio in sanita." Mimeo. Commissione tecnica spesa pubblica Ministero del Tesoro.

1987. "Il settore privato e la razionalizzazione del SSN," in M. Rey (ed.), *Efficienza ed efficacia nella produzione dei servizi sanitari*. Milan: F. Angeli.

Grant, R. M. 1983. "Appraising Selective Financial Assistance to Industry. A Review of Institutions and Methodologies in the UK, Sweden and West Germany." *Journal of Public Policy*, No. 3–4, pp. 369–98.

Grant, W. (v. libro italiano). 1983. "The Political Economy of Industrial Policy," pp. 118–37 in R. J. Barry Jones (ed.), *Perspectives on Political Economy*. New York: St. Martin's.

Grant, W., and McKay, D. (eds.). 1983. "Industrial Policies in OECD Countries." Special issue of *Journal of Public Policy*, 3, part 1.

Grassini, F., and Scognamiglio, C. (eds.). 1979. *Stato e industria in Europa: l'Italia*. Bologna: Il Mulino.

Graziani, A. 1978. "The Mezzogiorno in the Italian Economy." *Cambridge Journal of Economics*, No. 2, pp. 335–72.

Graziano, L. 1980. *Clientelismo e sistema politico*. Milan: F. Angeli.

Graziano, L., Bonet, L., and Girotti, F. 1984. "I partiti come struttura di controllo: il processo di formazione delle giunte," pp. 303–414 in ISAP, *Le relazioni centro-periferia*, 1. Milan: Giuffre.

Green, D. 1981. *Managing Industrial Change? French Policies to Promote Industrial Adjustment*. London: HMSO.

1983. "Crisis Management in France," in K. Dyson and S. Wilks (eds.), *Industrial Crisis*. London: Basil Blackwell.

Greenberg, W. (ed.). 1978. *Competition in the Health Care Sector*. FTC, Aspen System.

Guidotti, D. 1986. *Strategia generale e azione decentrata*. Milan: F. Angeli.

Havingurst, C. (ed.). 1982. *Deregulating the Health Care Industry*. Cambridge: Ballinger.

Hayward, J. 1984. "Les politiques industrielles et economiques," pp. 89–153 in M. Grawitz and J. Leca (eds.), *Traite de science politique*, 4. Paris: PUF.

Heclo, H. 1978. "Issue Networks and the Executive Establishment," pp. 87–124 in A.

King (ed.), *The New American Political System*. Washington, D.C.: American Enterprise Institute.

Heclo, H., and Wildavsky, A. 1974. *The Private Government of Public Money*. London: Macmillan.

Heidenheimer, A. J. 1981. "Secularization Patterns and the Western Extension of the Welfare State." Mimeo.

Hellman, Stephen. 1977. "The Longest Campaign: Communist Party Strategy and the Election of 1976," in Howard Penniman (ed.), *Italy at the Polls*. Washington: AEI.

Hibbs, Douglas. 1978. "On the Political Economy of Long-Run Trends in Strike Activity." *British Journal of Political Science* 8:153–76.

Hirsch, F. 1978. "The Ideological Underlay of Inflation," in F. Hirsch and J. Goldthorpe (eds.), *The Political Economy of Inflation*. Cambridge: Harvard University Press.

Hogwood, B. 1979. "Analysing Industrial Policy: A Multi-Perspective Approach." *Public Administration Bulletin*, No. 29, pp. 18–43.

    1983. "The Instruments of Desire: How British Government Attempts to Regulate and Influence Industry." *Public Administration Bulletin*, No. 2, pp. 5–25.

Hollingsworth, J. R., and Lindberg, L. N. 1985. "The Governance of the Economy: The Role of Markets, Clans, Hierarchies and Associative Behaviour," in W. Streeck and P. Schmitter (eds.), *Private Interest Government: Beyond Markets and State*. Beverly Hills: Sage.

Huntington, S. P. 1968. *Political Order in Changing Societies*. New Haven: Yale University Press.

Hyatt, H. 1975. "Protecting the Medical Commons." *New England Journal of Medicine*, No. 293.

Istituto Gramsci. 1962. *Tendenze del capitalismo italiano*. Rome: Editori Riuniti.

Jacobi, O., Jessop, B., Kastendiek, H., and Regini, M. (eds.). 1986. *Economic Crisis, Trade Unions and the State*. London: Croom Helm.

Johnson, C. (ed.). 1984. *The Industrial Policy Debate*. San Francisco: Institute for Contemporary Studies.

Jordan, A. G. 1981. "Iron Triangles, Woolly Corporation, or Elastic Nets: Images of the Policy Process." *Journal of Public Policy*, February, pp. 95–123.

Jossa, B., and Panico, C. 1985. "Banking Intermediation During the Italian Economic Crisis (1964–1984)." Paper presented at Conference on the Political Economy of Central Banking, University of Naples.

Jossa, B., and Vinci, S. 1981. "The Italian Economy From 1963 to today: An Interpretation." *Review of Economic Conditions in Italy*, No. 1, pp. 9–40.

Kalecki, M. 1971. "Political Aspects of Full Employment," in *Selected Essays on the Dynamics of a Capitalist Economy*. Cambridge: Cambridge University Press.

Kammerer, P., Bechtle, K., and Heiner, S. 1983. "Mercato del lavoro e mercato della vita." *Inchiesta*, No. 62.

Katz, R. S. 1986. "Party Government: A Rationalistic Conception," pp. 31–71 in F. G. Castles and R. Wildenmann (eds.), *Visions and Realities of Party Government*. Berlin: De Gruyter.

Kemeny, P., and Napoli, M. 1986. "Per un'analisi multidimensionale delle relazioni industriali a livello territoriale," in P. Kemeny et al., *Relazioni industriali e territorio*. Milan: F. Angeli.

Kircheimer, O. 1966. "The Transformation of the Western European Party Systems," in J. LaPalombara and M. Weiner (eds.), *Political Parties and Political Development*. Princeton: Princeton University Press.

Klandermans, B. 1989. "The Formation and Mobilization of Consensus" [in press], in B. Klandermans, K. Hanspeter, and S. Tarrow (eds.), *From Structure to Action: Studying Movement Participation across Cultures*. Greenwich, Conn.: JAI.

Klandermans, B., Kriesi, H., and Tarrow, S. (eds.). 1989. *From Structure to Action: Studying Movement Participation across Cultures* [in press]. Greenwich, Conn.: JAI.

Klein, R. 1984. *The Politics of NHS.* Burnt-Mill, Harlow: Longmans.

Korpi, W. 1983. *The Democratic Class Struggle.* London: Routledge and Kegan Paul.

Lacci, L. 1976. "The Changes in the Compensation of Employees and in the Returns Paid to the Other Factors of Production in Italy During the Period of Rapid Inflation Registered in the First Half of 1970s." *Review of Economic Conditions in Italy.* No. 5. pp. 414–34.

Lange, P. 1977a. *Studies on Italy 1943–75.* Turin: Fondazione Giovanni Agnelli.

  1977b. "La teoria degli incentivi e l'analisi dei partiti politici." *Rassegna italiana di sociologia,* 28, No. 4.

  1983. "Politiche dei redditi e democrazia sindacale in Europa occidentale." *Stato e Mercato,* no. 9.

  1984. "Unions, Workers, and Wage Regulation: the Rational Bases of Consent," in John H. Goldthorpe (ed.), *Order and Conflict in Contemporary Capitalism.* Oxford: Clarendon Press.

  1986. "The End of an Era: The Wage Indexation Referendum of 1985," in R. Leonardi and R. Nanetti (eds.), *Italian Politics: A Review,* Vol. 1. London: Frances Pinter.

Lange, P., and Garrett, G. 1985. "The Politics of Growth: Strategic Interactions and Economic Performance in the Advanced Industrial Democracies 1974–1980. *Journal of Politics* 47(No. 3):792–827.

Lange, P., Ross, G., and Vannicelli, M. 1982. *Unions, Change and Crisis: French and Italian Union Strategy and the Political Economy 1945–1980.* London: Allen and Unwin.

Lange, P., and Tarrow, S. (eds.). 1980. *Italy in Transition.* London: Frank Cass.

Lange, P., Tarrow, S., and Irvin, C. 1988. "Phases of Mobilization: Social Movements and Political Party Recruitment." Unpublished paper.

LaPalombara, J. 1964. *Interest Groups in Italian Politics.* Princeton: Princeton University Press.

  1965. "Italy: Fragmentation, Isolation, Alienation," in L. Pye and S. Verba (eds.), *Political Culture and Political Development.* Princeton: Princeton University Press.

  1987. *Democracy, Italian Style,* New Haven: Yale University Press.

Lehmbruch, G. 1984. "Concertation and the Structure of Corporatist Networks," in J. H. Goldthorpe (ed.), *Order and Conflict in Contemporary Capitalism.* Oxford: Oxford University Press.

Lehmbruch, G., and Schmitter, P. (eds.). 1982. *Patterns of Corporatist Policy Making.* London: Sage.

Lehner, F., and Shubert, K. 1984. "Party Government and the Political Control of Public Policy." *European Journal of Political Research* 12:131–46.

Lenti, L. 1981. "La mobilita della forza lavoro: splendori e miserie di una legislazione speciale," in Scamuzzi (ed.), *Riforma del collocamento e mercato del lavoro.* Milan: F. Angeli.

Lewin, L. 1980. *Governing Trade Unions in Sweden.* Cambridge: Cambridge University Press.

Lindbeck, A. 1985. "Redistribution Policy and the Expansion of the Public Sector." *Journal of Public Economics,* December.

Lindblom, C. E. 1977. *Politics and Markets.* New York: Basic Books.

Linder, S. H., and Peters, G. B. 1984. "From Social Theory to Policy Design." *Journal of Public Policy,* No. 4, pp. 237–59.

Lizzeri, G., and De Brabant, F. 1983. *L'industria delle telecomunicazioni in Italia.* Milan: F. Angeli.

Lumley, B. 1983. "Social Movements in Italy, 1968–78." Ph.D. thesis, Centre for Contemporary Cultural Studies, University of Birmingham.

Lundmark, K. 1983. "Welfare State and Employment Policy: Sweden," in K. Dyson and S. Wilks (eds.), *Industrial Crisis*. London: Basil Blackwell.

Magna, N. 1978. "Per una storia dell'operaismo in Italia. Il trentennio postbellico," pp. 295–354 in D'Agostini, F. (ed.), *Operaismo e centralita operaia*. Rome: Riuniti.

Magnifico, G. 1983. "Recent Aspects of Monetary Policy and Models of Monetary Analysis." *Review of Economic Conditions in Italy*, No. 1, pp. 9–32.

Maier, C. (ed.). 1987. *The Changing Boundaries of the Political*. Cambridge: Cambridge University Press.

Maillet, P. 1984. *La politique industrielle*. Paris: PUF.

Makler, H., Martinelli, A., and Smelser, N. 1982. *The New International Economy*. London: Sage.

Mannheimer, R., and Sani, G. 1987. *Il mercato elettorale*. Bologna: Il Mulino.

Manoukian, A. (ed.). 1968. *La presenza sociale del PCI e della DC*. Bologna: Il Mulino.

Maraffi, M. 1985. "Business Interest Associations in the Construction Sector in Italy." Dipartimento di Sociologia, University of Milan. Mimeo.

   1987. "Le politiche industriali." *ISAP Archivio*, No. 4.

March, J. G., and Olsen, J. P. 1983. "The New Institutionalism: Organizational Factors in Political Life." *American Political Science Review*, No. 78, pp. 734–49.

Marconi, P. 1986a. *I nodi critici della legislazione di politica industriale*. Milan: Centro di Politica Comparata Bocconi e FOR.

   1986. *La politica governativa per la ristrutturazione industriale: il Fondo per la razionalizzazione aziendale e interaziendale degli impianti siderurgici e il Fondo per l'elettronica dei beni di consumo e della componentistica connessa*. Rome: FOR.

Marshall, T. H. 1965. *Social Policy*. London: Hutchinston.

Martin, A. 1986. "The Politics of Employment and Welfare in Advanced Capitalist Societies: National Policies and International Independence," in K. Banting (ed.), *The State and Economic Interests*. Toronto: University of Toronto Press.

Martinelli, A. 1974. *La teoria dell'imperialismo*. Turin: Loescher.

Martinelli, A., Baglioni, M., Chiesi, A. M., and Maraffi, M. 1985. "The Organization of Business Interests in Italy. A Preliminary Report." Paper presented at Conference on the Organization of Business Interests, Florence, European University Institute, April 22–24.

Martinelli, A., Chiesi, A., and Dalla Chiesa, N. 1981a. *I grandi imprenditori italiani*. Milan: Feltrinelli.

Martinelli, A., Schmitter, P., and Streeck W. 1981b. "L'organizzazione degli interessi imprenditoriali." *Stato e Mercato*, No. 3 (December).

Martinotti, G. (ed.). 1985. *Politica locale e politiche pubbliche. L'esperienza delle giunte di sinistra*. Milan: F. Angeli.

Maynard, A., and McLachlan, G. (eds.). 1982. *The Public-Private Mix*. London: Nuffield Provincial Hospital Trust.

Melucci, A. 1980. "The New Social Movements: A Theoretical Approach." *Social Science Information* 19:199–226.

   1982. *L'invenzione del presente. Movimenti, identita, bisogni individuali*. Bologna: Il Mulino.

   1985. "The Symbolic Challenge of Contemporary Movements." *Social Research* 52:789–816.

   1989. "Getting Involved: Identity and Mobilization in Social Movements" [in press], in B. Klandermans, K. Hanspeter, and S. Tarrow (eds.), *From Structure to Action: Social Movement Participation across Cultures*. Greenwich, Conn.: JAI.

Merli, S. 1972. *Proletariato di fabbrica e capitalismo industriale: il caso italiano (1862–1904)*. Florence: La Nuova Italia.

META. 1986. "Finanziaria: il documento unitario FIOM, FIM, UILM," No. 9 (September), p. 24.

Ministero dell'Industria. 1984. *La gestione attiva della transizione industriale.* Rome.

Ministero della Sanita. 1985. "La gestione del SSN nel 1984." Rome. Mimeo.

Ministero del Tesoro. 1986. "Obiettivi e strumenti della manovra di bilancio per il triennio 1987–1989." Rome. Mimeo.

Mirabile, M. L. (ed.). 1985 *Le associazioni territoriali della Confindustria.* Rome: IRES.

Monti, S., Cesarini, F., and Scognamiglio, C. 1983. "Report on the Italian Credit and Financial System." Special issue of *Banca Nazionale del Lavoro Quarterly Review*, Rome.

Monti, S., and Siracusano, D. 1979. "The Public Sector's Financial Intermediation, the Composition of Credit and the Allocation of Resources." *Review of Economic Conditions in Italy*, No. 2, pp. 223–53.

Mutti, A. 1982. "Lo scambio politico nelle relazioni industriali." *Stato e Mercato*, No. 5 (August).

——— 1986. "La fiducia." Dipartimento di studi politici e sociali, University of Pavia, Pavia. Mimeo.

Mutti, A., Addario, N., and Segatti, P. 1986. "The Organization of Business Interests: The Case of the Italian Textile and Clothing Industry." Florence, European University Institute Working Papers, 86/205.

Nardozzi, G. 1981. "Accumulazione di capitale e politica monetaria," in G. Lunghini (ed.), *Scelte politiche e teorie economiche in Italia.* Turin: Einaudi.

——— 1983. *Structural Trends of Financial Systems and Capital Accumulation: France, Germany and Italy.* Brussels: Commission of the European Community.

Nardozzi, G., and Onado, M. 1980. "The Relation Between Banks and Enterprises and the Public Sector as Financial Intermediary." *Review of Economic Conditions in Italy*, No. 2, pp. 355–72.

Negrelli, S. 1985. "Regolazione post-normativa delle relazioni industriali nell'impresa in transizione." *Sociologia del lavoro*, No. 24.

North, D. C. 1977. "Market and Other Allocation Systems in History: The Challenge of Karl Polanyi." *The Journal of European Economic History*, VI, No. 3.

——— 1981. *Structure and Change in Economy History.* New York: Norton.

O'Connor, J. 1973. *The Fiscal Crisis of the State.* New York: St. Martin's Press.

OECD 1979. "The Case for Positive Adjustment Policies." Paris.

——— 1983. "Transparence et adjustement positif." Paris.

——— 1984. "Social Expenditure: 1960–1990; Its Growth and Control." Paris. Mimeo.

——— 1985. "The Role of the Public Sector." *OECD Economic Studies*, No. 4.

Offe, C. 1982. "The Attribution of Public Status to Interest Groups: Observations on the West German Case," p. 123–58 in Suzanne Berger (ed.), *Organizing Interests in Western Europe.* Cambridge: Cambridge University Press.

——— 1985. "New Social Movements: Challenging the Boundaries of Institutional Politics." *Social Research* 52:817–68.

Offe, C., and Wiesenthal, H. 1980. "Two Logics of Collective Action. Theoretical Notes on Social Class and Organizational Form," in M. Zeitlin (ed.), *Political Power and Social Theory.* Greenwich, Conn.: JAI Press.

Olson, M. 1965. *The Logic of Collective Action.* Cambridge, Mass.: Harvard University Press.

——— 1981. *A New Approach to the Economics of Health Care.* Washington: AEI.

Ouchi, W. G. 1977. "Markets, Bureaucracies and Clans." *Administrative Science Quarterly*, No. 25.

Paci, M. 1982a. "Per una nuova filosofia dell'intervento pubblico in campo sociale," pp. 245–52 in *La struttura sociale italiana.* Bologna: Il Mulino.

1982b. "Onde lunghe nello sviluppo dei sistemi di welfare." *Stato e Mercato*, No. 6 (December).

1984. "Il sistema italiano di welfare tra tradizione clientelare e prospettive di riforma," pp. 297–326 in U. Ascoli (ed.), *Welfare State all'italiana*. Bari: Laterza.

1985. "Prospettive istituzionali di riforma del sistema italiano di welfare," pp. 511–34 in M. D'Antonio (ed.), *La Costituzione economica, prospettive di riforma dell'ordinamento economico*. Milan: Ediz. Il Sole 24 ore.

1986a. "Stato sociale e redistribuzione del reddito," pp. 245–58 in C. Carboni (ed.), *Classi e movimenti in Italia, 1970–1985*. Bari: Laterza.

1986. "Il male sta nelle fasce sociali. I rischi della fissazione di soglie di reddito per le prestazioni sociali." *Rinascita*, No. 44 (November 15), p. 5.

1986c. "Il mercato e la sfida della cittadinanza sociale." *Politica ed Economia*, No. 2 (November), pp. 9–12.

1987. "La tutela pensionistica di base." INPS, Rome. Mimeo.

Palmerio, G., and Valiani, R. 1982. *La regolamentazione strumento della politica economica*. Florence: Le Monnier.

Papadia, F. 1984. "Estimates of Ex Ante Real Rates of Interest in the EEC Countries and in the United States, 1973–1982." *Journal of Money, Credit and Banking*, August.

Pappalardo, A. 1985. *Il governo del salario nelle democrazie industriali*. Milan: F. Angeli.

Pasquino, G. 1980. *Crisi dei partiti e governabilita*. Bologna: Il Mulino.

1985. *Restituire lo scettro al principe. Proposte di riforma istituzionale*. Bari: Laterza.

1986. "Party Government in Italy: Achievements and Prospects," in R. S. Katz (ed.), *The American and European Experiences of Party Government*. Berlin: De Gruyter.

Pedone, A. 1979. *Evasori e tartassati. I nodi della politica tributaria italiana*. Bologna: Il Mulino.

Peters, G. B. 1985. "The Structure and Organization of Governments: Concepts and Issues." *Journal of Public Policy*, No. 5, pp. 107–26.

Piore, M., and Sabel, C. 1984. *The Second Industrial Divide*. New York: Basic Books.

Piperno, A. 1984. "La politica sanitaria," in U. Ascoli (ed.), *Welfare State all'italiana*. Bari: Laterza.

1986. *La politica sanitaria in Italia fra continuita e sviluppo*. Milan: F. Angeli.

Piven, F., and Cloward, R. 1977. *Poor People's Movements*. New York: Vintage.

Pizzorno, A. 1974. "I ceti medi nei meccanismi del consenso," in F. L. Cavazza and S. Graubard (eds.), *Il caso italiano*. Milan: Garzanti.

1978. "Political Exchange and Collective Identity in Industrial Conflict," in C. Crouch and A. Pizzorno (eds.), *The Resurgence of Class Conflict in Western Europe Since 1968*, 2 volumes. London: Macmillan.

1981. "Interests and Parties in Pluralism," pp. 249–84 in S. Berger (ed.), *Organizing Interests in Western Europe*. New York: Cambridge University Press.

Poggi, G. 1978. *The Development of the Modern State*. London: Hutchinson.

Polanyi, K. 1944. *The Great Transformation*. New York: Holt Rinehart and Winston.

1978. "L'economia come processo istituzionale," in K. Polanyi (ed.), *Traffici e mercati negli antichi imperi*. Turin: Einaudi.

Posner, A. 1978. "Italy: Dependence and Political Fragmentation," in P. Katzenstein (ed.), *Between Power and Plenty*. Madison: University of Wisconsin Press.

Putnam, R. D. 1976. *The Comparative Study of Political Elites*. Englewood Cliffs: Prentice Hall.

Regalia, I. 1975. "Gli strumenti d'informazione del sindacato: Le assemblee." *Quaderni di rassegna sindacale*, 1 3:103–13.

1984. "Le politiche del lavoro," in U. Ascoli (ed.), *Welfare State all'italiana*. Bari: Laterza.

1985. *Eletti e abbandonati: Modelli e stili di rappresentanza in fabbrica*. Bologna: Mulino.

1987a. "Le politiche del lavoro." *Archivio ISAP*, No. 4.

1987b. "Non piu' apprendisti stregoni? Sindacati e istituzioni in periferia." *Stato e Mercato* 19:43–72.

Regalia, I., Regini, M., and Reyneri, E. 1978. "Labour Conflicts and Industrial Relations in Italy," in C. Crouch and A. Pizzorno (eds.), *The Resurgence of Class Conflict in Western Europe Since 1968*, 2 volumes. London: Macmillan.

Regini, M. 1980. "Labour Unions, Industrial Action and Politics," pp. 49–66 in P. Lange and S. Tarrow (eds.), *Italy in Transition: Conflict and Consensus.* London: Cass.

1981. *Il dilemmi del sindacato.* Bologna: Il Mulino.

1983. "The Crisis of Representation in Class-Oriented Unions: Some Reflections based on the Italian Case," in S. Clegg, G. Dow, and P. Boreham (eds.), *The State, Class and the Recession.* London: Croom Helm.

1985. "Relazioni industriali e sistema politico: l'evoluzione recente e le prospettive degli anni '80," in M. Carrieri and P. Perulli (eds.), *Il teorema sindacale*, Bologna: Il Mulino.

1987a. "Social Pacts in Italy," in I. Scholten (ed.), *Political Stability and Neo-corporatism.* London: Sage.

1987b. "L'amministrazione e il sindacato nell' attuazione delle politiche: Introduzione." *ISAP Archivio*, No. 4.

1988. "Industrial Relations in the Phase of Flexibility." *International Journal of Political Economy*, vol. 5.

Regione Lazio. 1984. "1984: L'assistenza sanitaria nel Lazio." Rome.

Regonini, G. 1984. "Il sistema pensionistico: risorse e vincoli," in U. Ascoli (ed.), *Welfare State all'italiana.* Bari: Laterza.

1985. "Le politiche sociali in Italia: metodi di analisi." *Rivista italiana di scienza politica*, December, pp. 335–77.

1987. "Le politiche pensionistiche." *ISAP Archivio*, No. 4.

Rey, G. 1982. "Italy," in A. Boltho (ed.), *The European Economy, Growth and Crisis.* Oxford: Oxford University Press.

Reyneri, E. 1979. *La catena migratoria.* Bologna: Il Mulino.

1985. "Le politiche del lavoro in Italia: verso la deregolazione strisciante o una nuova regolazione flessibile e contrattata?" *Prospettiva sindacale*, No. 58.

1987a. "Il mercato," in D. De Masi and A. Bonzanini (eds.), *Trattato di sociologia del lavoro e dell'organizzazione. Le tipologie.* Milan: F. Angeli.

1987b. "Politiche e mercato del lavoro," in CESOS (ed.), *Le relazioni sindacali in Italia. Rapporto 1985–1986.* Rome: Edizioni Lavoro.

Richardson, J. (ed.). 1982. *Policy Styles in Western Europe.* London: Allen & Unwin.

Richardson, J., Gustafsson, G., and Jordan, G. 1982. "The Concept of Policy Style," pp. 1–16 in J. Richardson (ed.), *Policy Styles in Western Europe.* London: Allen & Unwin.

Rimlinger, G. V. 1971. *Welfare Policy and Industrialization in Europe, America and Russia.* New York: J. Wiley & Sons.

1982. "The Emergence of Social Insurance: European Experience Before 1914." Mimeo.

Romagnoli, G. 1976. *Consigli di fabbrica e democrazia sindacale.* Milan: Mazzotta.

Ruggeri, G. 1984. "The Difficult Financing of the Treasury." *Review of Economic Conditions in Italy*, No. 1, pp. 9–30.

1985. "Notes on the Control of the Public Deficit in the Medium Term." *Review of Economic Conditions in Italy*, No. 1, pp. 37–74.

Ruini, C., 1981. "Disinflation and Productive Investments in the Government's Program." *Review of Economic Conditions in Italy*, No. 3, pp. 516–30.

Rusconi, G. E. 1984. *Scambio, minaccia, decisione.* Bologna: Il Mulino.

Sabel, C. 1982. *Work and Politics*. Cambridge: Cambridge University Press.
Salvati, M. 1981. "May 1968 and the Hot Autumn of 1969: The Responses of Two Ruling Classes," pp. 329–63 in S. Berger (ed.), *Organizing Interests in Western Europe*. New York: Cambridge University Press.
1982. "Strutture politiche ed esiti economici." *Stato e Mercato*, No. 4 (April).
1985. "The Italian Inflation," in L. N. Lindberg and C. S. Maier (eds.), *The Politics of Inflation and Economic Stagnation*. Washington: The Brookings Institution.
Salvemini, M. T. 1983. "The Treasury and the Money Market: The New Responsibilities After the Divorce." *Review of Economic Conditions in Italy*, No. 1, pp 33–54.
Sarcinelli, M. 1981. "The Role of the Central Bank in the Domestic Economy." *Review of Economic Conditions in Italy*, No. 3, pp. 433–54.
Sartori, G. 1966. "European Political Parties: The Case of Polarized Pluralism," in J. La Palombara and M. Weiner (eds.), *Political Parties and Political Development*. Princeton: Princeton University Press.
1976. *Parties and Party Systems: A framework for analysis*. Cambridge: Cambridge University Press.
Scamuzzi, S. (ed.). 1981. *Riforma del collocamento e mercato del lavoro*. Milan: F. Angeli.
Scharpf, F. W. 1977. "Does Organization Matter? Task Structure and Interaction in the Ministerial Bureaucracy," in E. H. Burack and A. R. Negandhi (eds.), *Organization Design: Theoretical Perspectives and Empirical Findings*. Kent, Ohio: Kent State University Press.
1982. "Der Erklarungswert 'binnenstrukturellen' faktoren in der politik – und Verwaltungsforschung," in J. J. Hesse (ed.), *Politikwissenschaft und Verwaltungswissenschaft*, Politische Vierteljaresschrift, Sonderheft 13, pp. 90–104.
1985. "Policy Failure and Institutional Reform: Why Should Form Follow Function?" Paper presented at workshop on The Structure and Organization of Governments. Paris: IPSA.
1986. "La trappola della decisione congiunta: federalismo tedesco e integrazione europea." *Stato e Mercato*, No. 17 (August), pp. 175–216.
Schmitter, P. 1974. "Still the Century of Corporatism?" *Review of Politics* (January).
1981. "Interest Intermediation and Regime Governability in Contemporary Western Europe and North America," pp. 285–327 in S. Berger (ed.), *Organizing Interests in Western Europe*. New York: Cambridge University Press.
Schmitter, P., and Streeck, W. 1981. *The Organization of Business Interests. A Research Design to Study the Associative Action of Business in Advanced Industrial Societies in Western Europe*. Berlin: Wissenschaftszentrum.
Schor, J. 1983. "Social Welfare Benefits and the Rise of Labor Militance: Reinterpreting the Strike Waves of 1968–70." Paper presented at annual meeting of Council for European Studies, Washington, D.C.
1985a. Changes in the Cyclical Variability of Real Wages: Evidence from Nine Countries, 1955–1980." *Economic Journal* 95:452–68.
1985b. "Wages Flexibility, Social Welfare Expenditures and Monetary Restrictiveness," in M. Jarsulic (ed.), *Money and Macro Policy*. Boston: Kluwer-Nijhoff Publishing.
Schor, J., and Bowles, S. 1984. "The Cost of Job Loss and the Incidence of Strikes." Discussion paper 1105, Harvard Institute for Economic Research.
Selznick, P. 1957. *Leadership in Administration*. New York: Harper & Row.
Senato della Repubblica, X Commissione. 1985. "Bozza di documento conclusivo della indagine conoscitiva sulla politica industriale." Rome.
Serrani, D. 1978. *Il potere per enti*. Bologna: Il Mulino.
Shonfield, A. 1965. *Modern Capitalism*. London: Oxford University Press.
Simon, H. 1947. *Administrative Behavior*. New York: Macmillan.

Siniscalchi, E. 1981. "Il sistema italiano di collocamento. La Legge 29-4-1949 No. 264 e i provvedimenti in materia di mobilita," in C. Marazia (ed.), *Istituzioni e politiche del lavoro nella Comunita europea*. Milan: F. Angeli.

Skocpol, Theda. 1985. "Bringing the State Back In: Strategies of Analysis in Current Research," in P. Evans, D. Rueschemeyer, and T. Skocpol (eds.), *Bringing the State Back In*. Cambridge: Cambridge University Press.

Smith, G. 1986. "The Futures of Party Government: A Framework for Analysis," pp. 205–35 in F. G. Castles and R. Wildenmann (eds.), *Visions and Realities of Party Government*. Berlin: De Gruyter.

Snow, D., and Benford, R. 1989. "Ideology, Frame Resonance, and Participant Mobilization" [in press], in B. Klandermans, K. Hanspeter, and S. Tarrow (eds.), *From Structure to Action: Social Movement Participation across Cultures*. Greenwich, Conn.: JAI.

Snow, D., et al. 1986. "Frame Alignment Processes, Micro-mobilization, and Movement Participation." *American Sociological Review* 51:464–81.

Soskice, D. 1978. "Strike Waves and Wage Explosions, 1968–1970: An Economic Interpretation," in C. Crouch and A. Pizzorno (eds.), *The Resurgence of Class Conflict in Western Europe Since 1968*, 2 volumes. London: Macmillan.

Spaventa, L. 1983. "Two Letters of Intent: External Crises and Stabilization Policy, Italy, 1974–77," in J. Williamson (ed.), *IMF Conditionality*. Washington: Institute for International Economics.

    1984. "The Growth of Public Debt in Italy: Past Experience, Perspectives and Policy Problems." *Banca Nazionale del Lavoro Quarterly Review* 37:119–49.

    1985. "Adjustment Plans, Fiscal Policy and Monetary Policy." *Review of Economic Conditions in Italy*, No. 1, pp. 9–35.

Stefanizzi, S. 1987. "Alle origini dei nuovi movimenti sociali: Ecologisti e donne in Italia, 1966–1973." European University Institute of Florence. Unpublished paper.

Steiner, J. 1981. "The Consociational Theory and Beyond." *Comparative Politics*, April.

Stokman, F. N., Ziegler, R., and Scott, J. 1985. *Networks of Corporate Power*. Cambridge: Polity Press.

Streeck, W. 1986. "Il management dell'incertezza e l'incertezza dei managers. Imprenditori, relazioni sindacali e riequilibrio industriale nella crisi." *Prospettiva sindacale*, No. 59.

Streeck, W., and Schmitter, P. 1985. "Community, Market, State – and Associations?" in W. Streeck and P. Schmitter (eds.), *Private Interest Government: Beyond Markets and State*. Beverly Hills: Sage.

Tarrow, S. 1977a. *Between Center and Periphery. Grassroots Politicians in Italy and France*. New Haven: Yale University Press.

    1977b. "From Cold War to Historic Compromise," in S. Bialer (ed.), *Sources of Contemporary Radicalism*, Vol. 1. Boulder: Westview Press.

    1983. *Struggling to Reform: Social Movements and Policy Change during Cycles of Protest*. Cornell University, Western Societies Paper, No. 15.

    1988. *Democracy and Disorder: Protest and Politics in Italy, 1965–1975*. Oxford: Oxford University Press.

Thygesen, N. 1982. "Monetary Policy," in A. Boltho (ed.), *The European Economy: Growth and Crisis*. Oxford: Oxford University Press.

Tilly, C. 1978. *From Mobilization to Revolution*. Englewood Cliffs, N.J.: Prentice-Hall.

    1987. "Twenty Years of British Contention." Center for Studies of Social Change, New School for Social Research Working Paper No. 52.

Titmuss, R. M. 1974. *Social Policy: An Introduction*. New York: Pantheon Books.

Tremonti, G., and Vitaletti, G. 1986. *Le cento tasse degli italiani*. Bologna: Il Mulino.

Trentin, B. 1986. "Un welfare a rovescio," pp. 60–7 in M. Regini (ed.), *Risposte alla crisi del welfare state: ridurre o trasformare le politiche sociali?* Milan: F. Angeli.

Treu, T. 1984. "L'accordo del 22 gennaio: implicazioni e aspetti giuridico-istituzionali," in CESOS (ed.), *Le relazioni sindacali in Italia. Rapporto 1983–84.* Rome: Edizioni Lavoro.

1985. "Concertazione e riforme." *Il Progetto,* No. 30.

U.S. Bureau of Labor Statistics. 1983. *Handbook of Labor Statistics.*

Vaciago, G. 1985. "Financial Innovation and Monetary Policy: Italy Versus the United States." *Banca Nazionale del Lavoro Quarterly Review,* No. 155, pp. 303–26.

Valiani, R. 1985a. "Efficienza delle istituzioni: il caso delle politiche industriali," pp. 258–71 in Confindustria (ed.), *Risorse per lo sviluppo.* Rome: SIPI.

1985b. "What solutions are There to Italy's Public Debt?" *Review of Economic Conditions in Italy,* No. 1, pp. 75–95.

Van Der Gaag, J., and Perlman, M. (eds.). 1981. *Health, Economics and Health Economics.* Amsterdam: North Holland.

Veneziani, B. 1985. "Intervento dello stato e relazioni industriali," in CESOS, *Le relazioni sindacali in Italia. Rapporto 1983–84.* Rome: Edizioni Lavoro.

Viale, Guido. 1978. *Il Sessantotto: Tra revoluzione e restaurazione.* Milan: Gabriele Mazzotta.

Vilella, G. 1984. *Governo e amministrazione nella recente politica industriale.* Milan: Giuffre.

Visco, V. 1986. "Welfare state: diritti irrinuniciabili e scelte tragiche." *Thema,* No. 1 (February), pp. 102–6.

Walsh, K. 1983. *Strikes in Europe and the United States.* New York: St. Martin's Press.

Weber, M. 1985. *La borsa.* Milan: Unicopli.

Weingast, B. R. 1979. "A Rational Choice Perspective on Congressional Norms." *The American Journal of Political Science* 23:245–62.

Wiener, N. 1954. *The Human Uses of Human Beings.* New York: Doubleday.

Wildavsky, A. 1984. *The Politics of Industrial Policy in American Political Cultures.* Washington: American Enterprise Institute.

Wilks, S. 1983. "Crisis Management in Britain," in K. Dyson and S. Wilks (eds.), *Industrial Crisis.* London: Basil Blackwell.

Williams, A. 1985. "Keep Politics Out of Health." Mimeo.

Williamson, O. E. 1975. *Markets and Hierarchies.* New York: Free Press.

Wilson, J. Q. 1980. *The Politics of Regulation.* New York: Basic Books.

Windmuller, J. P., and Gladstone, A. (eds.). 1984. *Employers' Associations and Industrial Relations.* Oxford: Oxford University Press.

Zolberg, A. 1972. "Moments of Madness." *Politics and Society* 2(Winter):183–207.

Zysman, J. 1977. *Political Strategies for Industrial Order: State, Market and Industry in France.* Berkeley, University of California Press.

1983. *Governments, Markets and Growth.* Ithaca: Cornell University Press.

Index